SOMETIMES FARMGIRLS BECOME REVOLUTIONARIES

SOMETIMES FARMGIRLS BECOME REVOLUTIONARIES

Notes on Black Power, Politics, Depression, and the FBI

FLORENCE L. TATE
AND JAKE-ANN JONES

Black Classic Press
Baltimore

Sometimes Farmgirls Become Revolutionaries:
Notes on Black Power, Black Politics, Depression, and the FBI

Copyright 2021 Jake-ann Jones
Foreword copyright 2021 by Greg Tate
Afterword copyright 2021 by Brian Tate
Published 2021 by Black Classic Press

Library of Congress Control Number: 2019948359
Print book ISBN: 978-1-57478-164-9
e-Book ISBN: 978-1-57478-165-6

Printed by BCP Digital Printed (www.bcpdigital.com)
an affiliate of Black Classic Press, Inc.
For a virtual tour of our publishing and printing facility, visit:
https://www.c-span.org/video/?441322-2/tour-black-classic-press

Purchase Black Classic Press books from your favorite book seller
or online at www.blackclassicbooks.com.

For inquiries or to request a list of titles, write:
Black Classic Press
PO Box 13414
Baltimore, MD 21203

Contents

Florence Tate and Jake-ann Jones

Notes and Acknowledgments

Florence Louise Grinner Tate kept a vast collection of press releases, articles, letters to the editor, communications from politicians and organizational leaders, flyers, essays, and other writings in a dozen or more boxes stored in her Sarasota, Florida, garage. The journal from which much of this book's content is taken was kept in the study she shared with her husband Charles in their home. She kept her FBI files, bound with a photo of Stokely Carmichael on the cover, on an end table in their living room.

Between 2010 and 2013, Florence and I sat, walked, and, on occasion—like, on the way to a movie or a doctor's visit—drove with a tape recorder in the "on" position perched on the seat between us to recover what seemed like hundreds of hours filled with memories of her past. Sometimes, she clearly enjoyed the process of sharing stream-of-consciousness recollections of her eighty-plus years. Other times, she strained dutifully to chip away at the huge granite block of her past, unearthing less-savory memories. Sometimes, dates were foggy, and she ruefully reminded me about her escalating memory loss—much of it from age, some from the electroconvulsive treatments she endured for many years, hoping to ward off or diminish her recurrent bouts of depression. Toward the end, she would glower at me in near resentment as I repeatedly asked her to cover and re-cover old ground I needed to hear more of.

Sometimes, Florence refused to talk about the past at all. Instead, she would insist we turn to Facebook to see who was up to what, where, and when. Other times, we'd call her sister Lucille or her oldest friend Josephine to help her recall or correct a memory. Still other times, she would chuckle with glee as she strained to orchestrate a three-way call with Miriam and Dick Meisler, Paul Delaney, LaVerne McCain Gill, or another old friend. It was fun to listen in while they prodded each other's memory to get to the facts of an event—or, at least, their closest shared approximation of it.

When Florence talked with me about publishing her memoirs, she often did so with a wistful sigh, adding: "If I'm still alive to see it..." Of course, I always pooh-poohed her despairing sentiments and immediately changed the conversation to a more upbeat discussion. For example, I'd ask her what fantastic outfit she planned to wear to a book party being planned by her friends Mae Jackson and Kay Shaw, two ladies who really knew how to throw a party. She'd stare at me sternly and say, "OK, now, Jake, you have to promise to get this book out when I'm gone!" I would, of course, respond with a baleful gaze and shush her negative vibes, wanting to hear none of it.

In the end, that's what this book is: me, trying to fulfill a promise. This book was sewn together in a manner that can best be described as an incomplete collage of Florence Tate's life on the planet. To be sure, there was a lot of material to choose from but even with all we had, a lot was undocumented and therefore missing.

Florence insisted that her years growing up on a rural Tennessee farm—her earliest memories—made her who she was. She balked at my suggestion that we call the book *The FBI's Most-Wanted Press Secretary*, my nickname for her, and a title that I and others found catchy. "But that's just a small part of who I am and who I was," she protested. "I don't want folks thinking that part of my life was the most important to me!"

Her husband Charles agreed, "It needs to say that she was a revolutionary because THAT'S what she was," he'd bark at me.

"I don't know," Florence would muse, "maybe something like *Eads to Angola* or *My Life from the Farm to the Movement*. Something..." Then she would sigh and roll her eyes, already done with the conversation. In the end, the two longtime lovers and best friends won out. I retitled the book to honor the only title suggestion Florence and I shared in common. I wish she and Charles both were here to see that I honored my promise.

Some of the people whose commentary and perspectives are included in this book were interviewed after Florence passed away in 2014. (Charles passed four years later, in 2018.) I would like to send immense waves of gratitude to her friends and "co-laborers in the struggle" who agreed to share their memories and insights from the years they spent living and working alongside Florence and the Tate family. Her longtime friend, Miriam Meisler, greatly helped in the completion of this work, serving as an early reader; unfortunately, her husband Dick also left the planet sometime between Florence's and Charles' passing. Writer and party-planner extraordinaire Mae Jackson was a wellspring of spiritual support, eagerly awaiting the book party-to-come in Florence's honor! Additional contributors and supporters included: Charlie Cobb, Lamin Jangha, Paul Delaney, Michael Tarif Warren, Josephine Bridges, Juadine Henderson, Hedi Butler, LaVerne McCain Gill, Joan Thornell, Mark Smith, Malik Chaka, Thomas Porter, Eric K. Easter, Julia Jones, Doll Gordon, Kalama Ya Salaam, Dr. Howard Fuller, Kay Shaw, and Omo Misha McGlowan — whose words and photographs provided profoundly robust views of Florence's colorful and vibrant life. I heartily thank them each for their participation, as I know Florence would, if she were still here.

I also wish to thank poets Asha Bandele and Ethelbert Miller for offering words of support and recommendations for this project. Hettie Jones also deserves thanks for her consideration and advice. The friendship and advice of author and filmmaker Bridgett Davis was invaluable, as was that of the following: Cedric Johnson, author of *Revolutionaries to Race Leaders, Black Power and the Making of African American Politics*, for his kindness and for sending me a copy of his brilliant research; Jefry Andres Wright for his lovely photographic images; and Nana-Ama Danquah, author of *Willow Weep for Me: A Black Woman's Journey Through Depression*, for her early words of encouragement.

Many hugs to the Tates's "Sarasota Family," with whom I spent time with during my frequent and prolonged sleepovers at Florence's and Charles's Florida home: Vickie Oldham, for her pies and all-around fierceness; artist John Sims; Dr. Joyce Ladner; and especially Ralph and Che Barnett, for the hospitality and friendship they showed me and the Tates.

My deepest appreciation goes to the remaining members of the Tate family for sharing sister and mother with me: Lucille Knowles,

Geri Augusto, Greg Tate, and Brian Tate. Their faith in this project never wavered. Thank you.

Of course, I must give big shout outs to the Black Classic Press (BCP) family, especially BCP's esteemed publisher, W. Paul Coates, whom Florence pointed me toward early in this process. It was her wish to find a home for her story with a Black publisher; and I'm so grateful and thrilled BCP, with the support of team members Natalie Stokes–Peters and April Chenier, offered just that. Much respect also to BCP editors Rosalyn Coates, Lynn Suruma, and D. Kamili Anderson for working around the hybrid nature of this book and keeping it on point.

Finally, I must extend special shout-outs to my personal support system, the people who were there for me in countless way throughout the years it took to complete this project: Alexis Morton, Kenya Morton–Numan, Julius and Vivian Morton, Mitchell Bleier, Mark Hayward, Brigitte Hayward, Dudley Findlay Jr., Andrietta Syms, Beverley Williams, Elisa Koizumi, Gabe Tolliver, Sharon Pendana, Al Santana, Michael Gonzalez, Sandye Wilson, and Gregory Thomson. Just your listening, sometimes, meant so much—and enough. I would also like to thank two women who stepped into the space left in my life after Florence moved onto her next assignment: Leah Clendening and Gwendolyn Reese, who have both performed as supportive mentors and 'godmothers.'

This book is dedicated to ALL the future revolutionaries and to the memory of my parents: Julius Hamlet Morton and Judith Mary Jenkins Morton. I hope I'm honoring everything you gave me before you traveled on. I hope also that you've hooked up with Florence and Charles and are having a good laugh behind my back.

Last, to my sons/suns River Quinton Hayward and Sky Alexander Hayward: you are the bass and drums of my entire beat.

Jake-ann Jones

FOREWORD

GREG TATE

There is a time when you think of your mother's existence and your own as indivisible. You are constant objects of attention and affection in each other's lives. She wakes you in the morning for school, sometimes by ambush, ripping away your warm blankets, exposing you to the arctic elements—or so they seemed on certain Ohio winter days. She made you breakfast, sent you off to the schoolhouse, prepared all those nightly family dinners.

And even though she had two other kids, Big Sis Geri, Baby Bro Brian, you never felt like it was a shared relationship in which whatever mother-child thing they had going on with her overlapped with your own. And you dug that because kids are mad-selfish with their mothers.

I recall wanting her devout and undivided attention so much so that whenever she was on the kitchen phone, which had a long cable, I would wrap it around her legs while she was talking until she realized she was being cocooned in one spot by her ball-and-chain of an elder boy-child, who'd have to unwrap her before she could freely move again.

In any event, as years went by and you grew from child to tween, you realized you did have one rival for your mother's affections, and it wasn't your dad but this thing called "The Movement," which had both an abstract and a human dimension. It actually existed in at least five dimensions simultaneously, and it was protean. It took on many forms and appeared in many places throughout the house.

There also were "Movement people" to contend with. They visited regularly. Some spent the night after long hours holding court on the living-room couch and chairs. Some stayed even longer—for days, weeks, even months at a time. Some you came to realize were Movement celebrities, people whose names loomed above others:

Stokely Carmichael (nee Kwame Ture), H. Rap Brown, Eldridge Cleaver, Amiri Baraka. These were people who also became lifelong friends alongside lesser-known members of SNCC and CORE and The Black Panthers.

The Movement had a life outside the home too, and sometimes it meant one or both of your parents had to leave town to attend a March on Washington, a marriage between Carmichael and Miriam Makeba, a Black Political Convention in Gary, a Pan-African Cultural Festival in Nigeria. The Movement was also multidisciplinary. It defined your mother's bookshelf, the Sunday morning heavy rotation of her vinyl selections: recordings of Malcolm X's speeches; the music of Nina Simone, Aretha Franklin, Pete Seeger, and Otis Redding; the soundtrack from *The Harder They Come*; twelve-inch singles by Fela Kuti.

And as the years went by, there were her travels with Dad throughout the Caribbean and Africa. There was wall art from Ethiopia, Haiti, Nigeria, Egypt. The Movement produced t-shirts, buttons, and posters that also turned up over the house.

And because you were a prodigious reader, you read everything that came in the house under her Movement-supporting aegis: Baldwin, Baraka, Giovanni, Sanchez, Alice Walker and Toni Morrison. You learned she had favorite writers outside of the Movement camp too, her Great White Men of Literature: Updike, Cheever, Le Carre, Roth.

Mom also loved Hollywood—the old movies and the new—and loved to watch The Oscars. As a family, we regularly went to the drive-in in Dayton and, before the movie-ratings system advised parents, she exposed us to some really adult fare: Kubrick's *Clockwork Orange*, Peckinpah's *Straw Dogs*, Frank Sinatra in *The Detective*, Lee Marvin in *Prime Cut*. In later years, I can recall the two of us going to see *Three Days of The Condor*, *Devil in a Blue Dress*, and, at my insistence, *Blade Runner* (though she always let me know she didn't like or understand sci-fi flicks, and *Blade Runner* didn't alter that opinion one whit).

And while Mom would sometimes tell us she thought Elijah Muhammad got it wrong when he declared the white man to be the devil when it was really that white woman, she loved many a screen siren of Old Hollywood. Faye Dunaway's performances *in Bonnie and Clyde, Chinatown, Network*, and *Mommy Dearest* mightily impressed her. She once described her favorite kind of film as "something modern, in an urban setting, with a bit of violence and sex," but since Paul Newman was also on her list of favorites, I'm sure *Butch Cassidy and the Sundance Kid* was still modernist enough for her cinematic palate.

At a certain point, as I entered into adolescence and discovered jazz and the concepts of hip and cool, I realized Mom and Dad were the epitome of those terms, as were many of their friends in post-revolutionary Washington, DC. Actually, I came to realize this by getting to know some of my other friends' parents and those friends' reaction to my parents' stances and cosmopolitanism–also by realizing that many of my parents' best friends were folk half their age and only a few years older than myself.

As with many an angst-ridden teenager, this realization of my parents' sophistication occurred when I was trying to cut the umbilical cord and rip my alienated, oat-sowing self from the happy family circle. Or maybe it was not always so happy since by then I was well aware of Mom's ongoing war with cyclical depression, which would strike her down in winter with a force that would leave her slumped in a darkened living room and given to crying jags that sometimes lasted all day.

Over the years, we pieced together her possible "triggers": child of divorce, abandoned to relatives for long or short periods, loss of my sister's companionship to Africa, being the only woman in a household full of men whose rampant hetero-masculinism could no longer be disciplined or restrained… Who knows? All the same, even if we were little pains in the ass and miniature male-chauvinist piglets, she still came to every performance by my spoken-word band, The Six-Legged Griot Trio, and Brian's punk-rock unit, Brickhouse Burning—even in sketchy 1970s downtown-DC venues at two in the morning.

What I did come to understand as I got older was that Mom's depression was as much a defining member of our family engagements as the Movement and my parents' cool factor. Because Mom's depression was cyclical, she would always rise from the lower depths and perform gargantuan tasks like serving as the press secretary of her old Movement friend Marion Barry before and after his first election to office. It was Marion who would recommend her to his buddy Jesse Jackson for his epic presidential campaign.

The political field of battle energized Mom because it was her natural environment as a "people-person." And she was drawn to it not as someone who simply enjoyed the company of folks but as someone who was able to read a roomful of high muckety-mucks instantly and immediately discern all the ways folk high up on the totem pole signified status, character, style, phobias, anxieties, affinities, and ambition. Her fluidity in that realm and her ability to create professional intimacy with the various players on a campaign trail—traits that would magically and momentously lead the Jackson campaign to Syria on a diplomatic mission and a presidential plane lent by Ronald Reagan to free a U.S. airman—are well on display in Jake-ann Jones's fantastic telling of Mom's extraordinary story.

Even when Mom took to describing herself as "a retired revolutionary and grandmother," she maintained a phenomenal presence on social media as an organizer and counselor of lost and found souls on Facebook, where she became The Mother of The Matrix to her many online constituents, some of whom have even introduced themselves to me on the street. On the site, folk still address her spirit as a personal and political confidante.

We are all blessed that Mom's voice, still overflowing with much-needed warmth and wisdom in print and in our heads, will be reactivated by the publication of this memoir/biography: a book of Florence Louise Tate's life equal to her fierceness in elegance, intellect, integrity, and *SOUL*!

Acrid fumes and the sound of gunfire.
It is 1976 in southern Angola, and I'm pressed against the doorframe of a shanty on the edge of a field. Twenty or so yards away, soldiers slide along the ground on their bellies as bullets fly above their heads. It's a deadly training exercise, and it's terrifying to watch.

My interpreter speaks over the barrage of gunfire in broken English, translating for the young Portuguese-speaking woman beside her who, in turn, interprets for the Lingala- and Umbundu-speaking women with us: "This is how they must train. They must be prepared. If they cannot dodge the bullets...they die."

Soon the girls, members of LIMA (the League of Angolan Women), lead me away. We pass wire-and-wood pens holding chickens and a few goats; then travel through planted rows of maize, beans, and sweet potatoes. As we settle down in a field just beyond the farm, the musical voices of the women momentarily transport me to my own childhood in rural Tennessee...

As we trade halting scraps of conversation above the now-distant shellfire, gesturing in our patched-together language, I'm entranced by the rich, easy laughter of my young guides and taken by their easy, unadorned beauty. I wonder if they are as jarred by the complexity of their lives as I am. The grim reality of their country's civil war clashes with the pastoral beauty around us.

In the warm haze of Huambo's afternoon heat, various memories of moments I'd experienced along the way to becoming an ardent Pan-Africanist and well-known activist shift in and out of my mind. At this moment, however, I am mostly still awestruck by my present surroundings.

How had I ended up here...surrounded by these gentle and brave young sisters fighting for their country? Some of them were as young as I had been when I'd left the South as a young, single mother, barely more than eighteen at the time.

How and why on earth had Florence Louise Grinner Tate traveled all the way from Eads to Angola?

In the echoes of those sisters' voices, something whispers:

Because sometimes, farmgirls become revolutionaries.

This is how it happened.

Florence Tate at age 12

Florence Tate (year unknown)

From the FBI FILES ON FLORENCE TATE:

SAC, Cincinnati [sic] (167 — 1293)

January 14, 1969

Director, FBI

FLORENCE LOUISE TATE

RACIAL MATTERS — BLACK NATIONALIST

Florence Louise Tate, a 38-year-old Negro female who resides with her husband in Dayton, is a representative of the Black extremist SNCC in Dayton and a close friend of Stokely Carmichael.

She is included on the Agitator Index.

CHAPTER 1

SEEDS

It's a Sunday morning in Dayton, 1965. Outside my bedroom window, there are signs that my neighborhood is on the move. Black church-going families dressed in their most respectable attire (hats, gloves, jackets, and ties) are on their way to ask God for another week of fortitude, self-restraint, and a roof overhead.

This morning, my family is headed to church as well. It's not going to be just another day of listening to the sermon and smiling politely at the other—mostly white—members of the Unitarian church we joined more for its politics than anything else.

"Florence…you coming?" Charles calls from downstairs. I can hear him trying to hustle our sons Brian and Greg out of the house and into the car.

"Hold on!" Quickly patting my short natural into a soft halo, adding a dab of lipstick, and clipping on my favorite pair of earrings, I can't deny my excitement. After hurrying to the car to help settle the boys in the back and sliding in next to Charles, one look tells me that beneath his calm exterior, his anticipation matches my own.

Only a night or so before, Reverend Harold J. LeVesconte—the progressive, pro-integration pastor at First Unitarian Church—had called to ask "a favor" of our family. "Mrs. Tate, perhaps you know that Stokely Carmichael is currently on a speaking tour, and we've invited him to come here to Dayton. He'll be here at the church this Sunday, along with one of his colleagues, and they need overnight accommodations." Reverend LeVesconte might have paused momentarily, but I'm sure he already knew my answer. "Mr. Carmichael has specifically requested to stay with a Negro family," he continued. "I was wondering, could you all accommodate him during his visit?"

Charles and I were two of a handful of Blacks attending the church, and LeVesconte and many of the white members who had supported his efforts at integration were aware that we were heavily involved in Civil Rights Movement activities in Dayton and beyond. In fact, the organization we helped form, the Dayton Alliance for Racial Equality (DARE), greatly admired the work that Stokely and the Student Nonviolent Coordinating Committee (SNCC) were doing in the South. Stokely, as SNCC's chairman, was encouraging a new philosophy: Black Power.

It also made sense that Stokely would want to spend as much time as possible with the Black folks who lived in the communities he was visiting, and it couldn't be any more divinely designed as far as I was concerned.

LeVesconte didn't need to ask twice. "Well, of course, we'd be glad to have him, and he can stay as long as he likes," I replied, delighted at the prospect of getting to know this new leader of the Black youth movement that was shaking up the country.

Stokely's name was already well known to many Blacks and whites across the nation, and I expected the church to be full that Sunday morning. Unitarians were known for being open-minded and more socially conscious than many other denominations, but how would they react to this radical young firebrand? My curiosity was also piqued because it was apparent that the Movement was branching off into two very different paths, and SNCC's less "polite" strategy continued to make more and more sense to me.

"I can't wait to hear more about this Black Power stuff," I assert as the car pulls closer to the church.

Charles nods. "Sure seems we've gotten as far as we're going to, doing it the way we have been," he sighs, speaking of integration and the current nonviolent, direct-action movements. We both feared that we had come to the end of what could be accomplished by pushing for integration and were fully ready to hear a more self-reliant and self-assertive message.

As we enter the church, I'm convinced that Stokely will be sharing his cry for Black Power. Chuckling to myself, I anticipate that his vigorous proclamation of SNCC's new direction will fill much of the congregation with dread.

It was hard to sit through the opening rituals. I try not to be conspicuous as I search for Stokely among the pews filled with liberal, highly educated, and largely integrationist-minded whites.

Reverend LeVesconte finally finishes his opening notes. When he introduces Stokely, the whole atmosphere of the church seems to change as the tall, caramel-complexioned young man strides to the pulpit, extremely collegiate and attractive in a suit and tie.

I'm immediately struck by Stokely's appearance; his head is clean-shaven and not in a style that many men sport, unless they lose their hair from old age or sickness. Later, I learn that Stokely had earlier been jailed in Alabama, where his head was shaved, supposedly as a precaution against head lice.

Before he begins, Stokely looks over his audience, his eyes piercing. It might have been my imagination, but many of the white folks in the pews around me look apprehensive. The silence in the church is heavy, but as Stokely's clear, strong voice reaches us, his first words are a surprise:

There is but little virtue in the action of masses of men. When the majority shall at length vote for the abolition of slavery, it will be because they are indifferent to slavery, or because there is but little slavery left to be abolished by their vote. They will then be the only slaves. Only his vote can hasten the abolition of slavery who asserts his own freedom by his vote.

Stokely pauses deliberately, allowing the impact of his words to resonate. "That," he continues, "is taken from Henry David Thoreau's 'Civil Disobedience,'…written over a century ago, after his arrest and jailing for his refusal to support the system of slavery and warmongering being carried out by the leaders of the United States government.

I find myself completely mesmerized as Stokely proceeds to eloquently compare Thoreau's treatise on civil disobedience with the nonviolent protests of King and Gandhi—even managing to tie in a quote or two from Ralph Waldo Emerson. This was a potent touch, as Emerson has always been considered by the Unitarians as the most "revered figure in the Unitarian movement." Throughout Stokely's speech, I can hear the white folks around us murmuring to one another under their breath, clearly stunned by this erudite young man.

Surprised by his choice of topic, I find it amusing to surreptitiously take in the apparent confusion on the faces of the white folks. Am I imagining their collective sigh of relief? After all, liberal or not, they most likely expected him to appear breathing flames—and he most certainly was not.

As Stokely ends his remarks by encouraging each of us to do our part in striving for the lofty goals set forth by Thoreau, he is met by rousing applause. It appears he has gained far more support with this less-fiery approach than he would have with an incendiary speech. My thoughts about his success are confirmed when the offering plate is passed. The white folks seem to be more generous than usual, though fully aware that their contributions will support the work of SNCC and its new focus on Black Power, a focus Stokely had cleverly held as the ultimate focus of his sermon. This was classic Stokely, as I was to learn later. With tactical brilliance, he always carefully considered how best to connect with his audience, never underestimating the power of his words nor his ability to impact his listeners deeply.

Years after that first meeting, I received the voluminous FBI file filled with references to, and accusations about, my dealings with Stokely, SNCC, and DARE and my associations with the many other community and political organizations I worked for. I felt it to be a testament to my decades of work in the Civil Rights Movement throughout the Midwest, and alongside proponents of the Black Power Movement. The file was also a reminder of my experiences with Pan-African and African liberation activities both abroad and in the U.S.

These very same activities ultimately resulted in my coming under the scrutiny of the U.S. government and caused me to be branded as a "rabble-rouser" and "agitator." I'd been linked to organizations and people labeled as "seditious" and deemed a "threat to internal security"—all terms used in the FBI's Counterintelligence Program (COINTELPRO). These terms were used repeatedly in the FBI file compiled over a number of years to describe me and my activities.

To me, the file also symbolized the many years I spent in partisan politics, including my time as press secretary in the early part of Jesse Jackson's historic 1984 presidential campaign as well as the excitement and coalition-building I experienced working alongside DC's mayor Marion Barry during both his initial run and his first year in office. Although one friend joked while perusing its pages, noting, "We need to call you the FBI's Most-Wanted Press Secretary!" the FBI file only told part of the story. And not even the *truth* of the story, most of the time.

I prefer to think of its contents as reminders of the roads I've traveled from Eads to Angola—from my life as a farm girl, to my life as a freedom fighter or, in my husband Charles' lexicon, *a revolutionary*.

After receiving my FBI files and sifting through the copied pages of classified memos, newspaper articles, and case reports, I gradually realized how closely my comings and goings had been monitored. I was astounded by the depth of detail captured to track the minutia of my life, a project on which the government had seen fit to waste taxpayers' dollars. It was shocking to read how low they would go to bring discord into my personal life for the sake of halting my political work.

Although I had not been politically active for a while and considered myself to be retired, reading the file caused me to wonder just how much privacy there was in "retired" life. Would the FBI ever stop watching me after almost two decades of surveillance? The last pages of the dossier seemed to recommend that my file be closed, as I was mainly considered a "housewife" in DC at that point. But the file made me wonder how long they had watched my comings and goings and listened in on my conversations. *Had my phone been tapped all that time?*

I recall an incident that occurred two decades earlier. Charles and I were working with DARE and were on our way to a "get out the vote" event in Cleveland. I called Mother, grateful that she was around to help since her recent relocation to Dayton. Although my mother wasn't big on the Civil Rights Movement, she'd come to realize how important the Movement was to me. We'd been estranged for many years, so after decades of struggling with difficult emotions toward her, relying on her as a support had become a very different, but welcome, experience.

After a bit of small talk, I brought up the weekend. "Well, Mother, I was wondering… could you keep the kids while Charles and I run up to Cleveland this Saturday? We'll be back by Sunday night, not too late."

Like most Black activists of the time, we had to work during the week, but our evenings and weekends could quickly become filled with various meetings, picketing, and leafleting. As the years went by, when more activism was required, I became more and more reliant on my oldest child Geri to take care of her brothers after school or on weeknights and on Mother for the weekends.

"I'm sure I can, but I'll let you know later this evening," Mother assured me.

Suddenly something on the line distracted me. I pressed my ear into the headset, listening intently. "Wait…do you hear that?" I paused, straining to identify the hollow crackling that had begun to distort our telephone connection. "I hear something strange."

Before Mother could reply, I loudly announced into the odd, familiar echoing, *"Whoever that is—can you please hang up? I just want to talk to my mother!"*

Silence. A few seconds later, there was a strange series of clicks.

Mother sighed. "Louise,"—the name my mother and all my other relatives had called me since childhood— "what is *going on?*"

I ignored her question, not wanting to remain on the line any longer than necessary. "It's OK, Mother. Just call me back when you know for sure about the weekend."

Hanging up, I thought: *they're getting mighty bold. What next?*

This wasn't the first time I had heard telltale sounds indicating a wiretap had been placed on my phone, nor would it be the last. More than anything, it was a reminder that even my most private communications were at risk of being intercepted and exposed.

Reading the file was also a chilling reminder that those doing the intercepting were powerful enough and had the means and the authority to keep me on their radar all these years.

People have asked me, "What made you risk the privacy of your life, your family's life? What drove you to spend so many years working with organizations and entities that would be viewed as threats, possibly criminals, and often unseemly or caught encouraging violent government overthrow?"

I'm sure most people, if they dig deeply enough, will find those experiences early in life that profoundly impacted them, shaped them, and laid a path their life would follow. At least, I feel this is the case for me.

I believe I can identify the seminal events that led me to become involved in the Civil Rights and Black Power movements, and ultimately to become the activist I became. There are three experiences that stand out: two of those experiences occurred during my childhood. The third occurred when I was an adult, was shared nationally by way of the TV screen and would be a pivotal event in U.S. integration efforts.

The first took place in my early childhood. I have a memory of Daddy, my great aunt Mama Annie, "cousin" Eddie Lee, and me back home in Eads, Tennessee, clustered around the open-hearth fireplace in the front room. We had no central heating; in the evening, we'd put logs on the fireplace and sit around the hearth to stay warm until we went to bed. In those days, it was not uncommon during the winter to see spots on children's legs where blisters formed from sitting too close to the fire. Depending on the season, we'd roast sweet potatoes or pork kidneys on the fire. The year was 1939, and I was three or four years old, not yet in school.

Daddy and Mama Annie were talking in hushed tones, as Mama Annie, a big boned, nutmeg-toned woman, sat peeling fruit to be preserved in mason jars for use in pies, jams, and jellies. Her husband, Papa Elvin—farmer, landowner, barber for the town's white men, and deacon at the church—was conspicuously missing, as he often was in the evenings when his workdays on the farm were done. At night, he was more than likely to be found in the home of his lover, the albino we called "White Effie," who lived in a small cottage at the edge of his large plot of land.

As Daddy and Mama Annie conversed, occasionally Eddie Lee, who was really my Mother's cousin, chimed in. Eddie and my mother had been raised together by Mama Annie when their own mothers, Mama Annie's sisters, died in the 1918 flu pandemic. Although I was young and couldn't understand much of what was said, I could tell that it had something to do with our cousin, twenty-year-old Jesse Lee, whom I remembered faintly from family gatherings. I knew that something bad had happened to him and also that it had to do with white people and Black people. It was later I realized the three of them were discussing Jesse Lee's lynching in nearby Arlington, Tennessee, at the hands of a mob. Over the years, I was to learn more details that I was too young to understand at the time.

Jesse Lee and his mother were sharecroppers on Mr. Wilson's property in Arlington. Jesse was regarded as smart, being both literate and numerate, and capable enough to deal with the sharecropping accounts. His father, my mother's first cousin, wasn't around. I don't know if he was dead or gone. The Wilsons owned the general store and the cotton gin. The sharecroppers would get supplies from the store all year on "credit." At the end of year, when their crops yielded, they would square up with Mr. Wilson, who also owned the land they farmed.

On this particular day, Jesse Lee had gone to the general store to square away his mother's account. Mrs. Wilson, who was clearing the books, gave him a figure that didn't match the one Jesse had calculated, and they exchanged heated words over the matter. It seems that Jesse Lee must have been feeling a little spirited that day, because Blacks didn't normally contradict white folks, even if the Black person was right and the white person was wrong.

In any case, things apparently escalated to a point where Mr. Wilson heard the commotion, came in, and threw Jesse Lee out of the store, shouting after him, "Boy, I'll have you killed." A short while later, on the same day, Mr. Wilson called Eddie Lee—who was just a boy of ten or so then, and who worked odd jobs in the store—and sent him to "catch" Jesse Lee.

Eddie Lee, frightened and unaccustomed to disobeying white men, did go out to find Jesse Lee. But while the story is unclear about the details leading up to his capture, Jesse Lee was eventually taken by several white men. They beat him almost to death, bound him up, tied him to the back of a pick-up truck, and dragged him up and down the street right in front of the store and around the nearby farming community of Arlington before leaving his dead body in the field, where he was found.

Jesse Lee had been my mother's and Eddie Lee's favorite cousin. Eddie Lee began to drink soon after that and remained an alcoholic for most of his life. Eddie would continue to live there on the farm doing odd jobs long after the rest of us—Mother, Father, my little brother Junior, and I—were gone, and he was still there years later when both Mama Annie and Papa Elvin died. I believe that what happened to our cousin Jesse Lee crippled Cousin Eddie for life.

Over the years, I heard the elders talk about Jesse Lee's swollen and beaten corpse. In my imagination it ballooned and decayed into a grotesque, grisly, and barely identifiable monstrosity. It was an image that I could never, ever, completely erase from my mind. So, from the time of Jessie Lee's lynching, I began to see color and race. I began to recognize people whose skin I'd paid no particular attention to before as "white" or "Black."

We lived across the way from some white sharecroppers (they worked on somebody's dairy farm), and I had played with one of the little girls in that family without realizing or being conscious of her race. After hearing about Jesse Lee, I realized that white people were to be feared. In my mind, lynching became the most vicious symbol of white hatred toward Blacks—not just a horrifying possibility, but an ever-present danger. I became conscious of lynching as the violent response of whites against those of my color if we got on the wrong side of them. To this day, I associate pick-up trucks with white mobs. If I see several white people in a pick-up truck, a "danger" warning immediately goes off in my mind.

It was a time when southern Blacks lived in constant fear. It wasn't just discrimination, it was *sheer terror*. Any group of white men, any police officer you might see—in fact, any white man at all—was a reminder of their Jim Crow-enforced and state-sanctioned might and right to rule over our lives. So, we kept to ourselves, as best we could…and worked…and survived.

To this day, whenever I recall my childhood on the farm, Jesse Lee's lynching comes to mind. I can never remember the good times with Mama Annie, Papa Elvin, my brother, or anybody else without thinking of the lynching. It's not the dominant thing, but it certainly laid a primary and significant brick in the foundation of who I was to become.

The second incident affecting my awareness of the painful realities surrounding racial difference occurred a few years later. I was probably around six years old. It was my first *personal* encounter with the dynamics of race and, like hearing the story of Jesse Lee, it also occurred in "the Big House."

I had been born in the two-room "Little House," which had been built by Papa Elvin for Mother and Daddy when they married. But when Junior was barely two, Mother disappeared. We didn't know where she went, she was just gone. Soon after that, Papa, Junior, and I went to live with Mama Annie and Papa Elvin in the "Big House" on the hill.

In addition to farming his vast properties, Papa Elvin was also a barber for white men. He only cut white men's hair because back then a Black barber couldn't barber both Black and white men. If he was going to cut white folks' hair, he couldn't use the same clippers on Black folks. He had to choose: it was "either/or"—and "either" must have been more profitable.

Although barbering was chiefly Papa Elvin's side occupation, mostly performed on weekends, since he was farming during the week—it was still interesting that those white men would come into our house to get their hair cut. Normally, Black folks didn't have white folks coming to their house for anything. And unless you were working for them, you didn't go to white folks' houses for anything. But something made it acceptable for white folks to come to Papa Elvin to have their hair cut. I don't know what kind of understandings, relationships, or agreements made such an unusual break with the social code of segregation acceptable, but acceptable it was. Papa Elvin's fair skin, straight hair, and extensive property holdings may have made it so. Whatever it was, that arrangement was another reason I suspect that Papa Elvin's parents were near to white.

His old-fashioned barber chair was set up in the front bedroom where he and Mama Annie slept and where he kept various shaving creams, colognes, combs, brushes, and scissors. That room was also where his wooden Philco radio was kept. Most people in the area didn't have radios, so they would come to our house to listen whenever Joe Louis beat the white boxers—our vicarious experience of victory over white racism.

The incident in question had to do with a little white girl who accompanied her father to have Papa Elvin cut his hair. On that day,

I was playing with that customer's daughter, who was about the same age as I was. As we giggled and teased each other, she pulled one of my plaits.

Because I was always feisty—quick to give my brother and cousin a good punch if it seemed necessary, usually without consequence—I'm sure my response was something tantamount to an "Oh *really?* You ain't getting away *with that!*" Physically, I retaliated by pulling her stringy blonde hair, to which she screamed holy murder.

Did she suspect that her cries—those of a little white girl "set upon" by a Negro child—would draw a quick and aggressive response by her father? Perhaps.

Instead, my swift punishment came from another set of hands. Papa Elvin dropped his precious clippers on the floor and, within what seemed to be seconds, appeared near where we were playing at the foot of the bed.

Large and powerful, he leaned over and slapped me—hard. "Don't you *ever* hit a white woman again!" he hissed, his voice low but filled with emotions that I couldn't understand at the time. *"Don't you ever hit a white woman again!"* I was shocked...frightened...and confused. *What white woma*n? I wondered. Was he talking about that pale, silly little girl sitting next to me, her own eyes now wide with surprise at Papa Elvin's merciless retaliation for my crime? That slap at the hands of my beloved Papa Elvin confirmed a suspicion that had begun to grow in me after the story of Jesse Lee: *White people can do anything they want to you, and you are supposed to take it.*

That literal "slap in the face" stayed with me, another bit of proof regarding the imbalance of power between Blacks and whites in my child's mind. Years would pass, and my anxiety regarding both Jesse Lee's lynching and Papa Elvin's brutal response to my innocent horseplay with that white child would grow into a general cautious suspicion regarding *anything* involving white folks.

There was a third and final crisis that cemented in my mind the hatred and vile disregard whites had for Black people. It was that episode which would ultimately set my feet on the path of activism.

It was 1957, a year in which several seminal historical achievements occurred, both in the burgeoning Civil Rights Movement and in the integration of Blacks into new facets of American society. That year, the Southern Christian Leadership Conference (SCLC) was founded and beginning to organize. The country saw Perry H. Young become the first Black person to pilot a commercial airline flight on New York Airways. Martin Luther King Jr. gave his first speech at the Lincoln Memorial during the Prayer Pilgrimage, the biggest civil rights demonstration up to that point, with an estimated 25,000 to 30,000 in attendance. Althea Gibson broke the color line and won international tennis tournaments including Wimbledon and the U.S. Open. And, in spite of Senator Strom Thurmond's twenty-four-hour filibuster, Congress passed the Civil Rights Act of 1957.

Yet, while Blacks were making these inroads into many areas of American life, in the deep South another drama, that of the Little Rock Nine, was about to play out. I wasn't the only witness to be changed by that moment. It was a much-televised, heart-wrenching ordeal. If you were to ask even the most disinterested Blacks of a certain age how this wretched chapter of American history affected them, more than a few of them would say "It made me feel like getting out there and doing something." That's exactly how it made me feel.

At the time, I was married to Charles, the love of my life, and I was the young mother of a sweet, bright, eight-year-old daughter and a brand-new baby boy. Always a workhouse, Charles was a wonderful provider, and had finally managed to get a good job at Gentile Air Force base in Dayton, Ohio. We were poor as church mice, living in a tiny house on Gramont Avenue, but we were happy—as happy as we believed Black folks anywhere could be during those times.

Yet here I was, only weeks after the birth of my second child, and I was witnessing a scene that filled me with outrage for Black children across America. Cradling my newborn son Gregory to my breast, my eyes were pinned to the TV as I watched clips of the grim, beautiful countenances of Minnijean Brown, Elizabeth Eckford, Ernest Green, Gloria Ray, Terrence Roberts, Jefferson Thomas, Carlotta Walls, Thelma Mothershed, and Melba Pattillo as they made their way through a mob of more than a thousand angry white protestors.

That evening the newscaster described the drama surrounding "the Little Rock Crisis." On September 4th, Governor Orval Faubus deployed the Arkansas National Guard to block the nine Negro children who had been selected to integrate the school from entering Little Rock Central High School. Prayer vigils, national and international outrage, and even threats from President Dwight D. Eisenhower still hadn't helped the integration effort. It appeared that it would take strong action on Eisenhower's part to defeat the anti-desegregationist tactics.

My heart hurt watching that tragedy unfold on television. It was so much injustice for those children, barely older than my oldest child, to endure. I turned to Charles, shaking my head in disbelief, rocked by an outrage I couldn't describe. "Look at them, Charles...they're spitting on them!" I was so upset I was trembling. "Those brave little kids, facing that mob of nasty, screaming white folks...it just makes me sick."

My mind was whirling as I watched the Little Rock Nine courageously march into that school. "What am I doing?" I thought, full of self-reproach. "Those young people are out there braving all that injustice and hatred. I know how those hateful white people terrorized us, but here I am in safe, nice Dayton, not doing a thing to help the cause!" I fumed, as baby Greg stirred in my arms. "I ought to be doing something. I ought to be doing something about this whole racial thing! I mean, if those kids can do that, braving that mob to integrate that school, then I can certainly find some way to get involved." Nearby, my daughter Geri, precocious and polite, watched me curiously. I didn't have the words to explain my emotions, but I made a promise to myself, hugging baby Gregory tighter: "I am going to find a way to do my part!"

The seeds of frustration that had been planted during my childhood in Jim Crow Tennessee were given a heavy dose of fertilizer, courtesy of Arkansas' Governor Orval Faubus and nine impossibly brave young souls. Today, when I'm asked about the "how" and "why" of my journey toward activism, those three memories stand out, even among many others. The family tragedy of Jesse Lee's lynching has remained with me. By the time Emmett Till was killed in 1955, I was in my early twenties and had moved to Cleveland, away from the Deep South, but the visceral horror of fourteen-year-old Till's lynching felt personal. To this day, whenever I hear of violence against Blacks, I still think of Jesse Lee.

The bruising of my flesh at the hand of Papa Elvin was a shock to my childhood self that marked more than my cheek. It left me with a deep sense of the injustice perpetuated against Black bodies in the name of upholding white supremacy. And much later, the brutality enacted against the Little Rock Nine shook me to my core as a young mother filled with anger at those who would abuse children in such a way. Those three life events became the germinating seeds of my desire to change our circumstances, to defend my people at all costs from a society that continues to slap us down, literally and figuratively. It would still be several years before I could finally act on my promise. But I, like many Blacks, was becoming tired of simply turning the other cheek.

Henry Grinner

Florence drum major at Manassas High School
(1944 or 1946)

Mama Annie

Papa Elvin as a young man

From the FBI FILES of FLORENCE L. TATE

The following description of Florence Louise Tate was obtained from various records:

Name: Florence Louise Tate
Sex: Female
Race: Negro
Nationality:American
Date of Birth: June 29, 1931
Place of Birth: Memphis, Tennessee
Height: 5'4"
Weight: 135 pounds
Build: Medium
Hair: Black
Residence: 333 Westwood, Dayton, Ohio
Former Residence: 529 Gramont, Dayton,
Ohio
Employment: Housewife
Former Employer: Dayton Daily News; Ohio
Bell Telephone Company; Alcoa Industries,
Incorporated; all Dayton, Ohio.
Marital Status: Married
Husband: Charles Edward Tate
Education: High school graduate and
attended Le Moyne College

CHAPTER 2

GROUND

The FBI had some facts wrong.

I was actually born in the town of Eads, about 30 miles outside of Memphis, Tennessee, on June *21*, 1931. I grew up in deep rural country with rich Black earth, wild grass fields, and no electricity. The Tennessee Valley Authority (TVA) electrification project hadn't reached us yet.

I was born at home and delivered by a midwife. There was no such thing as hospital births for Black people in that part of Tennessee back in 1931. I was Mother and Daddy's first child. They were barely out of high school when they married, two seventeen-year-olds thrown together by fate.

My mother, Callie Francis, was an orphan. She was taken in by her Aunt Annie, her mother's sister, whom I called Mama Annie (although she was actually my grand aunt), after her parents died in the worldwide flu epidemic of 1918. Mother grew up on the farm in Eads with Mama Annie's husband, my Papa Elvin (actually my grand uncle), her brother (my Uncle Jim), and her cousin Eddie Lee.

Meanwhile, Daddy was growing up in the home of his mother, my Grandmama Ida, and his stepfather, Grandpapa Joe, in nearby Arlington, Tennessee. Grandpapa Joe wasn't Daddy's real father. Nobody ever knew who Daddy's father was, because Daddy was conceived and born in Baton Rouge, Louisiana, where Grandmama Ida had gone to teach school for a while. She'd eventually returned to Arlington with a baby named Henry—my father—who Grandpapa Joe raised as his own after they married.

Grandpapa Joe was Papa Elvin's brother, so Mother and Daddy grew up as cousins. Not kissing cousins, as they weren't related by blood, but they saw each other often enough and eventually went to high school together at Barrage Chapel, the sleep-away high school that all the Black teenagers in the region attended.

Somewhere along the way they married, and I came along. But while their marriage might have been inevitable, their differences were ultimately insurmountable. Years later, it became apparent why my father, a serious-minded educator, and my mother—a lover of excitement, beautiful clothes, and many men—couldn't stay together. There were stark differences in the way Mama Annie and Grandmama Ida raised them. Although it wasn't discussed in terms of class differences, there was definitely a clashing of ways.

One day, without apparent warning, Mother just up and disappeared. I was not yet four, and my brother wasn't even two.

Whenever I asked where my mother was, Mama Annie would just say, "Well, we don't really know where Callie is." This "not knowing" would occur again over the years whenever Mother popped in and out of the picture. Nobody ever knew "where Callie was" until she showed up unexpectedly after an absence of months or sometimes years.

Mama Annie was the one who told me that my mother was a very beautiful woman and that, even from an early age, Mother aspired toward more than a life on a country farm. She wanted to be glamorous.

"Even as a little girl picking cotton, she would come home from the field and use my red paper roses from the living room, and she would spit on the roses and paint her lips with them," Mama Annie would tell me.

I only remember my mother coming back to Eads a couple of times after she left. It would be during holidays like Easter and Christmas. I remember that she brought me little dresses and shoes during her infrequent and brief visits. But Mama Annie never talked badly about my mother. As a matter of fact, she talked about her fondly, reminiscing about "when Callie was coming up…" or "when Callie did this…" or "when Callie did that…." It was obvious that Mama Annie had a soft spot for my mother.

"Your mother likes the big city," Mama Annie would say, by way of explanation. "She doesn't like this small, slow place," she'd tell me.

In Mother's defense, on her deathbed she told me (although it was more like an absent-minded memory she was recalling), "I tried to get Grinner"— that was my father, Henry Grinner—"to move to the city, and he just wouldn't move." I later understood that this was her way of explaining to me why she left Eads…and us.

After Mother's desertion, Daddy had his hands full trying to handle Junior and me alone in the Little House; but it soon became clear that he couldn't take care of us by himself while teaching at the schoolhouse down the road. So, we moved up to the Big House, where Mama Annie assumed the responsibility of tending to us.

Within the next year or two, my father was made the principal of the Bartlett School in Oak Grove, which, being twenty or thirty miles from Eads, was still considered somewhat of a distance away. He moved there and eventually met and married another schoolteacher, Malinda Dorsey. Very soon he too became a distant figure. So, basically without warning or explanation, my brother and I were left at the Big House to be raised by Mama Annie and Papa Elvin—abandoned, as I came to think of it.

After Daddy departed, I don't remember him coming back to see us at the farm. If he did so, it was very infrequently. But I do remember going to see him in Arlington where he lived with his new wife and baby daughter—my darling sister Lucille, who would become my best friend.

During those visits, I came to understand that my father was an important person in his community. He was a deacon, well-loved not only in his church but by his neighbors and the many teachers and students he influenced. He was held in high esteem and addressed as "Professor Grinner" by both Blacks and whites alike. He was a brilliant conversationalist, teacher, an avid reader, member of the NAACP, and a very good joke teller. Daddy was also a gifted cartoonist who made extra money painting signs.

My father was also what was called "a race man." I remember visiting the Bartlett School over the years, where I would sit in on my father's classes, awed and adoring, listening as he taught Black history, Black literature and poetry, and Black politics.

Along with politics, it seemed clear my love of learning and letters came from his side. My father had gone to college, and he had become a teacher and principal. His mother, Grandmama Ida, had also gone to college and had also become a teacher and school principal.

When I was young, I'd often wondered why nobody else's parents or grandparents that I knew had gone to college. But years later, a cousin went to the National Archives and found all the records, including my paternal great-grandfather's veteran papers, and it all came together.

My Grandmama Ida had to have been born just as Negroes were coming out of slavery, and my great-great-grandparents would have definitely been slaves. Her grandfather and my great-great-grandfather, Henry Thomas, fought with the Union in the colored troops brigades during the Civil War. Great-great-grandfather's name is listed among the 220,000 other Black troops who served, whose information is included in exhibits housed in the African American Civil War Memorial Museum in Washington, DC. According to stories, he escaped from the plantation and traveled up to the District of Columbia, where a Union camp was located. He eventually was sent to a camp in Virginia and joined a unit that took care of calvary horses. After the war, he was discharged as a veteran, returned to Tennessee, and got a veteran's pension. That was how he was able to send his children to college.

My great-great-grandfather couldn't read or write, but upon his military discharge, he was asked a series of questions, most of the answers to which were recorded on a form that someone—a clerk, presumably—filled out for him. According to my cousin, one of the questions on the form was "Who is your father?" His answer (as written by the clerk): *"I think my master is my father."* Where the form asked for a signature, he had written the obligatory "X"—the universal signature of slaves and illiterate workers who couldn't write.

Although Grandmama Ida and my father were college graduates, they were still simple people who grew up and lived in the country, went to school, and returned to their rural roots to teach. They never lived in the city or "learned city ways," but they were educated and clearly held different values and beliefs than Mama Annie and my mother, Callie.

During my childhood on the farm, Mama Annie had told me that Grandmama Ida wanted me aborted because she didn't want my father to come out of school and get married. I suspected, however, that she meant get married to Callie, specifically. Mama Annie would never have let Callie have an abortion or, as they called it, "kill the baby."

"We didn't want to kill the baby"—meaning *me*—was her way of letting me know that she had saved my life. In other words, if it had been left up to Grandmama Ida, I guess I wouldn't even have been here. Although Grandmama Ida was born in Tennessee, she had gone to Baton Rouge to teach. "Ida learned all of that voodoo stuff down there, and she knew how to do things that would kill a baby," Mama Annie asserted. "But I wouldn't let her make Callie do it."

In any case, I was born and, for a short time, I had a mother and a father...and then I didn't. But the lessons I learned from my father— and later those I gained attending Memphis' historic Manassas School,[1] where our principal, James Ashton Hayes, conducted Black history programs throughout the year—gave me a thorough grounding in both the pinnacles of achievement of Black people and the horrors of slavery and racism experienced by our race. Both men instilled in me a deep, abiding passion for anything having to do with Black culture and Black politics. And although I didn't know it at the time, they gave birth to my evolving race consciousness.

Despite feeling abandoned by my parents, I consider myself very fortunate to have grown up in the country because I think—in fact, *I know*—that it played a large part in grounding me. That foundation gave me what some would later call frankness, honesty, and what I believe is just basic human decency.

After both my parents left, I grew up on the farm alongside my little brother and a cousin named Jewelle, who was not much younger than I was. It was a near repetition of how Mother had grown up years earlier along with her brother and their cousin Eddie Lee.

Papa Elvin's farm was made up of the Big House, which had a living room, dining room, two bedrooms, a kitchen, and a front and back porch; the cotton house, where he kept cotton picked from his fields until it went to be ginned; the smokehouse, where the pigs and hogs were slaughtered, cured, and hung; and pens that held cows and chickens. There was also an orchard with peaches, pears, and apples;

---

1   This primary-through-twelfth grade school was conceived and built by Blacks in 1899.

Blackberry bushes; and a persimmon tree in the front yard. I'll never forget the taste of persimmons because when they were ripe, they were so good and sweet and juicy, but if you bit into one before it ripened, it would turn your lips inside out. There was also a pond with fish and a water well and a garden with all kind of vegetables: corn, potatoes, sweet potatoes, turnips, and turnip greens. I learned a lot as I watched Mama Annie plant the garden. I watched as the vegetables grew and I learned when and how to pick them. Mama Annie would can the harvested fruits and vegetables for the winter and put them in the cellar.

For bread, there were the biscuits Mama Annie would make for breakfast or cornbread that was made from corn grown on the farm that would be ground to meal. Everything was homemade—cakes, pies, ice cream, everything. Mama Annie kept the cakes and the pies that we would have for dessert on Sunday in the corner of the dining room in a little triangular cupboard wedged against the walls. We didn't have dessert with our regular meals, but on Sunday we would have coconut cake or peach or apple pie made with fruit from the orchard.

Mama Annie also made homemade plum wine and peach brandy by putting the fruit in a jar with lots of sugar and letting it ferment for the whole year. It was customary to serve wine and brandy along with cake during Christmas visiting time. The brandy would be kept under the bed. As kids, we would sneak under the bed and take sips of it. Mama Annie would, of course, be able to tell that we had sipped the brandy and she would yell, "You kids been in that brandy again!"

Life on the farm was entirely self-sufficient. Everything we ate came from the farm. I didn't know anything about store-bought food. There was no need to go to the store to buy anything, although sometimes we'd go to the store to buy "store-bought candy" or a soda pop with the little change Mama Annie gave us from her apron pocket.

Mama Annie was a real farmwife, responsible for doing farm work from sunup to sundown: feeding the livestock, gathering the eggs, milking the cow, and trying to keep the Big House, where we all lived, clean. She was also a businesswoman, and she made extra money by selling supplies such as extra eggs and butter and "church candy" bought wholesale from Gray's Creek Baptist Church.

Mama Annie didn't have children of her own. She lived through a very unhappy marriage with my Papa Elvin, mostly because of White Effie, the albino girl he'd built a house for on a portion of his property and stayed with much of the time.

Although other people in Eads had much less than we did, it did not matter much what one's parents had or didn't have. All the Black people lived together in the same, truly segregated community, with no "race mixing." Blacks and whites did not mingle, fraternize, or socialize. In our community, we had our own everything: Black churches, Black schools, Black everything (except the country store).

I remember that even our doctor was a Black man, Dr. Thomas, who had what they called a "circuit." Under Jim Crow, Blacks didn't go to a white doctor or hospital. Dr. Thomas lived in Memphis, but once a month or maybe once a week during seasons of illness, he would come to each house with his little Black bag to see if "everybody was alright in there" and to check on whether anybody needed medicine for a cold, the croup, rheumatism, or pellagra. He also would have quinine for malaria, which still affected many people in our area.

Aside from the poor white sharecroppers who lived across the highway, Eads was an almost totally Black community. We supported each other, before integration, and even if some of us struggled, we were able to take care of most of our needs without integration.

Within the boundaries and economic limitations of racially segregated Eads, we, as children, were protected. We were basically at home with our families, in school, or at church. We didn't step outside the Black community. It was only the adults who interfaced with whites regularly and had to confront the racism that created segregation.

On occasion, Papa Elvin and Mama Annie would go to Memphis to do some shopping. Most of the people we knew didn't go to Memphis. It was a big thing, going there. Most just went to the little store by the train tracks in Eads. If they had a little more money, they would also shop at the dry goods store in Arlington. Mama Annie and Papa Elvin always had more than the rest of the people around us. While other folks had only wagons and horses, Papa Elvin and Mama Annie always had a car. And once in a while they would drive to Memphis to the Black &White department store or to the more upscale Bry's.

It was taking those trips to Memphis from Eads with Mama Annie and Papa Elvin that introduced me to the larger reality of segregation. The irony was that, while segregation meant that there was no socializing between Blacks and whites—no close social contact, no interracial contact in schools, churches, restaurants, or movie theaters—Black people could go into grocery stores and department stores and spend their money.

Of course, you couldn't try on clothes, as there was rarely a Black-only dressing room. And some department stores didn't even have colored-only bathrooms, so you had better hope you didn't have to use the bathroom when you shopped there. The segregated department stores—Gerber's, Bry's, and Goldsmith's—also had segregated cafes that Blacks couldn't go into. At some point, Goldsmith's finally opened a small space in the back where Blacks could have a little sandwich or something, but we couldn't eat in their dining room. So, after shopping, we would all go to eat at the North Memphis Cafe on North Main Street, where all the Black folks from the countryside generally went. It was probably white-owned, as most things were, but only Black people ate there.

North Main Street was where the then so-called "colored" folks went to spend their money. Normally, we'd never go to the other end of Main Street—South Main Street offered nothing for Black people, for the most part. We could walk down there, but generally speaking, we'd be like tourists—just looking, not really having anything to do. It was just understood that *that* part of Main Street wasn't for us. It was through these early outings that I would truly come to understand segregation as a toxic and noxious system that Blacks were just expected to accept and submit to.

When I was eight years old, my mother finally came to get me from the Big House. I was glad and excited to be going with her because I had been missing her for so long. I don't remember how I felt leaving my brother Henry and my cousin Jewelle or leaving the home where I had lived with Mama Annie and Papa Elvin since I was little more than a toddler. I don't remember anything but being thrilled that Mother had come for me.

The fact was that I really had no idea who this woman was that I was going off to live with or where she was taking me. I didn't know anything about my mother or her life. And she didn't know anything about me—or about raising children.

Mother took me to a house on Manassas Street in North Memphis, where she lived with Mr. Jamison, an older man whom she had "married" and set up housekeeping with. The way I saw it, Mr. Jamison was the man she left us for. They'd met while she was still in Eads, at what they called the annual "association"—that is, when all the Baptist churches in the surrounding counties would gather for a convocation of church officials. When my mother met Mr. Jamison, a deacon at Gospel Temple Baptist Church, she was twenty-five and very beautiful. He was in his fifties (at least) and always smelled of liquor. Mother wanted to get out of the country and, while I won't say that Mr. Jamison lured her or that she lured him, their coming together was the way she ended up in Memphis.

Mr. Jamison's mother, Mama J., and his grandson Bobby lived with him. His six-room house was painted white and had nice front and back yard. It was, by the standards of the time, a proverbial "house with a white picket fence." It also bordered an alley, which was a new, citified word for me.

Mr. Jamison was the rent collector for all the little three-room, shotgun houses with tiny front yards in the twelve-to-sixteen square blocks of Manassas, Wells, Tully, and Marble Streets. A white woman named Liz or rather, "Miz Fisher," owned the houses. I remember her coming by on Saturdays. She would pull up in her Black Model-T Ford, and he would hand her an envelope filled with rent money. I first thought the little houses must have been slave shacks, but later discovered they had been army barracks during the Civil War, and Mr. Jamison's big white house was where the commanding officer once lived.

My mother was always, until the day she died, a meticulous housekeeper. Bobby and I were not allowed in the living room or the dining room. We could play in our room—the room we shared with Mama J., that is—or in the yard or in the alley. Bobby and I slept together on a rollaway bed, head-to-toe and toe-to-head. Our room, much like Mama J. herself, was dark and musty. She was a heavy, gray-haired old lady and mean as a snake.

Reverend Kemp was the fire-and-brimstone preaching pastor at Mr. Jamison's church. Gospel Temple was only a stone's throw from where we lived, and we went to church every Sunday. In fact, we went three times, starting with Sunday school, followed by the 11 a.m. service, and finally, the 6:00 p.m. Baptist Young People's Union. Sometimes, we also attended services during the week. Mother and Mr. Jamison would go together. Mama J., Bobby, and I would follow. I dreaded those services.

The devil became a real person and hell a real place for me during the three years we lived with Mr. Jamison and attended services at Gospel Temple Baptist Church. I have held onto those feelings ever since. The overbearing religious indoctrination made me feel trapped and uncomfortable, feelings that subconsciously lingered into my adult life and crept into my parenting style years later, resulting in my ambivalent relationship with the church to this very day. When suffering from my deepest bouts of depression, I told countless psychiatrists that my lingering and very real fear of going to hell was the one thing that kept me from suicide.

I hadn't been living with Mother very long before a feeling of disillusionment sunk in. Though initially I was very excited about being with her, before long I started to suspect that she didn't really want me there. I felt unwanted, as if I was in her way, and I was pretty much treated that way. Mother neglected me emotionally and physically. She never hugged me or told me she loved me or complimented me about anything. She never checked on my homework or seemed to care at all about my general well-being. We rarely talked the way I wanted us to. Basically, she was curt, distant, and intolerant—and that was at her very best.

Mother loved to dress up, and she was the most beautiful woman at Gospel Temple, where she sang in the choir. She did not dress me nearly as well, and I was always ashamed of the way I looked compared to her. Once Mother overheard some of her choir members talking about how well she dressed and how shabbily she dressed me. It was only then that she took me shopping at Sears & Roebuck's for school clothes and for Sunday clothes like my friends had.

I remember my mother whipping me for small things like, for instance, if she caught me reading a book instead of cleaning. My mother was not one for sitting around reading books. I had to be up cleaning or doing something like that, and she wanted everything cleaned in a very particular way. I had to be down on my hands and knees, scrubbing the floors and floorboards long and hard until they looked just right. If she didn't think I'd put enough labor in, I'd surely get a whipping.

Getting whippings came to an end when I was about twelve, however. I can still remember the last one. My mother got the strap and came toward me, but I had had enough. "Oh, no, uh-uh, you're not doing that to me anymore," I'd snarled, holding my arm in front of me to protect myself. By that time I was a big girl and stood eyeball-to-eyeball with her, so I was able to grab her by the wrist and stop her from hitting me. I'm not sure what lightbulb turned on for my mother, but something in her changed that day, and she never tried to hit me again. I was still a minor and still under her rule, but she seemed to realize that she couldn't physically discipline me anymore and seemed to have a different kind of respect for me after that.

We lived with Mr. Jamison during my third-, fourth-, and fifth-grade years. During my sixth-grade year, something happened between Mother and Mr. Jamison, and she sent me to live with Uncle Jim and Aunt Pina.

After sending me to their house, Mother disappeared again. Of course, it reminded me of how she had left me with Mama Annie and Papa Elvin when I was little more than a toddler. This time I was almost a teenager, but I realized it was my mother's pattern. "Go pack up your stuff and go to Aunt Pina's," was Mother's way of letting me know she was about to take flight.

Without asking any questions, I packed up my little parcel of belongings, walked to the bus station, and rode the bus over to Aunt Pina's. I didn't know when I'd see Mother again, and I didn't ask. I just knew I'd have to make my way on the bus, or walking, from Aunt Pina's to school and back. I lived with Aunt Pina and Uncle Jim during my sixth- and seventh-grade years.

I felt almost homeless through much of my childhood, shuttling back and forth between family members. When I lived with Mama

Annie and Papa Elvin, my Aunt Pina, who taught school, would sometimes come and take me for the summer. Aunt Pina was my father's stepsister, Grandpapa Joe's daughter by a former marriage. Grandpapa Joe was also Papa Elvin's brother. Aunt Pina, Daddy, Mother, and Mother's brother Jim all grew up together. Eventually, in the same manner Daddy married Mother, Aunt Pina ended up marrying Uncle Jim. So going to live with Aunt Pina and Uncle Jim signified the comfort of family on both sides. Even if it wasn't *my* home, it was a home where I was welcome. Still, I wondered again why Mother had ever come to get me.

But there was one good thing in my life that I came to excel in and rely on: school. Manassas Elementary and High School was a place where I was able to shine, and it fostered the love of learning that proved to me that I was, indeed, my father's child.

During my childhood years in Memphis, the Manassas school became the only consistent thing in my life. I excelled in school. I was very smart and must have had a winning personality because all the children liked me, as did the teachers. In many ways, Manassas became a substitute for family. The teachers were like parents, the principal was like the father of the school, and my classmates and other students stood in for my brother Junior and cousin Jewelle, both of whom I'd lost after moving with Mother to Memphis.

At Manassas, the faculty and administrators made it a point to make us kids feel good about ourselves and recognize us for our achievements and talents. I couldn't wait to get to school, and I would be sorry when school was out for the summer because school was where I felt loved and appreciated.

Mr. Hayes, our principal, brought a parade of great Negroes to Manassas: saxophonist and bandleader Jimmie Lunceford, groundbreaking educator Mary McLeod Bethune, and heralded opera singers Roland Hayes and Dorothy Maynor. Assembled in the school's large auditorium, we'd gather to hear these inspiring and eminent guests discuss their experiences and share their talents.

Mr. Hayes would always present us to the guests, proudly expressing how beautiful and smart we were, and leading us—students ranging from the first through the twelfth grade—in a song. "Look at how beautiful they are, in every shade of our race, from lily white to cockroach brown," he'd grandly pronounce. He would then lead us in the popular song, *"Let Me Call You Sweetheart,"* directing us to follow his pencil baton with our heads as we sang. It was one of our favorite rituals.

Mr. Hayes was a strict disciplinarian who strongly believed in order and manners. Each classroom teacher had a "permit," a thick wooden 4" x 6" block with the teacher's name on it. This block was given to a student when he or she needed to leave the classroom for any reason such as going to the bathroom, drinking from the water fountain, or being called to the office. If a student was caught in the hallway without a permit, he or she would get "strap-licks" on an extended hand. We also got whippings for being late for school, talking back to teachers, fighting, or running up and down the stairways. There were no disorderly clumps of students scurrying from here to there. We marched in orderly fashion and to the rhythm of military anthems playing through the halls when changing classes, going to assemblies, or being released for recess. You didn't just "turn the corner" at Manassas, you made a military swivel, performed with precision. And we loved it! Somehow, all of this made school more fun.

I still remember the names of my teachers from the third through twelfth grades. All were good, many were outstanding. My most memorable teachers include Miss West, my third-grade teacher and my first teacher at Manassas. She was responsible for my being called Florence rather than Louise, the middle name my family had always called me. To this day, only my close relatives and long-time friends still call me Louise.

Miss Martin, my fifth-grade teacher, was brown-skinned, freckled, with a short bob, and proper speech. She had us memorize lots of poems, and we wrote our own in her class. One day she beat my legs so badly, they bled. She seemed determined to make me cry in front of a group of boys who were in the hall practicing for a musical performance. But my little boyfriend, Edward Lewis Smith, was in that group—and I was determined not to cry. Miss Martin kept beating me until I think *she* got scared. Today, she'd be hauled into court for child abuse and rightfully so. I was used to being disciplined with a paddle or a strap, but this went beyond discipline into cruelty. Forty years later, I saw her at the wedding of a friend's daughter and she said, "I bet you don't remember me, do you?" Giving her a cold eye, I replied tersely: "Oh yes, I remember you" —and kept on moving.

Miss Boyd, my seventh-grade English and homeroom teacher, was skinny and severe. She ingrained in her students the history of the English language, the rules of grammar, and how to dissect a sentence. Miss Sylvers, my eighth-grade math and homeroom teacher, had me double-promoted to the ninth grade.

Then there was Miss Threat, an algebra teacher in whose class I met my lifelong friend Sara, mother of Judge Jayne Chandler; and Mr. Weed, my eleventh-grade chemistry teacher who was rotund, funny, and wacky. He had chemical signs and symbols posted on the walls all around his classroom. He spent his time teaching only the A- and B-grade students, totally ignoring the other students. He would tell the others, "Just come to class, bring your book, look around the room, and get your basic C," before turning his attention to the five or ten of us who he decided were smart enough to command his attention.

Miss Fingal, my eleventh- and twelfth-grade English literature teacher, was the organizer and director of the Speakers and Writers Club, of which I was a member. My tenth-grade biology teacher was Mr. Williams, who later became well-known as "Moohah," the program director at the first Black radio station in Memphis: *WDAO: Home of Rufus Thomas, BB King, Johnny Ace, Booker T and the MGs, Carla Thomas, Al Green, and the Memphis sound!"* Of course, there was also Miss Ross, the librarian, Mr. Hayes's "special friend." She was the costumer and director for majorettes in the band and the drum-and-bugle core. I was the drum major for both during my time at Manassas. I was also chosen as "Miss Manassas" when I was in the eleventh grade. Miss Ross was a friendly, wonderful woman, and we were always wondering why Mr. Hayes didn't marry her.

I also remember Mr. McDaniels, who was the bandmaster for both Manassas and our arch-rival: Booker T. Washington School. He produced outstanding marching bands and jazz orchestras at both schools. From Manassas emerged talented jazz musicians Frank Strozier, Edward Lewis Smith, Calvin Jones, Andrew Goodrich, several college band directors, and a number of music teachers. From Booker T. Washington hailed Phineas Newborn, a genius at the piano.

I felt safe and appreciated at Manassas, more so than I ever did living with my mother and whatever "husband" she was with. So, no matter where I was living, I would find a way to get to that school. While most children in the neighborhood walked to the school, I would usually been seen getting off at the nearest bus stop to attend my beloved Manassas.

Mother re-appeared and brought me back to live with her when I was in the eighth grade. We roomed with a woman in the same neighborhood as Mr. Jamison's house. We were there for a few months before Mother "married" Mr. Cole, an older gentleman just down the street. Then we moved in with him. I'm not sure there were any real marriages or divorces going on during these relationships. I do know that I was ashamed of my mother's behavior.

My oldest friend, Josephine Bridges, was a confidante and source of comfort for me during those years. Josie, who became a record producer for the renowned Stax record label, witnessed my despair and frustration while I lived with Mother.

Josephine Bridges: *I met Florence when I was in third grade; she was in the fourth. Florence was extremely smart. She skipped the fifth grade and went to the sixth grade, then skipped the seventh grade and went to the eighth. She was really smarter than the teachers, I think. She had a wonderful personality and was a pretty girl. She was the drum major of the band, she was in the literary clubs, French club, everything—because she just surpassed everybody.*

Florence had a really rough time 'cause she was living with her aunts most of the time—anywhere that she could live, basically. Florence was just out there. She would go home with different ones of us and eat dinner 'cause she had no certain place every day to eat, no home to go to.

I remember one time we went up to the library to get our library cards. The librarian said, "OK, just give me your mother's name." She must have looked it up in her address files because I got my card. Another girl named Betty was with us and the librarian asked her for her mother's name; after she looked it up, this girl also got her card.

But when it came to be Florence's turn, the librarian said, "Give me your mother's name." "How about Callie Grinner?" Florence said, and the librarian looked in her files and said "No, I don't see that." "How about Callie Jamison?" Florence tried again. "No…," the librarian said. "Well, how about… Callie Branch?" Again, the librarian said, "No," and Florence must have tried six names. And then she said, "Well then, just forget it!" After we dropped Betty off along the route home, Florence started to cry. "Everyone else can get a library card but me 'cause I don't even know my mother's name, she's had so many husbands!" I remember that really did hurt her. It was just sad.

I remember one time—we were in about the eighth or ninth grade—and Callie told me, "Josephine, your teeth are beautiful, so pretty and white. But Florence, your teeth are rotten across the front, don't you smile with your bad teeth." She didn't even realize that it was insulting.

Callie also had the prettiest house: clean, neat, and immaculate. But Florence only had a small bedroom with just a bed in it–the worst looking room, nothing in there. And Callie's was beautiful… but she couldn't see anything wrong with that. Florence didn't want to stay there, mostly because once when she was there, she bumped into this man in the hall who was wearing her robe as he was going to the bathroom.

Still, despite all she went through, Florence was one of the most popular girls in Memphis.

Mother always loved decorating a house, and she fixed Mr. Cole's up like a doll's house. It had two bedrooms, a tiny living room, dining room, kitchen, and a bath. I slept on a day bed in the dining room. The other bedroom was a guest bedroom, but we never had guests, and I wasn't allowed to have friends in the house, except for Lloyd—a boy at school who I liked and who liked me—and who, for some reason, my mother seemed to find agreeable.

Mother stayed married to Mr. Cole until I was in the tenth grade. Then one day she decided that, once again, it was time to move on. Since moving on with me was not a part of her plans, she must have thought of Lloyd as one way to get me "off her plate."

"If y'all are so in love, why don't you get married?" she spouted out one day when Lloyd was visiting. I was shocked; Lloyd was seventeen, and I was fifteen. I'm not sure what answer we gave her, but I knew I wasn't planning on marrying anyone at fifteen. Not long after asking us that, she told me to get my things together, that I was going back over to Aunt Pina's. I guess I took too long to get it together, and she couldn't wait because I came home from school one evening and she was gone. She'd split…and left me there with Mr. Cole. A few days after she left, Mr. Cole—who had always been kind to me—tried to molest me. That was all I needed. Once again, fifteen and alone, I quickly hit the road, escaping to Aunt Pina's. I would complete my tenth- and eleventh-grade years there, in the safe confines of her and Uncle Jim's home.

Florence and her mother, Callie 1950

Florence and Sarah McKinnie

CHAPTER 3

UP NORTH

Mother reappeared in Memphis in 1947, my senior year of high school. This time she was married to Cornelius House—a very good-looking man whose light skin and curly hair made it impossible to determine his race. They met while he was in the Navy and she was working in the kitchen of the naval base in Millington, a service town about eighteen miles from Memphis. Mother and Mr. House were living in the Foote Homes, a housing project in South Memphis that was generally considered to be a very good place to live in those days. The two-story, red brick apartments had yards and gardens, a commons for every three u-shaped apartment complexes, and a social center where community activities and teenage dances were held.

Foote Homes was in close proximity to Booker T. Washington High School, the archrival of my own Manassas High. Since she lived closer to Booker T., when Mother came to collect me from Aunt Pina's she expected me to complete my senior year at that high school. Of course, this became a huge point of contention between us.

Before this, we had always lived in North Memphis, which wasn't as urban or sophisticated as South Memphis. This difference also applied to the schools. Although, for the most part, Black children were poor everywhere, those whose parents were professionals— doctors, lawyers, and teachers—lived in South Memphis and went to Booker T. Washington.

Booker T. clearly had an advantage in terms of facilities and resources. Thinking back, I attribute that to Mr. Hunt, its principal. Mr. Hunt appeared to be what I would consider your basic accommodationist. He'd "toe the line" and avoided bucking the system in any way. Perhaps this earned him favor with the white superintendent and the all-white board of education.

Perhaps this is why Booker T. had an actual shop facility where the boys could learn welding, while Manassas had a little shed where the boys went to learn carpentry. It might also explain why Booker T. had a football field and stadium, while the boys at Manassas had to play on the same grassy playground that the other students used for recess. Booker T. also had a school of cosmetology, where girls could learn how to do hair and makeup. We didn't have anything like that at Manassas. Plus, the band at Booker T. would get new instruments and new uniforms, and the girls in the marching troupe had new boots. At Manassas, our instruments were hand-me-downs from the white schools that sent us their leftover equipment and used instruments.

This unequal treatment and disparity in resources was probably the basis for the long-held rivalry between the two Black schools' football teams. It was always a big event when they competed against one another. The games were always played at Booker T. since they had the stadium and the football field. While we didn't have access to the same quality of resources, our team still won sometimes, and our band was just as good as their band!

At Manassas, our principal, Mr. Hayes, would do what had to be done to keep his job and to keep our school open. He followed the rules and regulations, but he also subverted authority and rebelled in various ways. Under his leadership, the focus at Manassas was about instilling pride in who we were and giving us a sense of individual value. As far as I was concerned, Booker T. Washington could have whatever it had, but I still loved Manassas. There was never any jealousy about what they had versus what we had; it was just a recognition that we were different in terms of resources.

Very few parents of Manassas students were professionals. The school was located in North Memphis, which had been settled by ex-slaves and their descendants. The residents of North Memphis were, for the most part, people from rural backgrounds. I'm sure my initial transition to the city from Papa Elvin and Mama Annie's farm had been somewhat eased by those circumstances. If I had gone to a different school when I'd first come to live with Mother, my transition might have been more difficult. It helped me feel more comfortable, coming from the country, that Manassas was a school in the middle of a community settled by rural people.

That is why, when I was brought to live at Foote Homes, I put up a real fight to remain at Manassas, even though I lived within two blocks of Booker T. Washington High School.

My mother opposed me on this because I would need carfare every day to attend Manassas. "Why do you want to go all the way over there? You could throw a pebble and hit Booker T.!" she insisted. "I'm not going to Booker T. Washington! I'm going to Manassas, even if I have to walk all the way there!" I protested loudly. Eventually she gave in, and she and Mr. House came up with that seven cents from somewhere. And so, I took the bus, making two transfers, all the way across town back to Manassas.

By then, as a teenager, Mother couldn't do anything to me physically anymore. I was as tall, if not taller, than her; but she still did things to me that I considered mean. Since Mother didn't believe in having me "sittin' around," a favorite assignment from her was to wax and polish the floors. Mother was so proud of her genuine hardwood floors (which every apartment in Foote Homes had) that she made sure I got down on my hands and knees and waxed and polished those floors almost daily or else she made sure I was washing the windows or scrubbing the walls—just doing something, anything, to make sure I stayed "busy."

To escape, I would sneak off somewhere to read a book. Mother was not a book person; Daddy was the book person. With the exception of a Bible that she acquired later on, my mother didn't own any books. If I wanted to read, I had to go to Edna's, a girl I'd made friends with, who lived in the house across the alley.

Throughout my school years, Mother only allowed one or two of my friends to come visit me at the house. Although we had a telephone, I wasn't allowed use it. If I tried to talk on the phone, she would hang it up right in the middle of my conversation.

By then, I was a senior in high school with a busy social life centered around Manassas. I also had a few friends at the Foote Homes: Edna, who lived across the alley, and my lifelong friend Joyce. I regarded my Manassas friends as my family, especially Sarah McKinnie, Josephine, and another girl, Barbara; and I depended on them for emotional support. Soon, I also had a new boyfriend: Leon Morris, the captain of the football team.

Young people, I was to learn much later, will look for love in the outside world when they do not receive it at home. Cute, smart, and popular, I got pregnant in the twelfth grade. I was about three months along when I graduated, although it didn't show. Leon and I got married in the late summer of 1948 and I went to live with him and his family in Lemoyne Gardens. Lemoyne Gardens was another garden apartment project, but it was not as nice as the Foote Homes.

Leon started working at United Parcel, which was in the vicinity of where we lived. Since Lemoyne College was just across the street from Lemoyne Gardens, I started college there that fall on the scholarship I'd received upon graduation from Manassas. I'd received scholarships from several other colleges, including Talladega and Fisk, but it was no longer feasible for me to attend any of those colleges. I was a student by day and a pregnant wife by night. My high school friends, Sarah and Joyce, also enrolled at Lemoyne, and I enjoyed my classes and the social life of the school. I was popular and excelled in my studies.

When the first semester ended for the Christmas holidays, I knew I would not be returning in January. Instead, I prepared to celebrate the birth of my beautiful daughter Geri. She was born at John Gaston Hospital on January 29, 1949. I was seventeen.

The following fall, I resumed my studies at Lemoyne. By then, it was apparent that my marriage to Leon was on the rocks. We simply were not on the same wavelength. He had been a high school football star when I was a drum major for the high school band. Once that connection was erased by age and changing social circles, it became obvious that we had nothing else in common. Our relationship really deteriorated when Geri was about six months old. Leon made the serious mistake of trying to slap me around-—for the first and last time. I got up, got my daughter, and got right out of there. We went back to stay with Aunt Pina and Uncle Jim, and that was the end of that marriage.

After leaving Leon, we stayed at Aunt Pina's and Uncle Jim's for a time while I gathered my wits and considered the best course of action now that it was just me and Geri. I needed a housing option that allowed me to get to school and offered some opportunities for work. My friend Sarah had an aunt who had a house near Lemoyne, and I took a room there. The new location allowed me to walk to school. I was also able to find part-time work as a babysitter for friends of Dr. Goldberg, my English professor.

In January of 1950, my Alpha Kappa Alpha Sorority sister Cleo introduced me to her youngest brother, Charles Tate, who had transferred to Lemoyne from Oakwood College in Alabama. I was separated but not divorced, but that didn't keep Charles and me from being together all the time or as much as possible. We fell in love.

Charles Tate: *Florence had met my older sister, Cleo, at Lemoyne. Florence was one of the highest-achieving students to come out of the Memphis public school system and was so bright and talented. Cleo was part of a group of the highest-performing students on the campus. Florence was pulled into the relationship with my sister because she had that love of learning that my sister had.*

Florence and I had several classes together. She saw that I was always serious about learning and about school. She admired people who she felt were smart; and I was confident, studious, but not nerd-ish. I loved to party. I could go to the party and then I could go to the classroom and run it 'cause I would do the homework—and she saw this. Not too long after we started seeing each other, I took her home and introduced her to Mama and the whole sixteen-member Tate family. Everyone else was living in the projects or renting a place, but we owned a home. My father had a business, and that put us in a very small percentage of Black folks in the community., My mother and aunt ran our household. They both had maybe eighth-grade education, but they loved learning. So, I took Florence to the house, and from the moment she got there she was accepted as one of the family. She and my mother and aunt hit it off because they were all on the same page with this love of learning. Here were older women who had a love of learning and deep reservoirs of literature and other things, and I think Florence experienced—and felt—what she had missed. And so, it was sort of the idealized family for her. She could go there whether I was there or not. So, I think that was important to her and helped her to fight off some of those demons from her own family's past.

Charles was sending himself to school by working at night at white restaurants and country clubs. On his off night, we would go to Tony's, the top restaurant-club for Black people in Memphis. At Tony's, you would be sure to run into friends and other young (and not-so young) people out to have a good time enjoying good food, music, and spirits. Most of the time, Charles would cop a bottle of champagne to celebrate our night out.

Life with Charles was exciting. School, however, was not. I was still making all A's and B's, but I was getting fed up with the redundancy of the classes, which had different names but seemed to cover the same tired materials. Not to mention, the teachers were the same for many of them. I was bored out of my skull.

During my junior year, the one subject that was challenging, and for which I had an excellent teacher, was American History. Dr. Johnson considered me one of his best students, but he was very demanding. I'm not sure whether I was being petulant or had finally decided teaching was not for me. Perhaps I was simply worn out by the challenges of school, work, and single motherhood; but when he gave me a D on one of my papers, I decided that was it. I quit!

In 1952, life took a decisive turn when Charles was drafted into the Korean War.

Charles Tate: *I did what a lot of Black boys who had not had an opportunity to get out of the community they were born into did. I had finished three-and-a-half years [of college] and only had a semester to finish when I went into the army in 1952. But I had this desire to see something beyond what I knew, and the way I could do it was to join the army.*

I was drafted, and under the draft laws you serve[d] two years as a draftee. I had a two-year tour to serve. They sent me down to Fort Sam Houston in San Antonio, Texas, where they did all the training for medical, dental, and other technicians. I went into the dental training [program] and came out with a dental technician specialty. Then they shipped me off to Korea.

Charles and I were so young, and, unable to negotiate the distance, we eventually drifted apart. Alone with Geri and with Charles gone for two years, which sounded like forever to me at that young age, I wanted out of Memphis. I believed I could establish a better life for my daughter and myself outside the South, and I chose to do what many southerners had done and were continuing to do during the years of the Great Migration: to take my chances in the North.

I had a friend named Emily McKissack who had moved to Cleveland. Emily had lived down the street from me in LeMoyne Gardens. She was still in high school when I was attending LeMoyne and Geri was a little baby. When Emily finished high school, she moved to Cleveland to go to nursing school and was living there with her sister Inez and brother-in-law Robert.

After finding out how to reach Emily, I talked it over with Aunt Pina, who agreed to care for Geri for the few months it would take me to find a job and establish myself in Cleveland. I arranged to stay with Emily, Inez, and Robert. Emily also arranged a job for me as a nurse's aide at the world-renowned Cleveland Clinic, where she worked.

On the day of my departure, I said goodbye to my little girl Geri and left Aunt Pina's and Uncle Jim's with my proverbial box of fried chicken to board the train for the overnight ride to Cleveland. I wore my best outfit: a powder-blue suit with a poodle cloth jacket, my white felt hat with Black grosgrain ribbon, Black patent-leather heels, white gloves, and pearls. I don't remember meeting or talking to anyone on the train, although I must have. I do remember that the train cars were still segregated until you reached the Mason-Dixon line.

Emily and a friend were waiting for me when I arrived at the huge Cleveland Terminal Towers. I had never been in a really big city before, and I was overwhelmed both by the size and the hustle and bustle. As we moved through the terminal, it greatly surprised me to see white women on their hands and knees scrubbing the floors. I had never seen white women do physical labor. I had seen them in the shops as sales ladies, but that was the only work I'd seen them do. Therefore, the sight of white cleaning women was quite shocking to me. When I mentioned it to Emily, she told me that those women were "DP's" or displaced persons—Eastern European women who came or were sent to Cleveland as refugees in the aftermath of World War II.

As soon as possible after settling in with Emily, Inez, and Robert— each of whom was gracious, hospitable, and welcoming—I began training as a nurse's aide. Cleveland Clinic had patients from all over the world. One patient, a white South African, told me that in his country I would not be a Negro, but would be called "colored." According to him, Black Africans were like dumb animals and could not learn as whites and coloreds did. On one occasion, he pointed out to me that the way I had picked up a glass at his bedside could not be done by Black Africans because their fingers were too thick, more like "animal paws." He said that my fingers were graceful and slender, like those of whites! I knew he was lying, that this could not possibly be true, but I didn't disagree with him as I was trained not to cross white folks. I was twenty years old at the time.

Another patient was a good-looking, curly-haired Greek man who spoke no English, but who was apparently attracted to me. His face lit up with a smile whenever he saw me. One day when I entered the room, he smiled earnestly and spoke in broken English: "Florence, *give me some pussy.*" I was shocked and unable to imagine what had led to that crudity. I reported his remark to Miss Myers, our head nurse, and asked never to be sent to his room again. She liked me, and I wasn't. Later on, I decided that he must have asked some staffer or patient how to tell me that he liked me in English and was unwittingly duped into making the offensive proposal.

Yet another patient was a white boy of about seventeen or eighteen years old who'd been shot by a policeman as he and some other teenagers ran from the scene of some mischief or crime. He was the last one trying to climb the fence and didn't stop when the policeman called "halt." He was shot in the back and spine and was left paralyzed, probably for life. I remember being puzzled because he and his parents were so nice. I hadn't known many nice white people. It was also the first time I realized that policemen could be brutal indiscriminate of race.

During this time, I worked the day shift and Emily worked the night shift, so I seldom saw her, Inez, or Robert. I didn't know anyone else and was so lonely I wanted to die! I remember once being on the bus coming home from work and fighting the urge to turn to a fellow passenger and cry out about how lonely I was.

Later that summer, I did meet a boy. Bob was attractive, intelligent, and a student at Kent State University. We went to several movies; he also took me down to Kent and tried to teach me to play tennis. When I knew him well enough to open up a bit, I told him about my daughter in Memphis. He was incredulous, and after that I could tell that he viewed me in a different light. I assume he'd seen me as a naïve and innocent "little southern girl," and finding out that I was a single mother who'd already been married caused his charming personality to do a 180-degree flip-flop. His polite and respectful behavior changed almost immediately, quickly ending our budding romance. We stopped seeing each other but, years later, when Kent State became the site of the student rebellion that ended in a massacre by the Ohio State National Guard, I thought of Bob and wondered how he'd fared in life.

Soon thereafter, I decided to try to get work in a department store. Living in Memphis, I always thought it would be so glamorous to be a cosmetics-counter sales lady, and I believed that "up North" I would have that opportunity. It never occurred to me that there was also job discrimination up North or discrimination of any kind. Back home in Tennessee, the North was always thought of as the "Land of Milk and Honey." I was so sure my life would be one without discrimination, Jim Crow, or segregation in the North. How little I knew!

I applied to several different stores and was interviewed and tested but never hired. One day, I applied to Sterling-Lindner, a major department store in downtown Cleveland, dressed in my very best. After taking the test, a middle-aged white lady came out and told me that I had scored higher than any applicant she had ever tested.

"But I'm going to do you a favor, and let you know right now that department stores don't hire coloreds as sales ladies," she informed me with an apologetic shrug. Thinking back, I realized she was right: during my time in Cleveland, I'd only seen Blacks hired to clean at the department stores or work in the kitchens of the department store restaurants Blacks couldn't eat in or, if you were a man, you could only operate the elevators at the stores. I sincerely thanked that white woman before leaving the human resources office. She had jolted me back to reality—the reality that I was "up South" rather than "up North."

After living with Emily for a while, I began anticipating the moment when I could bring Geri up to join me. At the same time, I realized that I needed to live someplace where there was someone who could take care of her while I worked. So, I went to live with my friend Sarah's older brother Alex, his wife Gloria, and their children, Mark and Ellene.

Alex, whom we called "Junior," worked in the downtown post office, and Gloria was a housewife. They had an extra bedroom and lived on a nice street in a good neighborhood near a good school. It was perfect for me and Geri! In addition, through his contacts at the post office, Junior was able to facilitate my taking the civil service exam.

In those days, working at the post office was considered a top-notch job for Black people. The postal service employed many Black men, and a smaller number of Black women, who were college-educated professionals denied the opportunity of working in their chosen professions. Junior had a degree in journalism from Western Reserve University (now Case Western). His friends, the Cooper twins, also worked there. They had doctorates in industrial psychology. Black lawyers, accountants, and engineers wound up at the post office and made the most of it. So, I felt privileged when I passed the test and got a job there. I made a number of friends while working there, including Janet Harris, a pretty girl who lived in my neighborhood. Janet and I became known as the post-office beauties! We worked the four p.m. to one a.m. shift, which in time would become a pain in the neck since it killed our chances of having social lives.

I was so glad when, late that summer, Geri arrived with Sarah, who was enrolling at Western Reserve University to get her masters in library science. I was so happy to see my sweet, polite, intelligent girl! Aunt Pina hadn't wanted to let her go, but I insisted. Ironically, Aunt Pina had actually offered to take me to Dr. Thomas for an abortion when I'd first become pregnant with Geri, but with the innate wisdom of a seventeen-year-old, I'd indignantly refused, saying, "I want to have *my* baby!" Aunt Pina quickly fell deeply in love with her. She'd always wanted children but had been unable to get pregnant, and she begged me repeatedly to "give" Geri to her. No way was I giving my baby girl away! Geri started kindergarten that fall, and I continued at the post office for almost a year.

Sometime between 1954 and 1955, I got the call that Charles was back from Korea, safe and sound. He'd finished his degree in Lemoyne, gotten my information from Cleo, and tracked me down to tell me he was moving to Cleveland to live with his Uncle Elihu, his father's brother. I sent Geri to Memphis to spend that summer with Aunt Pina. I moved into my own small apartment on the third floor of a house owned by an elderly Black woman because I wanted to experience living by myself. It was the first time I'd lived alone, and I savored every minute of it. Charles and I started seeing each other again, and we had a ball in that third-floor apartment that summer!

Of course, when it was time for school to begin and for Geri to return, I had to leave the fun of the apartment and get back to reality. I needed a new place to live and found a home with a woman named Miss Grahame, who lived in Emily's neighborhood. Geri would be able to go to the same school, and Miss Grahame would help watch her while I was at work.

By that time, Emily had left Cleveland Clinic for a job at the Cleveland Public Library as a lending assistant. Frustrated by my hours and the monotony of my job at the post office, I applied to the library as well and was hired as a lending assistant at the Sterling Branch Library in the city's Hough area. There, I became friends with a white girl named Shani Kaislov, the children's librarian. It was really the first time I had ever socialized with a white person. We even went to the movies together. Sometimes we would double-date; she would bring her boyfriend Ernie and I would bring Charles. Once, I was upstairs in the library staff lounge lying down on the sofa, and Shani came up and stretched out beside me. She meant nothing by it; we were friends, but I'll never forget how it literally made my skin crawl to be in such close proximity to a white person.

Around that time, I learned from Charles' sister Cleo that while Charles was in the army and stationed in New Jersey he had become engaged to a girl there. I confronted him about it and told him he needed to let this woman know about us. He quickly and formally broke off that engagement and he and I began talking about getting married.

Charles was having problems finding a suitable job, even as a veteran and a college grad. Willing to do whatever he could until he found more appropriate work, he went to work for the Cleveland Trust Bank polishing the enormous amount of brass that adorned the doors and handrails at the bank's entrance. I used to bring the library fine deposits from Sterling Branch Library down to Cleveland Trust. Young and silly—I was all of twenty-two or twenty-three—I would approach the bank from the opposite side of the street so I could laugh at Charles with his very dignified, sharp self, polishing brass!

He later took a job at a metal factory making widgets of some sort while he waited to hear about the status of his civil service application. Finally, he heard back from the U.S. Civil Service 5/7/9 program, a career-ladder entry program for college graduates. He was hired and found out he would be stationed at Gentile Air Force Station, on the Wright-Patterson Air Force Base, outside of Dayton, Ohio. He left that summer.

I was alone and lonely again. I met another young man named Joseph Hornell. Joe and I became very friendly, and he said wanted to marry me too! Geri liked him a lot, and she went everywhere with us.

Charles would return to Cleveland on most weekends, and sometimes I went to Dayton to visit him. Soon, I had a real love triangle on my hands! Ultimately, Charles won out, and we married on the weekend of October 1, 1956, in Indiana.

Leaving Geri in the care of Sarah's Aunt Ruby for a week, Charles and I found a small apartment on Forent Avenue in Dayton, in the house of a man whose wife had left him. After our move, I got Geri situated into third grade at Wogaman Elementary. With Charles off to work at Gentile every day, I started job hunting with assistance from the Urban League.

The Urban League had opened up branches in many of the major cities, including Dayton. The organization helped Black people who were moving from rural areas to the city and Black southerners seeking to escape Jim Crow racism. One of its major programs focused on getting white corporations, offices, and factories to hire Negroes. It chose only the most qualified and presentable applicants to present to those potential employers.

As a fresh-faced young wife and mother who had reentered the workforce, I was interviewed by the folks at the Urban League. My subsequent visits to the organization ensured them that I'd been fully groomed for the mission, with full knowledge of the importance of my role. When the day came for my last interview, I was sporting my best office-ready outfit, neatly straightened coif, and the mandatory pearls.

The Urban League representative seemed pleased. "We've found a placement for you," he informed me. "The position is as a secretary for the chief engineer of Globe Industries. A very good job, a fine opportunity. I know you'll do fine," he continued. "Just get there five minutes early and dress appropriately. Remember to go the extra yard. Avoid confrontation and, whatever you do, always be polite and professional. You're an articulate young lady, and you should fit in well. Good luck, and make us proud."

As a major Dayton corporation, Globe was responsible for manufacturing parts and widgets for the motor industry. The Globe building was in the industrial part of town, which was inhabited by nothing but white folks. Although they had a few Black men working in the factory, they had agreed to hire one Black person in the administrative pool: me.

Occasionally, I would ride the bus to Globe with a Black factory worker—a very nice guy who, like me, loved Fats Domino's music. We both listened to one particular radio disc jockey who could be counted on each Monday to play Domino's hit, "Blue Monday," as we reflected on our lack of excitement about facing another long week at Globe:

Sunday mornin' my head is bad
But it's worth it for the time that I had

But I've got to get my rest
'Cause Monday is a mess...

At Globe, I worked for Jim, an affable-enough guy whose small, enclosed office was right in the middle of the factory. I was introduced to the workings of the office by Shirley, the bubbly white secretary who worked in the next office over. If she had any reservations about me, she must have gotten over them quickly because we soon became office friends. She adored me and couldn't stay out of my office, which was lucky for me because my typing was atrocious—a fact that somehow had slipped under the Urban League's radar. If Jim had to have something that had to be typed really well, I'd get Shirley to do it; otherwise, I struggled along satisfactorily with all the minor typing assignments. I *could*, however, take dictation and managed to uphold the standards set forth by the Urban League.

I was also very popular among the women working in the factory, most of whom were lower-class whites from the South or the mountains. I suppose my southern manners and mores appealed to them. One of them, Dottie, would often come by my office because she was dating Stanley, another company engineer, so I soon had a friend in the plant as well as the main office. When I left to have my son Greg in 1957, I was given two baby showers: one at someone's home and one in the factory since office and plant workers didn't mix. By the time I left Globe, everyone there had warmed to me. I guess you could say it was a successful experiment in the company's so-called workplace-integration project.

We had moved from Forent Avenue to a two-bedroom garden apartment on Stewart. Charles, ever industrious even at twenty-seven years old, worked out a deal with the white building owner to serve as the resident manager in exchange for our rent. He was still on the 5/7/9 path at Wright-Patterson, but when he wasn't working he would collect rents and settle the neighbors' squabbles. Most of our friends were Charles's work friends. They were all nice people, but not ones I would have chosen or that I had an affinity for, but I had yet to make friends of my own in Dayton.

We lived on Stewart for a couple of years. Geri and Greg shared a bedroom, but I began to feel the need for a house of our own. We found a little house on Gramont, and I was really excited to have achieved the "American Dream": home ownership. The house had two bedrooms, a large kitchen/dining space, a living room, bathroom, and a full basement with another bedroom downstairs. It also had a front porch and a small, fenced-in backyard.

I had been hired to work at Ohio Bell Telephone Company, where I was another "first Negro": its first Black service representative. The job consisted of answering customer calls regarding their bills and service, dealing with moves and transfers, and selling new equipment. Once again, the white women adored me, and they were forever inviting me to parties, lunches, and baby showers.

While at Ohio Bell I became pregnant with Brian, and once again I received a giant going-away party and baby shower. Still, when I returned home to await Brian's birth, it occurred to me that although I'd been in Dayton for four years I had no friends of my own. I'd been so busy with my Bell Company social life that I had allotted no time to participate in the kinds of activities that would enable me to meet other young Black women with whom I might be compatible.

There was, however, someone Charles knew from Memphis: Charles Bailey, who had moved to Dayton with his wife Sally, and we had become friendly. The "two Charleses," Sally, and I did lots of things together; but when Bailey was drunk he abused Sally, so they weren't always fun to be around. Still, I would be glad Sally was only a phone call away because she probably saved my life. That was when, a month after Brian's birth, I suffered a sudden stroke that changed everything for my family—and left an entirely different "me" in its wake.

Florence and Charles

Florence and Geri

CHAPTER 4

STROKE

The onset of my clinical depression had its roots in the debilitating stroke I suffered just one month after the birth of my third child Brian in 1960. At the time, I was a healthy, twenty-nine-year-old mother of two with no history of health issues. Brian arrived to happily round out our little family. He was the sweetest, calmest baby. He is still a sweet-natured and loving individual.

Back then, it was normal for a mother to stay in the hospital with her newborn baby for two weeks. Afterward, she would go home and spend another two weeks in the house with the baby, who normally didn't leave the house until he or she was six weeks old.

Nothing had gone awry during my pregnancy or during the weeks I spent at home following Brian's birth. To celebrate the one-month "freedom pass" that meant I could finally leave the house, Charles and I decided to celebrate with a movie.

That Friday night, we hired a sitter and went to see the movie, *Elmer Gantry*. While in the theatre, I suddenly began to feel very cold. It was August, however, and it was hot outside, but the theater was air-conditioned, which made it comfortably cool for most people. Still, I felt strangely frigid. "Charles," I whispered into his ear, "I'm freezing cold." He put his arm around me and hugged me a little tighter, without thinking much about it. I returned home, feeling a little funny but experiencing nothing alarming.

The next morning, I was in the basement bedroom, which we had fixed up for Geri since the upstairs bedrooms of our little house were now full with Greg and baby Brian in one room and Charles and I in the other. While standing barefoot on the linoleum-covered floor and talking on the telephone with a friend, I became aware that, while I could feel the linoleum under my right foot, I had no sensation at all in my left foot. "That's odd," I thought, hanging up the phone. I pricked my left leg to see if it too was numb. It was.

Now I was worried. I hurried to the kitchen and got an ice cube out the freezer and ran it up and down that leg. Nothing. I told Charles and, although it was a Saturday, we decided to call Dr. Daniels, the doctor who delivered Brian. When he answered the phone, I explained what I was experiencing. "It sounds like it might be a blood clot," he said. "Come in to see me Monday morning."

Although the lack of sensation was worrisome, I had enormous faith and trust in doctors, so I assumed that if Dr. Daniels told me to wait until Monday to come in, then whatever was happening wasn't urgent. So, I waited through the rest of the weekend.

On Monday morning, I was awakened by the baby's cry. Charles, who had to be at work at Gentile Air Force Base by seven a.m., had left around six a.m., taking two-and-a-half-year-old Gregory to nursery school. By that time, Geri had also left for school.

Hearing Brian's cries in the next bedroom, I tried to get out of bed to nurse him. I felt myself listing to my left side. "What is wrong with me?" I thought, grabbing the side of the bed to steady myself. I couldn't hold myself up, and I was overcome by dizziness. It was such an odd feeling. No matter how many times I tried to stand up straight, I couldn't.

I felt like I was about to pass out, and I was worried about Brian, whom I couldn't get to. I couldn't stand, let alone walk. "I'll never get Charles at work," I thought, "Who can I call?"

Although we knew a number of people, there was only one person in our circle that I knew wasn't working and who might be home: our friend, Sally Bailey. I called her and thankfully she was home.

"Sally, I don't know what's wrong with me," I remember mumbling into the phone when she answered. "I can't stand up straight, I keep falling down, and I feel like I'm going to faint." "Florence, you don't sound good!" Sally exclaimed. By that point, my speech was probably already being affected. Calling Sally was the last thing I remember about that day. Later, I learned that she had called an ambulance and had managed to reached Charles at work.

When I came to, I was in the hospital emergency room, vomiting bile. I tried to open my eyes to see what was happening around me, but the room was in motion and kept swirling around me. I had to close them again to keep from experiencing extreme dizziness. From that point on, the next two weeks was a foggy, fractured memory.

I remember being in a semiconscious state. I couldn't talk, and I couldn't see anything, but I could hear everything being said. At some point, Charles must have contacted my other family members. I remember my mother being at my bedside. She was feeling up and down along my left side, crying, "She's cold, she's cold! My child is dying! Go get the doctor!" I also remember hearing my brother somewhere farther off, crying, "Louise…my sister, she's going to die!"

Sometime later, a new doctor was brought in to work with me. Dr. Hughes, the younger half of Hughes and Hollister, the city's best and most respected neurological practice, had somehow been secured to treat me. He visited daily, checking on my stability and progress. I learned later that he decided not to do anything invasive after an arteriogram revealed that a blood clot had lodged in my carotid artery. At some point, I remember him saying, "Surgery is out because the area [the clot] is in is too delicate. I'm going to try to dissolve it." I remember wanting to see what Dr. Hughes looked like. At some point, I managed to open my eyes and find him in my greatly impaired field of vision.

That was early fall, right before the Kennedy-Nixon election contest. I was able to see a large "Kennedy" button affixed to Dr. Hughes's lapel. He was voting for Kennedy, in Dayton—a conservative town in a conservative state—with the Ku Klux Klan virtually next door in Indiana! That alone told me he was cut from a different cloth than most of the white people that I knew.

Initially, though I could hear Dr. Hughes talking to me and asking me questions, I couldn't respond. Later, when I was able to speak, I told him, "I knew you were a good doctor when I saw the Kennedy button." He just laughed at that. I later learned that he was also a Unitarian, so I just adored Dr. Hughes.

During my semiconscious state, I was still able, at times, to hear much of what was going on around me. Conversations about the upcoming elections, discussions between my doctors and relatives, and the comings and goings of nursing attendants would pierce my stupor.

Some things I heard stayed with me, including the words of Dr. Daniels when he'd stopped by to see me one day: "She might be better off dead," he said, probably speaking to a nurse. "Better that than for her to be stuck in a wheelchair, always watching her young family walk out the door."

Dr. Daniels's careless words forced me to face my mortality at the age of twenty-nine. I remember thinking in that hospital bed: "If I get up from here, I'm going to do everything that I want to, that I can, when I can—because, hey, I may be young, but death can come at any time!" I still believe that Dr. Daniels's statement about death, heard in my semiconscious state, had a great impact on me when I regained full consciousness. It has stayed with me to this day.

Although the doctors could never determine what caused my stroke, they surmised it was the clot. "Does she have high blood pressure or edema?" I remember them asking. "Had she fallen and hit her head?" The answer to all their questions was "No." However, they seemed to believe that even if the blood clot had loosened after childbirth and somehow traveled to my brain, a month had passed since the delivery and it shouldn't have taken that long for a clot to reach my brain.

Apparently, at that time, strokes were very uncommon in people my age. I was considered and treated like a medical phenomenon. Even Dr. Hughes later told me that he had never experienced such a case in a person so young.

The clot, lodged in my carotid artery, affected mainly my left side, rendering it numb and destroying my inner-ear equilibrium, which controls balance. This resulted in my initial inability to stand up straight. The stroke caused facial paralysis and the contortion of the left side of my mouth as well as a drooping left eye. I was in that semiconscious state in the hospital for two weeks. Gradually, under Dr. Hughes's care, I regained consciousness.

When I first spoke again, my voice was extremely high-pitched, almost like a child's. When I was strong enough, I began physical therapy. I had to learn to walk again. Fortunately, my therapist, Gwen Washington, was wonderful. During those weeks, I would often look in the mirror and say, "Lord, if you'd just let my eye not droop…" In time, my eye did regain its proper shape and muscle tone.

Later, I thought, "Oh Lord, if you'd just let my mouth not be twisted." Again, in time, the muscles around my mouth returned to normal. Being young worked to my advantage; I was able to bounce back from the stroke with no long-term physical impairment.

After physical therapy and a return to semi-normal physical condition, I was discharged from the hospital and sent home to return to my life and my roles as wife to the ever-patient, ever-caring Charles, and as mother to Geri, Greg, and three-month-old Brian. But I was soon to discover that nothing would be the same again. Clinical depression would make its appearance, changing my life forever. The person I had been, and the life I'd had before the stroke, would become but a memory.

My lapse into terrible states of inertia and despair started sometime after the stroke. I returned home from the hospital to find myself unable to nurse my precious baby Brian, whom I so wanted to hold in my arms. A sense of unease began to sweep through me. I wasn't in any pain. Nothing was hurting, nothing physical, at least. I just had a bad, bad feeling… I felt as if some ambiguous but overpowering hazard was stalking me. It got worse over the next year. Still, nothing bad was happening to or around me, and my husband and my children were fine.

Geri, a big girl by now, would go off to school while Greg went to an all-day nursery. In my still-fragile state, Charles' Aunt Bea came down from Flint, Michigan, to help us. The house was so tiny that I soon felt uncomfortable with her there, and I implored Charles to send her away. I have always felt somewhat bad about that decision.

Unable to identify the cause of this new anxiety, I considered going to see a doctor, wondering if it was somehow related to the stroke and subsequent hospitalization. Soon it progressed to a point where I was so despondent that I found it hard to put one foot in front of the other. "I can't move," I'd tell Charles, as he was going off to work.

By this time, Brian was two-and-a-half years old. Charles would leave me sitting on the couch, in the blue-and-white checkered housecoat I wore daily like a hospital gown. When he returned from work, I'd still be sitting in that chair, unable to account for the time or for what I'd been doing or thinking, aware only of an exhausting and ongoing agitation.

I made appointments and saw one doctor, then another, and another; but without any physical symptoms, none of them could provide a diagnosis. One doctor, the husband of a friend, upon hearing of my complaints one evening remarked, "Well, it sounds like that old-fashioned melancholia...but that hasn't been around for a long time." Another doctor told me, "Oh, Florence, you just need a job." A third doctor actually said, "You must have Lumumba Fever"—a poor joke, referencing the short but meteoric political career of Congolese prime minister and freedom fighter Patrice Lumumba. That doctor, who somehow knew of my political inclinations, thought it was a humorous remark. It wasn't...and I was left no closer to a resolution for my growing sense of foreboding agony.

"Are you in pain?"
"Are you suffering?"
"Is your husband drinking?"
"Is he beating you?"

These were the kinds of questions they continued to ask me, and my answer was always the same: "No." Then, inevitably, they would inquire somewhat impatiently: "Well...can you describe what you're feeling?"

But that was part of the problem. I couldn't describe it, beyond telling them, "I just feel *so bad.*"

Finally, in desperation, I went back to Dr. Hughes, the neurologist who had treated me during my stroke. If anybody could help me, I was sure it would be him. Dr. Hughes hospitalized me twice, ordering a full workup, special exams, even bone marrow extraction—a painful and traumatic experience. Nothing. As with the other doctors, he could not provide a diagnosis for my problems.

My panic seemed to grow with every negative result. I continued to press and badger Dr. Hughes for new tests. Finally, one day on the phone—after my second round of hospital exams had yielded nothing, and I had worked myself into tears—Dr. Hughes cleared his throat and said: "Mrs. Tate, I think you need to see a psychiatrist."

It was as if someone had slapped me across the face. His words hung in the air like an indictment. I hung up, deeply offended. "That man thinks I'm crazy!" I told Charles in hurt disbelief. "Just 'cause he can't find out what's wrong with me…" I huffed. But inside, my hopeless discouragement mushroomed.

Dr. Hughes's words left a terrifying question in my mind. I was in the Midwest in the early 1960s, and the term "clinical depression" had yet to become a standard diagnosis, and my condition was to remain a painful mystery for almost three years. During that time, I was so desperate to find something or somebody who could help me that I went to several ministers. One was an old white minister. I even allowed him to give me some kind of intelligence test.

I remember once getting dressed to go somewhere. I was sitting on the couch, waiting for Charles and the children when something inside of me seemed to break just as we were getting ready to go out to the car. "Charles… Charles!" I blurted out in anguish, "Why didn't y'all just let me die? I wish I was *dead!*" Charles was clearly stumped and taken aback. He just couldn't understand how bad I really felt.

Perhaps that was because, during the spring and summer months, whatever had been hovering over me would seem to just lift and go away like nothing had ever happened. During those months, I was able to do the expected, everyday things with Charles and the kids. I cooked and made big dinners. We went to parks and took road trips to Cleveland and Columbus. During one of those trips, we learned that Geri was prone to car sickness, so we arranged for her to stay with Mother during later car trips out of town. Otherwise, we were a "normal" family, and I wouldn't have to be concerned about my "condition" until it came back again.

The third winter the "terrible darkness" occurred, in 1962, I consulted with Dr. Johnson, a Black doctor we knew socially. I asked him to come by and see me for himself, at my home, so that he could see what a mess I was. My theory was that when I went to a doctor's office, cleaned up and pulled together, I looked much more "normal" than I actually felt—leading them to dismiss or minimize the significance of my cry for help. In reality, I was trapped in one of my downhearted, dispirited cycles.

Dr. Johnson soon visited me. He took one look at me wearing that damned blue-and-white checkered housecoat and said, "My God, girl, what's the matter with you?" "I told you," I sighed. "This is way I am, *all the time*, during these spells."

On another day soon after, feeling semi-suicidal, I called him again. "Dr. Johnson, I'm coming over there, and you're going to have to do something for me or I'm going to kill myself!" I cried, hugging myself tightly. I felt as though I would fly to pieces if I didn't literally hold myself together. Hearing my desperation, he told me to come to his office that evening. Once there, I repeated my suicide threat. "Girl, don't you kill yourself in my office! It will be bad for my business!" He spoke with the dry humor that was characteristic of him: "You think you can hold on until the morning?" I told him I thought I could.

The next morning, Dr. Johnson called to tell me he'd arranged for me to see a psychiatrist. A *white* psychiatrist. There was no Black psychiatrist in Dayton at the time, at least not one that Dr. Johnson knew of. Ordinarily, outside of a hospital situation, if you were Black, you went to a Black doctor. If you were white, you went to a white doctor. Dr. Johnson made whatever arrangements had to be made for me to see this psychiatrist; but because medical "race-mixing" just wasn't done, I had to go see him after hours when he was certain none of his white patients might see me.

During my visit, the psychiatrist, armed with the expertise and experience that the regular medical doctors I had gone to previously lacked, questioned me carefully. At the end of the session, he sat back, nodded, and picked up his phone.

"I'm going to arrange for you to be admitted for treatment," he gently informed me. "You see, Mrs. Tate, what you have is depression. And it seems, in your case, to be extreme enough that I'm going to recommend electroconvulsive therapy, to begin immediately."

As unnerving as his words were, his diagnosis offered me a consolation I had been seeking during those three years. Finally, the frightening condition I had desperately sought to understand had a name: *depression.*

Over the next two weeks, I received a series of electroconvulsive therapy treatments. Within days after my last treatment, I was shocked (no pun intended) to find that I felt like my normal self again. It was as if the treatments had completely reset my brain's wiring—which, in a way, they had. With a prescription for Elavil to help "smooth out the rough edges," the psychiatrist said, I was discharged to return to my family and my life.

Throughout the years, I have been treated by a number of psychiatrists and prescribed a variety of medications and therapies, yet I have continued to experience the "six months on, six months off" pattern of depression that has marked my life. I was also to return for electroconvulsive therapy every seven to ten years for several decades because eventually my depressive states would become so severe that *only* the electroconvulsive therapy could lure me from the edge of my near-suicidal state—that, and my deep-seated fear of going to hell.

Over the years I told my doctors that, even though I often thought about it, they didn't have to worry about me trying to commit suicide because being brought up in Gospel Temple Baptist Church had truly put the fear of the flames in me. I can still see the intimidating scowl on Reverend Kemp's face at Mr. Jamison's old fashioned, hell-and-damnation Baptist church to this day. In that church, everyone knew that killing oneself was the only unpardonable sin. If you killed yourself, you would surely be damned to spend eternity in the fiery pit with the Devil.

While in the throes of my illness I would often think: "Being like this is already like being in hell. If I commit suicide, I'll spend eternity feeling this horrible—and be on fire too!" That idea was so terrifying it nipped all thoughts of suicide in the bud, invariably leaving me to decide, "No, not that! I think I can hold on another day."

I told Charles of my fears and, during the worst times, when I swore I wanted to be dead, he would remind me, "Remember what you said about the Devil and being in hell? Well, just hold that thought!"

My indoctrination at Gospel Temple was so overbearing that as a young teenager I remember protesting: "If I ever get out of here, I'm not ever going to church again!" I'm not sure whether by "here" I was referring to Mr. Jamison's house or Memphis or Mother's presence. But being forced to go to Sunday school, eleven o'clock service, Baptist Young People's Union meetings, and multiple weekly meetings, where I was constantly reminded of God's wrath and the Devil's blazing eternity, convinced me that I wasn't going to put any of that on *my* children.

Perhaps another kind of introduction to religion, a more spiritually centered one, would have helped me in my battle with depression. But my ambivalence toward religious institutions ultimately undermined my ability to find faith in a merciful God and offered no alternative to my seasonal spiral downward.

By early 1963, with the treatment of my depression somewhat stabilized, I felt deep in my gut that I could no longer just stand by and watch the courageous acts of the southern protesters—led by Martin Luther King, the SCLC (Southern Christian Leadership Conference), and the SNCC (Student Nonviolent Coordinating Committee)—and do absolutely nothing. I knew I needed to find a way to become involved in the Civil Rights Movement. In the Movement, I found something that gave me a commitment to a cause and a belief that I never truly found in a church.

After meeting Stokely at the Unitarian church and becoming involved in the Civil Rights Movement, there was simply no room for church in my life. It wasn't that I believed you couldn't be in the church and in the Movement too. In fact, some of the people in the Congress of Racial Equality (CORE) and the Dayton Association for Racial Equality (DARE) were churchgoers and through their membership made small differences in their spiritual communities when they could. Additionally, my contact with ministers in town who were supportive of the Movement was vital, as they could be called upon to offer their sanctuaries for events and gatherings when needed.

But the church was simply no longer a part of my life, and I never felt the need to go back. "The Movement is my church," was a favorite saying among those of us working in the struggle. The Movement was *my* church; it was a church that sustained me. I would spend the next several years deeply immersed in work that helped bring Dayton and the surrounding areas fully into the cause: Civil Rights for Black people throughout the land.

CHAPTER 5

DAYTON CORE

Once I felt able to rise out of the energy-sapping fog of depression to which I'd been captive for more than two years, I looked for ways to get engaged with my community. During that time, I became an assistant Girl Scout leader for an all-Black Girl Scout troop after attending a leader-recruitment meeting at the home of VerDree Harris, who would become a lifelong friend. VerDree was also responsible for bringing me into the Alpha Wives.

My husband Charles was an "Alpha" (a member of the Alpha Phi Alpha fraternity), and through VerDree and some other young wives I'd made friends with—Vivian Reese and Marilyn Ivory— I soon found out that living such a constricted life in Dayton might be made more bearable if one was the wife of an Alpha. And if you were, you'd certainly want to be in the Alpha Wives. So I joined and did whatever the other Alpha Wives did, which was basically to host meet-and-greets, organize teas and other social events, gossip, and have lots of house parties. We just moved the party around from one couple's house to the next.

Later, I decided I wanted to do something more seriously meaningful, so I joined the League of Women Voters, a virtually all-white organization. As far as I could tell, I was the only Black woman in the Dayton chapter. We dealt with voter education and did leafleting—that is, we handed out flyers that provided information about community issues, candidates' backgrounds, and where they stood on these concerns. We also held forums during which the candidates could speak with members of the community.

Even then, I was trying my best to exercise my political wings where I could, but I knew there was far more for me to do. I just needed to find the right group of people working on behalf of the Civil Rights Movement in our area. I found what I was looking for in the Dayton chapter of the Congress of Racial Equality (CORE), which held open meetings every Wednesday night. When I finally attended a meeting, I fell upon a bunch of kindred souls, the kind of people I had long been hungering to have in my life. The headquarters of the Dayton chapter of CORE was in a little union hall on West Fifth Street in the heart of the Black community. We met there every Wednesday to decide what our activities would be for the week: who or what we would protest, picket, or select for a sit-in or for whom we would host public meetings and demonstrations.

To this day, I count those years spent in Dayton CORE as some of the best years of my life. The organization's membership included some of the best people I'd ever met: Tommy and Joyce Herring, C. J. McLin, Mildred Kerica (the local real estate mogul), Mrs. Francis, and, of course, CORE's executive director in Dayton and heroic leader, W. S. McIntosh. McIntosh—or "Mac"—was quite a character and a brilliant organizer. He was absolutely fearless. Although regularly lambasted in the papers as a rabblerouser, a crook, or worse, Mac knew just what would "tweak the beak" of the local white establishment and what would get our group some media attention, which would in turn draw more Blacks to our Wednesday night meetings.

Being labeled a communist, however, meant that some of the middle-class Black community looked down on Mac. They disparaged him continually with comments like, "Oh Lord, here's McIntosh and that foolishness he's doing again." But Mac was a former AFL-CIO labor organizer, skilled at assessing personalities, pitting cliques against one other, and exacerbating class tensions. He was equally versed in making compromises, stroking egos, applauding jobs well done, and inspiring others to greater action.

Mac's work in Dayton is renowned. He worked tirelessly for more than two decades to end discrimination, and his efforts resulted in Blacks being brought into city government, the integration of local lunch counters, and greater employment for Blacks in jobs that had been reserved for white people. In 1987, the City of Dayton and the University of Dayton established the W. S. McIntosh Memorial Leadership Award in his name, and in 1996 the Dayton City Commission renamed Riverview Park the W. S. McIntosh Park.

One of the Dayton CORE's greatest accomplishments was its push to integrate Rike's Department Store, the city's largest and best downtown department store. Rike's refused to hire Blacks for any sales or clerical jobs, and Blacks were certainly not considered for management positions. The few who worked there were in janitorial positions or performed other menial labor–in other words, we were not hired in positions where we would be seen by the public.

Still, our community patronized the store to the tune of millions of dollars annually, and we at Dayton CORE were determined that Rike's open up its hiring to include Blacks in all areas. We decided to make the hugely popular store our target. We had pursued many other venues before Rike's, but given the store's location, visibility, and economic and commercial weight in the community, taking an open stand against its hiring policies would be a big one for us.

So we picketed and marched outside the entrance to Rike's over a period of several months, but it was illegal to try to gain entry to the store, and anyone doing so could be arrested. We carried signs that read: "END TOKENISM AT RIKE'S," "YOU WANT OUR MONEY, WE WANT OUR JOBS," and "DIRECT ACTION IS WHAT IT TAKES!" We sang freedom songs, including Lucy Kinchen's classic, "Oh Freedom." *"And before I'll be a slave,"* we sang, *"I'll be buried in my grave, and go home to my Lord and be free."*

In one daring venture, several of us women of CORE, frustrated by the giant department store's steadfast refusal to open their hiring pool to Blacks, decided that picketing outside of Rike's wasn't enough. One Wednesday night, we proposed our plan to the rest of Dayton CORE, and we collectively agreed that a group of women would take our protesting to the next level. We would attempt to enter Rike's with our signs and songs, knowing full well that we would probably be hauled off to jail.

In a way, it was also a tactical plan. Part of our intention with any public act of protesting, marching, picketing, or sitting-in was about bringing attention to our actions. We sought both to raise awareness among Blacks and whites alike about what we were doing as well as to put more pressure on whatever entities we were protesting. By daring to enter Rike's Department Store holding protest signs and singing protest songs, we were "trespassing," consciously braving arrest and challenging the white establishment. We were playing out a strategy we hoped would lead to media coverage, perhaps even garnering us some time on the evening television news.

For the occasion, we decided to do something other than wear our normal "picketing" clothes. We wanted to make an impression. The majority of us were middle-class wives and mothers rather than young students or unemployed laborers. We wanted to let the management at Rike's know that, despite popular belief, we also cared, were impacted by their racism and discrimination, and were demanding justice—just like the rest of our people.

"I know," proposed Joyce Herring, an old pro at picketing, during our planning session. "Let's dress up!"

"Dress up?" I balked. "To go picket?"

"Yes," insisted Joyce. "Let's put on our best Sunday-go-to-meeting, child. Pretty dresses, big hats, string of pearls, good heels, and white gloves. We're going to carry those signs in our white-gloved hands. Do you hear me?"

It was a crazy idea, but we agreed it would certainly be different. For one thing, it would draw even more attention to us as we marched into Rike's singing spirituals and looking like we were on our way to an Alpha Wives brunch. We would trespass as a united front of style *and* substance. I recruited another adventurous friend, Jerrie Walker, especially for the occasion—the more the merrier for this party. Because we were all pretty much middle-class women with children in school, some of us having been to college and many with decent jobs, we wanted to make a statement: "Ok, you all have categorized Mac as a rabble rouser, an ex-communist, and someone not to be associated with. But look—we middle-class Black women are part of this group as well, so you can't label *all* of us!"

The protest went down just as we thought it would. Rike's customers were shocked, its sales staff was appalled, and the police were called. When the police came to arrest us, we did exactly as we'd been taught by our CORE trainers: we fell out. We had learned that when handcuffs are being put on you, you don't fight back—you just go limp! The police literally had to carry us into the paddy wagon, at which point we regained the ability to stand on our own (not wanting to be unceremoniously tossed in the back by frustrated cops!).

Let me tell you, we were a sight to see as we climbed in the back of the paddy wagon in our heels and hats!

The police took us to the station for booking, and then put us in a cell with a few other women who'd been picked up for whatever reason and who were quite fascinated by our presence and appearance. I know we were a sight to them—sitting up in jail in dresses and gloves. I'm sure they were looking at us like, "What the hell is *this*?" One drunken old lady kept demanding we answer questions that had no answers. I dared not eat the food or drink the water.

News soon spread about our protest. A crowd of people from Dayton CORE, along with families and friends who supported our cause, could be heard outside the jail demonstrating on our behalf. It definitely made us feel much better to hear our folks out there protesting our arrest for protesting.

Among them was my husband Charles. I had been trying to get him involved with our CORE activities from the time I'd started, but our Wednesday night CORE meetings conflicted with his regular Gentile Air Force Base golf club games, and I hadn't been able to pry him loose from that. But when I was finally "released" to him the next day, I could tell it was over for the golf club thing.

"That's it, Florence," Charles insisted after the CORE leadership handled the business of getting us women out of jail. "From now on you aren't doing any of this without me there with you!" He seemed grim, but I knew he was proud of me. And, as it turned out, my arrest and detainment were the catalysts that hurled him into the Movement. From that moment forward, he was an ardent CORE member and later a leader in the organization.

And of course, the whole ruckus did end up being televised on the evening news. Mission accomplished! Eventually, all of Mac's hard work and planning succeeded. After many months of protests, Rike's, along with several other stores on CORE's list, agreed to hire more Blacks and provide them with on-the-job training.

Mac was an astute politician and a "strong-armer" who knew how to isolate whoever was opposed to his wishes when it was time to reach a decision requiring group authorization. He could, and would, pit young against old, Black against white, educated against uneducated, and had no trouble showing an aggressive, sometimes even intimidating side, whenever it seemed necessary.

With so much at stake in terms of the future of justice for Blacks and because the Dayton CORE consisted of so many people with strong passions and convictions, the emotions of its members were often on edge. It was understandable that political "in-fighting" would occur within the group. As time passed, the political divide within the membership became obvious, and the chapter basically split into what would become the "McIntosh faction" and the "Maddox faction." Our general differences seemed to fall along lines of education and patterns of communication. Mac's group was, for the most part, more working-class and confrontational while John Maddox—a slightly built, acerbic, quick-witted, and articulate engineer who worked at Wright-Patterson Air Force Base—led with more college-educated, thoughtful rhetoric. Charles and I found ourselves in the latter group, having become social friends with John and Myrtle Maddox, who lived in the same neighborhood as we did. We later moved into their larger house when they moved to Italy.

Factions or no factions, Dayton CORE was nonetheless an excited and cohesive team when we attended one of the most thrilling events of the era: the March on Washington for Jobs and Freedom, which took place on August 28, 1963. We were excited about this venture all summer. Much planning went into our involvement in it. Committees were formed to arrange our transportation to Cincinnati, where we would board the overnight train to Washington, DC. Expense money was raised from our own budgets and from other supporters, including business people who were CORE members like Mrs. Frances, the realtor, and morticians Clarence Bowman and C. J. McLin. In the months prior to the event, we received regular communications from our national CORE directors James Farmer and Floyd McKissick. We discussed these communications at our Wednesday night meetings, along with logistics and plans to address unforeseen emergencies that might arise. We also prepared for any possible conflicts on the scene and were drilled on the fine art of getting arrested, including how to protect ourselves from billy clubs and other dangerous scenarios that might arise if we were confronted by police.

Most of all, we discussed how significant this march was and how important it was for us to be represented. Under Mac, we had been marching and demonstrating for jobs for Blacks in Dayton, now we would be joining thousands of others who were engaging in the same activities but on a national level. We hoped a national event showing how serious Black people considered the situation to be would provoke some kind of government support. We were seeking a mandate that would institute immediate change and sweeping reform in the American workplace, and we were willing to risk arrest and whatever else might come in response to our act of mass protest.

On the twenty-seventh of August, we traveled to Cincinnati to board the train for the long ride to DC. Along the way to our final destination, we talked, sang, ate sandwiches that some of the women had made for us, and slept. During the ride, the two factions pretty much clustered in their respective groups. Our party was made up of the Tates, Maddoxes, Duckers, Bowmans, Blunts, and Reeses. But I also spent time with Joyce, who was in the Mac faction. We had become good friends after the Rike's protest and subsequent jailing. Indeed, it was Joyce who'd first schooled me about picket lines: what to do and what not to do when picketing and protesting. She had taken me under her wing when I was new to CORE, reassuring me that there was "nothing to it" and encouraging me not to be afraid.

One of the non-CORE people accompanying us on the trip was Jim Fain, the editor of the *Dayton Daily News*. Jim had written editorials against our picketing Rike's because, as he saw it, Rike's was an upstanding participant in the business community, and why would we want to stir up trouble? "Race relations in Dayton are good," he claimed. Still, Fain's positions on the growing Civil Rights Movement were considered to be more liberal and progressive than those of many of his peers.

I made it my business to sit next to Jim on the ride to DC, and I engaged him for hours on a variety of topics regarding race and racism that had touched close to home in Dayton and were affecting America at large. My arguments stemmed from personal experience in the South and my political perspective from the viewpoint of a Black American. Fain responded with any number of the standard excuses, rebuttals, and opinions one would expect to hear from a liberal white person. "Colored people have achieved many of the things you all have been fighting for. One could say your protests have accomplished much in the way of integration, but don't you think now you're trying to push for too much without waiting for the lawmakers to implement the changes that already have been brought about by Dr. King and his SCLC? Maybe you're pushing the envelope too much, too soon."

"Maybe we, as a nation, just need more time to adjust," Jim suggested.

I countered, insisting: "But, by and large, Negroes in America are still not considered equal citizens, don't have equal rights, are not allowed equal justice, and certainly don't have equal access to jobs and economic stability. Why do you think this is called the March for Jobs and Freedom? Even in Dayton, you know many places still don't hire Negroes. We have to keep the pressure on!"

Our groups also prayed on the train ride—for our safety and for the safety of the thousands of others expected to arrive at the march. We heard that thousands of police and military forces would be stationed around the city and knew that, with so many Blacks assembled in one place, even the slightest infraction or perceived threat to DC's white establishment could become a lit match resulting in disaster.

Far from intending any ill consequences, CORE's leadership had ensured us that we were all almost utterly "brainwashed" regarding our behavior. They had left no stone unturned in stressing how critically important it was for us to go out of our way to be respectful, courteous, and polite. I remember being told in a training session in Dayton, "If someone steps on your foot, *you* excuse yourself…apologetically!" We prayed for peace, protection, and for our message to be delivered without retaliation or disruption by anyone who would stand in the way of what we meant to accomplish.

Finally, we arrived at the DC station. When our CORE group congregated on the platform, we were met by March organizers who had buses ready to take us to the Washington Monument. There was to be no marching through the streets, they told us. With thousands of marchers expected from across the country, the federal government had outlawed it, afraid the city would be overrun. Most government offices were closed, and workers had been cautioned to stay home and out of the city.

Approaching the Washington Monument, I remember being literally thrilled at seeing the flags rippling in the breeze. What a sight! I was still quite patriotic in my views, and my outlook was like that of most other Blacks attending the March. At that point, we only wanted to be given the opportunities that all other citizens had. We did not want to overthrow the government—at that point, at least. We simply wanted to be treated as fully vested and fully represented citizens of the nation.

When we de-boarded the buses that delivered us to the area near the monument, the point where we would be allowed to begin an abbreviated march, we were handed professionally printed signs supplied by Walter Reuther's United Automobile Workers proclaiming phrases like "JOBS AND FREEDOM!" We'd expected to see thousands of others, but the sheer number of Black people converging on the city was astounding...and empowering. Marching from the Washington Monument to the Lincoln Memorial, I felt great pride and excitement at being part of such a monumental historical event. Speeches, songs, prayers, and inspiring messages were delivered by various speakers. CORE's own leader, James Farmer—who had been imprisoned while leading a march in Donaldsonville, Louisiana, nine days earlier—sent an inspiring message that was read by Floyd McKissick. His speech included the famous statement that our marching, protests, and actions would not stop "until the dogs stop biting us in the South and the rats stop biting us in the North." And, of course, there was the thrill of seeing Dr. King and experiencing his legendary "I Have a Dream" speech firsthand.

As fate would have it, even among all those thousands of people, I ran into an old friend from my Memphis days: Calvin Rolark. It was especially moving to meet someone from my past at this march, which spoke so powerfully to and about our hopes for the future. Calvin would go on to found *The Washington Informer* newspaper a year later and become an important community leader and activist in DC.

Upon our return, we Dayton CORE members reconvened to recap the March during our regular Wednesday night meeting. We each expressed a deep sense of satisfaction and accomplishment at having taken part in such a momentous event. Mac, however, was not pleased with one very important part of the journey: the distribution of the sandwiches on the way to DC.

"My friends," he announced in his usual stentorian tone. "Some of us had baloney…and some of us had ham!" He was, of course, alluding to the quite well-defined schism within the group and the rising grumblings amongst the McIntosh and Maddox factions. Those of us who "had ham" knew very well who we were. We also knew that Mac was telling the truth. In the midst of planning and carrying out our projects and demonstrations in advance of the March, both factions had conspired to outwit one another. The conflict would soon come to a head.

Those of us in the Maddox faction decided that a democratic vote for new leadership should be held—never mind that it was McIntosh who had organized to bring CORE to Dayton in the first place. "He's too authoritarian," was a common complaint within our faction. "His tactics are too gruff," some asserted. "He gives us a bad name," said others. We viewed Mac's leadership style as outmoded and believed the group deserved the more "representative" leadership offered by John Maddox.

There were also recent allegations from some of the Jewish businessmen on Third Street that McIntosh was extorting money from them by threatening boycotts or picketing if they didn't contribute money to CORE. Third Street was the main street through Dayton's Black ghetto and the west side of the city, where the majority of Dayton's Black population lived. Most of the "economically strapped" Black folks shopped on Third Street, looking for bargains in the less-expensive, Jewish-owned thrift stores and second-hand shops. Any threat of a boycott thus portended a grave possibility for the Jewish merchants who did business there. Irrespective and regardless of our politics regarding Blacks and whites, we Maddox-faction members rationalized, we weren't extortionists and had no desire to be viewed that way.

We decided that until a vote could be arranged, perhaps McIntosh needed to be better occupied during the day. One of our members located a suitable position we felt would "complement his talents." When informed of the opportunity, however, McIntosh replied: "My friends, I don't need a job. Civil Rights is a full-time job." Clearly, he was a man ahead of his time! But his response did nothing to assuage our growing feeling that a change was going to have to come…and soon.

Ultimately, we decided to move forward with the election. We marshaled our forces, lobbied the neutrals, and managed to get an election date. We made sure that all our supporters from the Dayton CORE chapter were on hand on the day of the vote. When we trucked into the little union hall, we were flabbergasted: we were greeted with printed ballots and huge voting machines that Mac had procured from the board of elections and, most shocking of all, he had rounded up several busloads of CORE "voters" to secure his election. Mac had outdone us at our own game! We had totally underestimated his ability to ensure that victory would be his and his potential to mobilize a crowd—without us.

Through it all, however, there was never animosity or nastiness.[2] Truth is, we truly appreciated McIntosh's genius. Nonetheless, his leadership style made us "intellectuals" uncomfortable. Despite the internal conflicts, we at CORE continued to protest, demonstrate, hold rallies, distribute leaflets, conduct voter-registration drives, picket, boycott, organize forums on fair housing, and hold community meetings. Yet, we all knew that our days as one group working together were numbered.

It was during those early CORE years that I developed press communication skills—writing bold and outspoken letters to the city's newspapers that called attention to the latest outrages in our communities and the injustices of white supremacy. CORE had taught me the arts of protesting, picketing, leafleting, and agitation—as well

---

2   Later, after becoming a reporter for the *Dayton Daily News*, I was to find out that Mac had been the source of an untrue rumor regarding my having an affair with Jim Fain. I was shocked, but Jim—who told me about the rumor himself—had quite a chuckle about it. "I was kind of flattered at the idea you'd even have me," he laughed.

as getting jailed for standing up to discrimination. If my father had nurtured the seed of Black consciousness during my childhood, then W. S. McIntosh had trained my growing spirit of resistance through CORE's "Activism 101."

Eventually, our faction's disenchantment with Mac's leadership style reached a point of no return and we were ready to embark on a new road. At the same time, a bold, new philosophy— "Black Power" —was spreading, and increasingly I saw our changing methodologies as necessary to the progression of our work. Changing the game demanded new tactics. The time for "peaceful patience" had reached the end of its shelf life.

CHAPTER 6

DARE AND THE DAYTON DAILY NEWS

In 1964, DARE—the Dayton Association for Racial Equality—was established as a breakaway group from the Dayton CORE. At first it was an all-Black group, headed by John Maddox. Later, when the Maddoxes left for Italy, Charles assumed leadership. Original members included Minnie and Floyd Johnson, John and Myrtle Maddox, Clarence Bowman, Ed and Edna Blunt, C. J. McLin, George Ducker, and Jake Adams. We were later joined by several younger members after we opened the Dayton Afro-American Cultural Center.

Along with our Black membership came unexpected camaraderie with two people who would eventually become important to my life: Dick and Miriam Meisler, who I came to call "my only white friends." Dick and Miriam joined DARE along with a number of other white folks.

Aside from our work fighting discriminatory practices in public housing, DARE's first efforts in 1964 included going door-to-door in the heart of the Black community helping Lyndon B. Johnson (LBJ) get re-elected. Although many people accused him of having a typically southern white attitude about Blacks—which he probably did—Johnson also had the vision to grasp the necessity of a more inclusive America. He worked hard to pass the Civil Rights Act of 1964 and created the "Great Society" programs (including the "War on Poverty" mandate), which steadfastly made the elimination of poverty and racial injustice the major themes of his presidency. LBJ did whatever he had to do—back-room deal making, twisting arms, and hunting senators down, one by one—to get the Civil Rights bill passed. Of course, whatever positive is attached to his legacy was trashed by the Vietnam War. But he did a monumental thing for Black people in his fight for the Civil Rights bill as well as the Voting Rights Act of 1965.

DARE also worked in Cleveland to help get the vote out for Carl Stokes, who was running for mayor in 1965 and then again in 1967. Our friend Ruth Perot had become one of the executive members of the Cleveland CORE. At her invitation, DARE traveled there on weekends to assist in Stokes's campaign.

America had not seen many Black mayors since Reconstruction. After a handful took office between 1868 and the late 1880s, the rise of Jim Crow had put an end to Blacks holding public office in the South. The North had fared no better in bringing Blacks into political leadership.

When George D. Carroll took Richmond, California, in 1964, as the first Black elected mayor of a large American city since Reconstruction, it signaled another change in climate created by the Civil Rights Movement. When fellow Ohioan Robert C. Henry won the 1965 mayoral election in Springfield, proving to us that Carroll's election wasn't a fluke, we were encouraged even more.

Those of us working on Carl Stokes's losing mayoral campaign in 1965 returned to push for him in 1967, convinced he could win. His first bid had slipped beyond his grasp by a narrow margin of less than 200 votes, but we believed that, with more time to raise resources and awareness, he'd be able to garner the necessary votes the second time around.

During Stokes's second campaign, we worked tirelessly to get Black people registered to vote, going door-to-door to talk with them about their concerns and trying to convince them it was worth their time and effort to get to the polls. In some cases, we arranged transportation or drove voters to the polls ourselves, as public transportation was next to nil and polling centers were often placed in distant locations. Our efforts were rewarded in 1967 when Stokes won his bid for the mayor's office, becoming the first Black mayor of one of the ten biggest cities in America. At that time, Cleveland was being billed as "the best location in the nation," so his win was considered a major event for Blacks.

DARE also took part in community meetings following Dayton's first-ever "race riot" in September 1966. Toward the end of an oppressive summer, violence exploded on Third Street after the murder of thirty-nine-year-old Lester Mitchell. Mitchell was shot to death by white men in a pickup truck while he was sweeping the sidewalk outside his house on Fifth Street, just blocks away from west Dayton's Main Street. A frustrated crowd marched through the streets, voicing their anger at the inaction of the police immediately following Mitchell's killing and the sense that very little would be done to find his killer. Things eventually took a turn toward violence and looting. The mayor called in the National Guard. Charles, along with several other civil rights leaders, was arrested and made the papers for inciting violence after leading a protest calling for justice. As expected, no arrests were ever made, and Mitchell's murder was to go unsolved.

The following year, DARE participated in demonstrations and protests surrounding the 1967 death of Robert Elwood Barbee. Barbee, 41, was a Social Security Administration worker who was stopped by an off-duty police officer who claimed to see a large "bulge" in Barbee's pocket. When Barbee apparently tried to walk away, he was shot in the back by the white officer, who claimed Barbee had a gun. We knew Barbee personally, and anybody acquainted with him knew that this was a huge lie. He was a very refined and intelligent brother who had taken part in a DARE reading circle that focused on classic Black books. We knew he wasn't the type to carry a gun. Later, the police "discovered" the object in his pocket was a smoking pipe, which Barbee was known to carry.

The FBI's accounts of the rally include the following comments:

```
Florence Tate and her husband were
instrumental in the planning and organizing
of the rally and march in Dayton, Ohio, on
January 26, 1968, called "Black Labor Day.".

The "Journal Herald,", supra, carried an
article entitled, "Negroes March Quietly
in Collier Ruling Protest" on page 1 of the
January 27, 1968, edition. According to the
article Charles Tate, at the Rally, called
for a boycott of downtown stores. Tate stated,
```

"For Black people there'll be no Easter and Christmas in 1968.". Tate added "We shall boycott, we shall strike, and we shall shoot when we're threatened by white racists.".

Following the rally, marchers paused at the spot where Robert Barbee, a Negro, was shot and killed by Robert Collier, a Dayton detective, on September 17, 1967.

MEMORANDUM
CONFIDENTIAL

TO: DIRECTOR, FBI
DATE: 3/18/68
SAC, CINCINATTI DAYTON ALLIANCE FOR RACIAL
EQUALITY (DARE)
RACIAL MATTERS

On 1/26/68, at twelve noon a rally was held by approximately 200 to 300 Negroes at a grocery parking lot at Third and Conover Streets on the westside, which is a Negro community in Dayton, Ohio.

Following the rally, they marched on the sidewalk to Second and Ludlow Streets in the downtown area of Dayton. The marchers paused at the spot where ROBERT BARBEE, a Negro, was shot and killed by a Dayton detective on 9/17/67. On the return march through the westside of Dayton, the group passed the

```
Montgomery County Courts Building and the
Dayton Safety Building. The marchers "dropped
out" and were largely disbursed on arrival
at the point of origin. The PD considered the
march orderly, and no placards or signs were
carried. A few verbal exchanges occurred
according to the police between the younger
marchers and passersby, but no incidents
developed and no reports were made by their
department.
```

We were also very active in the movement toward the desegregation of schools and improving the education system in west Dayton. At one point we even ran Charles for the school board as an independent write-in candidate. He ran against C. J. McLin, a popular funeral-home owner who had been among the Macintosh Faction while we were in CORE. Charles lost the election, but we had a spirited time registering people to vote and canvassing streets, businesses, and bars.

One distinct memory of our canvassing stands out. While we were in one of the dicier neighborhoods, in one of the grittier bars, a patron asked the bartender for "seconds." Never having heard the term, we asked the bartender what it meant. He responded, "You pour everything that anyone has left over in the glass after finishing their drink into the same bottle," the bartender explained. "That's 'seconds,' and it's cheaper." I thought it was the most sickening thing I'd ever heard, but after passing out our flyers we left the bar with new insights into the depths of poverty in Dayton's ghetto.

During the summer of 1969, we carried out one of my favorite DARE actions. James Forman had just written his "Black Manifesto," and the tract had been formally adopted at Detroit's recent Black Economic Development Conference. Forman had barged into Riverside Church in New York to read the Manifesto's demands, which were addressed to "the white Christian churches and the Jewish synagogues." Like many pro-Black groups around the country, DARE decided to disrupt a Sunday service at the very large, proper, and all-white First Baptist Church to read the Manifesto. We marched in and, in unison, began to repeat Forman's entire script, beginning with, *"We the Black people assembled...are fully aware that we have been forced to come together because racist white America has exploited our resources, our minds, our bodies, our labor..."*

Given the location, the congregation, and the period, it was really quite a to-do. Needless to say, the churchgoers were appalled. The authorities were called, and several DARE members were jailed that Sunday afternoon. But invading the lily-white walls of that church with the demands of the "Black Manifesto" is still one of my most thrilling protest experiences.

Dick Meisler: *Florence was always informed about what "Civil Rights Movement-thinking" was, either from what she read or from the various people that she communicated with...and it went through various stages. There was one point when we felt that we needed to be community organizers and work with the social and economic problems and try to help people develop solutions rather than simply advocate for civil rights.... There was, of course, the time when the Black Power Movement came in, and Florence was very knowledgeable and up-to-date about those things.*

Florence was a source of information and philosophy for everyone about what was happening... and when I say that she was "the smartest person in the room," part of what that meant is that when something was happening, or new developments were coming along, or people were thinking in new ways, Florence not only knew about it—she had already done the thinking, had tried to sort out the issues, had tried to figure out really what's going on here, what's valid, what's just a fad... what's important. So that's one of the things she brought to the table.

Another thing she brought to the table was being a very good organizer.... If we were going out on a march, Florence knew where we were going. She told us what kind of clothes to wear. She told us if we were going to sing songs or not.... She provided a lot of organization for DARE and for what we were doing, down to the details.

Dayton was a strictly segregated city. The west side was all Black, and the rest of Dayton was all white. There was no integrated housing, and we were protesting the city's refusal to open the segregated public housing on Dayton's east side, which was in much better condition than the public housing in Black neighborhoods. The public housing in white neighborhoods also usually had available apartments, unlike the housing in west Dayton, which always had a waiting list.

As a mixed-race group, DARE stood out just by virtue of the fact that we were violating the status quo of the city's Black-white dynamic. We were also doing things in Dayton on behalf of the Civil Rights Movement that had not been done before.

> **Miriam Meisler:** *We were selling buttons in front of a super-market... and I'm going up to these people selling buttons—a Black button with a white equal sign across the width. And we were asking a dollar for the buttons. So, I go up to this old white guy, gnarled, and presumably not a wealthy guy... and while I was about 21, 22 years old, I looked about fifteen. I ask him if he wants to buy one of these buttons, and he says, "Ok, I'll buy your button." And then he asks, "Just one thing—why does it have an eleven on it?"*
>
> *I'm not sure we were raising consciousness... but we were out there, and it was not easy. I had never seen so much poverty. I remember one door opened. I knocked and the door opened... and we were right in the living room. It was probably a one-room apartment, and it was papered only with newspaper.... The walls were covered with torn newspaper.*

Though we were never afraid that we were going to be lynched or murdered like those young people had been in the South, the fact was we never knew what the reaction would be, depending on where we were. It was always a tense situation when we were out demonstrating, leafleting, or whatever we were doing because we never knew how we would be received.

These years comprised some of the most vital periods of my life. Today, I still think of things in terms of before, during, and after the Civil

Rights Movement. Although I haven't seen many of the people from DARE since that time, I'll never forget them. It was like a big family.

My close relationship with Dick and Miriam has developed over these many years—and we've remained committed to keeping our friendship alive, though we've been separated by geography and time and experiences. We know each other's children, their marriages, their sicknesses and deaths. We've experienced all of that with each other, and we've had great times over the years. But the original and initial bonding came during the work we did while in DARE.

While working with DARE my life took a fortuitous turn. I gained some notoriety during that time writing political "Letters to the Editor" that were published in the major Dayton newspaper, *The Journal Herald*. I shared my views on a number of subjects having to do with civil rights issues, and soon my name became well known in the newspaper circle.

Additionally, when the CORE group went to the March on Washington, we were accompanied on the train by Jim Fain, the editor of the *Dayton Daily News*, which was the sister paper of *The Journal Herald*. The *Herald* was issued in the morning and tended to be more conservative while the *Daily News* was the evening paper, known for being more progressive, or liberal, in its bent.

I'd made it my business to sit with Jim Fain on the way to the March on Washington. We discussed the pressing Movement-related current events, and by the time we got to Washington he was, in my opinion, a "convert." He was obviously affected by his experience because, after the March, the paper's editorial position on the ongoing struggle for Black equality in Dayton changed noticeably. The articles became much more sympathetic, actively covering the numerous issues concerning Black Americans and instances of racism in Ohio and across the country.

I had always been interested in journalism. I was the editor of my high school newspaper but had no training in the field. While working with CORE and DARE, however, my fiery "protest" letters were soon noticed.

April 25, 1964

DMHA Policy
Editor of The Journal Herald:

I would like to make some observations concerning the discriminatory practice of the Dayton Metropolitan Housing Authority in its administration of public housing in our city.

The practice of maintaining separate application files for prospective Negro and white tenants, and the placement policy of assigning Negroes primarily to West Dayton housing projects, and whites to Parkside Homes, Edgewood, and Summit Courts, is particularly despicable.

As a result of these two things, Desoto Bass has 100 per cent Negro occupancy, while Parkside Homes has two Negro families out of a total of 604 families; Edgewood Court has 123 white and 10 Negro families, and Summit Court has 120 white and 19 Negro families. These statistics are not accidental, but are the direct result of a discriminatory tenant placement policy...

—Florence Tate

August 1, 1964
In Dark Days
Editor:

You have printed several editorials
dealing with the unfortunate social violence
that has occurred in New York City, and in
Rochester, N.Y., and you rightfully voiced that
lawlessness not be allowed to prevail...

However... in these dark days for our
country, I would hope that a newspaper
such as the Journal Herald also would see
fit to try to convince white America of the
imperative need to be rid of the evil system of
segregation and discrimination which can only
destroy our country if allowed to continue.
While it is certainly necessary to deplore and
resist these orgies of violence, it is equally
necessary to stress the need to erase the basic
reasons for their existence.

Although it is not directly related to the
above, your reaction (June 29 editorial) to the
proposal of the Dayton Alliance for Racial
Equality to sit down with the "power structure"
of our city and talk turkey warrants some
comment too.

It seems that whenever a suggestion or
proposal is offered by a responsible civil
rights group (or any other group of concerned
individuals) that you would at least try to
give it the benefit of your omnipresent doubt,
before you start to impugn the motives of those
of those offering the suggestion.

We in the Dayton Alliance for Racial
Equality are fervently and constantly seeking
ways and means of attacking the problems of
segregation and discrimination that exist in
our city. We issued the invitation to some of
the most influential members of the Dayton

establishment to talk with us, along with other concerned individuals, to see if together we could explore conditions and discover areas of possible cooperation in tackling these problems, so that we could possibly avoid the kind of disaster that befell Rochester.

We certainly did not (indeed, would not and could not) intend our invitation to be seen as a threat. But a threat does exist, however, and shall continue to exist as long as civil rights groups which advocate change through peaceful nonviolent action are not even listened to.

—Mrs. Florence Tate

One day, I received a call from *The Journal Herald* about writing some more op-eds for the paper. I was surprised but had the distinct feeling it was a case of "keeping your enemy close." It seemed that perhaps the editors had decided—since I was determined to write with such frank vehemence—they'd better find a way to bring me "into the fold."

After all, this was a period when everybody was trying to recruit so-called "decent Negroes" to integrate their staffs, and it wasn't unheard of that a company would consider taking someone who had no experience, hire them, and provide them with on-the-job-training.

That call got my wheels turning, but I didn't want to work for *The Journal Herald*. If I'm going to work for a newspaper, I decided, I wanted to work for the *Dayton Daily News*. So, I called Jim Fain and told him about the call I had received from *The Journal Herald* and of my preference for a position at the *Daily News*.

Although he knew journalism would be new territory for me, the offer by his competitor encouraged Jim to consider me. "Well, Florence, I know you're not a trained journalist, but I have some books on journalism. Why don't you read them, get the fundamentals, and we'll give it a shot," he suggested.

My on-the-job training included accompanying experienced reporters for a month, observing and listening to their news-gathering techniques, assisting them at news scenes in any way possible, and writing my own practice versions of the stories when we returned to the newsroom. Whenever time permitted, a copy editor or a more experienced reporter would examine my copy and make suggestions for changes or edits. Along with my trusty *Reporter's Handbook*, I soon felt capable enough to go out alone, get the news, write my copy, and confidently hand it in to the city desk before the daily deadline.

I started working at the *Dayton Daily News* in 1964 or 1965. For a time, I worked the evening shift, from three or four p.m. to eleven p.m. or midnight. It was an almost all-white newsroom, except for one Black reporter, Paul Delaney, who had been recruited from Atlanta and had a graduate degree in journalism. Paul went on to become a much-lauded reporter at the *New York Times*. We had met before I arrived at the *Daily News* through various civil rights connections and, on starting at the paper, I looked to him for moral support and was glad to know he had my back as I began my career as a novice reporter.

The newsroom was also predominantly male, and the few other women on staff—white women—worked in a back room, relegated to the paper's society section and its "women's pages," which focused on weddings, births, parties, and anything that was considered to be within women's purview. All the frivolous stuff. But I was a general assignment reporter, and during my two-and-a-half years I learned to cover all the "beats": church and religion, business, the courts, policing, education, and, of course, civil rights. I quickly developed the distinct feeling that the other women on staff deeply resented my being out there with the men and covering the "hard news," especially as a brand-new hire.

Of course, I made gaffes in the beginning. On my very first writing assignment, I was sent downtown to cover a parade. My idea was to find something happening and get a good 'scoop'—but when I got to the parade, I quickly decided there was nothing worth covering. "Well, this is a bust," I grumbled, disappointed. "Nothing happening here worth writing a whole story about!" Without another thought, instead of going back to tell Jim or anybody else that there was no piece, I just went home. I didn't know that if you're on assignment for a story, you'd better come up with something because there will be a hole there waiting for your copy. Needless to say, when I went in the next day there was a whole lot of complaining and, in truth, if Jim Fain had not been my protector, I would have been gone because the guys in the newsroom were put out and beside themselves with annoyance. Fortunately, I learned from that experience and soon proved that I could do the work and become a very good reporter.

Another thing that aided me immensely in learning the ins and outs of news reporting was the daily lunch with my hard-boiled and cynical male colleagues. After hunkering down with them in their favorite "watering hole," and usually over alcohol, they would conduct a ritual review of the morning's news events. This often meant griping about what had been edited out of their copy and why, sharing the things they had purposely left out, and bragging about how they had skillfully snuck some no-no past "the desk."

It was while hanging out with Paul and the rest of the guys that I learned that the best stuff—the most "juicy" part of the news—often doesn't reach the newspaper. Copy that was too strong or upsetting could be discussed among those of us at lunch, but it would never make it past the desk. Far more experienced than I, they also schooled me on how to add more zest to my copy to make dull stories interesting, how to turn a good story into great story by making it "pop," and how to elicit provocative and/or or controversial quotes from important news sources.

I loved it! I relished being "in the know" and privy to the scandalous details that were well beyond what the general population of readers would digest in the morning tabloids. I became very popular with the guys, and it was only later that one of the white girls told me how jealous they were and how awful it was that they had been working there and had never been promoted.

Because of my involvement in the Civil Rights Movement and subsequently in Black Power activism, my insights, opinions, sensitivities to racial issues, and suggestions on news assignments and coverage were often solicited and accepted. I was frequently called upon to cover matters of particular interest, concern, or importance to the Black community. Additionally, given my Movement activities, I had direct access to all the local community leaders and activists as well as many of the national ones. It was during this time that I took Stokely Carmichael and Ivanhoe Donaldson to meet the editors at the *Daily News*.

Still, I managed to be both a "closet activist" and an "objective reporter" and was able to continue my Civil Rights and Black Power Movement activities without either being considered a conflict of interest. Maybe the editors were just happy to have a someone like me to send out on assignments. Not only was I able to connect with the Black people on the frontlines of those struggles, but I could also write a good story about changing race relations in Dayton from *within* both movements.

> **Paul Delaney:** *I was shocked that, being the activist that she was, being the revolutionary that she was, Florence could adapt and become a reporter in what must have been kind of a conservative setting for her, but she was an excellent writer. I was just amazed that she decided to make that change and come into that staid environment. She was a flaming revolutionary, but she adapted to daily journalism pretty easily. She was anticipated. She was known because she had already written several pieces for the paper before she was hired.*
>
> *She was not a journalist, but she picked up on it very quickly, and the surprising thing was that she seemed to like it. She moved into the newsroom and fell right into what journalism was all about. Obviously smart, she learned very quickly that she could not be an activist in the newsroom because the editor wasn't going to let her. So you could say she was two different people; on the outside, her activities were certainly different than what she did in the newsroom.*

I was working at the paper during the Dayton Riots of 1967, a period that came to be called "the Long, Hot Summer." Riots were breaking out around the country in other cities as well: Detroit, Newark, Cleveland, Cincinnati, Atlanta, Tampa, New York, Milwaukee, Minneapolis, Chicago, Birmingham, and Buffalo.

At one point, while covering the riots in Dayton, I ended up right in the middle of a group of young men who were dodging police activity, throwing bricks, and whatever else. I managed to pull one of the guys aside to interview and pose him for a picture. I queried him about his reasons for taking part in the riots, and he gave me a very "street revolutionary" speech about what he was doing. I found it somewhat humorous when, sometime later, while doing campus liaison work with SNCC at Central State sometime later, I ran into this same street revolutionary dressed as—and with the demeanor of—a clean-cut college student.

Two of the most exciting series of stories I wrote during my time at the *Daily News* were directly related to the social conditions Blacks were battling. One of those assignments—"Crown Point...a New Look"—was an in-depth series on living conditions in an all-Black, semi-urban slum adjacent to Dayton, in which one slumlord owned a large percentage of the grossly deteriorated housing stock and where municipal and county services were practically nil. With the help of a friend who was a highly trained sociologist, I devised a basic set of questions for a statistical, random-sampling survey and interviewed a third of the more than 300 households in Crown Point.

During the course of my investigation, I researched county and city records for deeds to determine the ownership and cost of all the Crown Point housing. I also interviewed local, state, and federal housing officials; local civil rights and social welfare leaders; teachers and students at the schools attended by Crown Point children; and former residents of Crown Point. All those activities enabled me to make the plight of Crown Point residents come alive on the front pages of the *Daily News* for a period of weeks.

Articles with titles such as "Many Crown Point Residents Old Settlers" (March 14, 1966), "They Solve Their Own Problems" (March 16, 1966), "Profiteering Slum Owners Thwart Law" (March 20, 1966), and "Residents Stress Leadership Needs" (March 21, 1966) appeared, accompanied by photos illustrating the neighborhood's deplorable conditions. The series offered a powerful depiction of the inner resolve of Crown Point's Black inhabitants as they faced daily struggles to maintain their humanity and dignity while living in the blighted neighborhood. Following publication of the series, officials moved to ensure that city slumlords bring their properties up to code. They also initiated new city and county services for garbage collection and street cleaning and began installation of additional sewer and water facilities.

Another series of articles of which I'm particularly proud was an expose I wrote on the Edison School, a vastly ill-equipped and thoroughly demoralized west Dayton public education institution. A telephone tip from a concerned teacher at the school prompted me to quietly slip into the facility one day (this was at a time when security at school campuses was next to nil). Peering into a number of the school's classrooms confirmed my source's claims of the lack of even the most basic resources. From what I could see, the only things in the classrooms were the teachers, the students, and, ironically, the ever-present American flag. There were no educational materials or motivational tools. No textbooks, bulletin boards, posters, pictures or even children's artwork could be seen. I also observed the principal, who was white, "disciplining" students in the hallway with two-inch wooden paddles, even though state laws forbade corporal punishment in schools.

I interviewed several Edison teachers during after-school hours and talked with parents, students, and the principal. When I submitted my first set of stories to the city editor, he expressed dislike for the "tone" of my stories and implied that I was being biased against the white principal on behalf of the Black students and parents. After several unsatisfactory revisions, in an attempt to "de-bias" the stories, and the passage of several weeks, the city editor informed me that he was not going to use them at all.

I was hardly about to let my investigations go unpublished! I used the organizing skills I had acquired during my work in the Civil Rights Movement and had parents, students, teachers, and other concerned members of the city's Black community telephone Jim Fain to inquire about the publication date for the Edison School stories. All that prompted Jim to come down to the paper's city room and find out for himself just what was going on.

Needless to say, with Jim involved, the stories ran. As a result of the stories, the local board of education began supplying the Edison School with textbooks and resources, the principal and teachers committed to make positive changes in their teaching and administrative styles, and the parents organized to monitor the school and its educational processes. Several months later, I made a return visit to the school and reported on the visible results of all these changes. It was extremely rewarding to be able to witness beneficial changes in existing conditions because of my investigative reporting.

It was a very exciting time to be learning the ropes as a journalist, and my experiences working for the paper would be invaluable years later when I became a press secretary. My years working as a reporter taught me how to develop good relations with various members of the press, assess the community's "thermometer" on issues affecting residents' wellbeing, and call attention to the gaps in policy that worked against the interests of what I was most concerned about: the Black community as a whole.

Charles Tate and Kwame Ture

Florence interviewing SNCC Field Secretary Charlie Cobb,
Dayton Ohio, 1966

Black Umoja 1967

DARE Fashion Show 1967

Integrating Ohio Bell Telephone 1958

Florence

CHAPTER 7

STOKELY, SNCC, BLACK POWER, BLACK UMOJA SOCIETY

By the time Stokely arrived in Dayton in 1966, one of the largest stories that year had been the shooting of James Meredith during his March Against Fear. Dr. King, Stokely, and others had voted to continue Meredith's journey while he recuperated in the hospital. Meredith rejoined the March as it entered Jackson, Mississippi.

It was during this march that the phrase "Black Power" exploded into the public vernacular. Stokely had been arrested on a stop during the March and, upon his release, had furiously and famously announced that he was through with being jailed.

This is the twenty-seventh time I have been arrested—and I ain't going to jail no more!… The only way we gonna stop them white men from whuppin' us is to take over. We been saying freedom for six years and we ain't got nuthin'. What we gonna start saying now is 'Black Power'![3]

Despite Meredith's shooting and the various squabbles and minor incidents of violence against protestors, the March Against Fear was considered a success, bringing as many as 15,000 individuals together in solidarity by the time of its culmination in Jackson. Many knew that the March was accomplished despite a tenuous set of allegiances undercut by a growing rift. The undertaking brought to the surface the friction between SNCC's anti-integrationist call for racial self-determination and independence and the SCLC's call for nonviolent, integrationist methods.

---

3   https://www.Blackagendareport.com/karen_spellman_sncc_Black_power; http://www2.iath.virginia.edu/sixties/HTML_docs/Texts/Narrative/King_What_We_Want.html.

Those of us working in Dayton were as eager as any to hear from Stokely exactly what was going on in the Movement around the country. Though we all loved, admired, respected, believed in, and were grateful for the work of Dr. King and SCLC, we had also started to realize that white people were only going to allow Blacks so much power and equality. We needed to hear what Stokely's Black Power contingent had planned.

After Stokely finished speaking at the Unitarian church that afternoon, Charles and I invited several DARE members to our home to meet with him and SNCC field secretary Ivanhoe Donaldson, who had accompanied him to Dayton. Our guests included Ed Blunt, well-to-do funeral parlor owner Clarence Bowman, John and Myrtle Maddox, George Drucker, and a few others. In this intimate setting, we felt we could better focus on the matters that most affected our interests. Our group was thrilled to have this controversial, outspoken national figure in our presence to share news about all the goings-on in the struggle around the country. We were open and indeed prepared to support this young yet seasoned activist, but we had many questions. For one thing, we wanted to know about the strategies and tactics Black Power would bring to coalitions and alliances like our own. We also wondered just how far SNCC's militancy planned to go and whether Black people in the Movement were expected to be ready to go that far as well.

As soon as we made our introductions all around, the questions began: "Stokely, what exactly is the present state of affairs between you and Dr. King now that SNCC is wholeheartedly embracing the Black Power stance? I heard rumor that some members of SNCC had even dared to say Dr. King could 'kiss their ass'!" "And what's become of Bob Moses?" (This question was referring to the inspiring SNCC leader who'd abruptly resigned, announcing that he was leaving the Movement and would never talk to another white person in his life.) "I heard the reason he's dropping the name Moses and going by Robert Parrish is really related to dodging the draft. Is it true?" "We heard that white folkses' donations are drying up now that SNCC is trying to oust its white members (on top of dropping nonviolence in favor of Black Power). Do you all think you can stay afloat without their money?"

Over the course of the next several hours, our visitors discussed the philosophy of Black Power with us, attempting to clarify its concepts. They described it as a way for Black people to come together to improve our communities and make decisions without interference by whites. Black Power alluded to the power we would engage and encourage to accomplish and seek out whatever we thought would heal and empower our people and communities.

By the end of their conversation, we were all very inspired and felt that we had a better understanding of where SNCC was headed. It was an enlightening and exciting evening, and everyone found both SNCC members friendly and likable. It was easy to see why people would be moved to follow Stokely's passion and determined vision.

Feeling welcomed and at home by their acceptance into our Dayton community and after meeting our DARE friends, Stokely and Ivanhoe decided to stay a few days more. "I'll tell you, Mrs. Tate, I had a feeling we were going to be alright when I saw you," Stokely confided as we two sat in my tiny dining room eating breakfast the next morning. "Last thing we expected was to see someone out here in Ohio with a natural," he laughed, referring to my newly adopted Afro hairstyle. "But when I saw you, I knew we'd come to the right place!" This made me very pleased with myself for being "ahead of the curve" and adopting the natural look before most women in Dayton even dared to stop pressing their hair.

Over the next few days, Charles and I engaged in round-the-clock discussions with Stokely and Ivanhoe about the efficacy of SNCC, CORE, SCLC, the various Civil Rights Movement agendas versus that of the Black Power movement and their impact on Black Americans, and the players backing each.

We also shared with them what we were doing with DARE, including our attempts to integrate Dayton's public housing. As we explained, when the city's public apartment dwellings first came about as a result of one of Roosevelt's Federal Works programs, they offered much-improved and affordable places for low-income families. They were undoubtedly a better alternative to the rundown shacks and shotgun houses into which Blacks from the South had been herded during their migrations north. Equipped with electricity, indoor heating, and plumbing, there were often long waiting lists to enter the public housing reserved for Black people in west Dayton. On the other hand, the white public housing—located in east Dayton—was more readily available. There were often vacancies, so whites rarely, if ever, went on a waiting list.

DARE was protesting the policies that kept Blacks out of housing reserved for whites and barred from participating on the board of the public housing authority. In truth, we had been told by many Negroes, in and out of public housing, that they didn't want to "live out there with those white folks," and it wasn't hard to see why. During our times picketing and protesting in the east Dayton projects, we'd been spit on, treated to thrown rocks, and threatened with aggressive racist taunts and threats.

When we shared this with Stokely, he seemed incredulous. "Why would y'all even be doing that?" he demanded. "That's precisely *not* what we should be aiming for—to live among a bunch of people whose interests are not our interests. No, you're using your efforts in the wrong way. We don't need to be begging white people to live in their derelict public housing. We need to figure out how to get more and better housing of our own!"

His words struck a resounding note. Charles and I already felt it was high time for Black folks to start "doing for self," and Stokely's ideas about what Black people should be seeking continued to turn my head around.

While they were staying with us, I took Stokely and Ivanhoe to meet Reverend Flanigan, the lone Black minister in Dayton who supported the more radical civil rights groups and allowed us to use his church for political and community events. I also took them to the Antioch and Central State college campuses to meet some of the student organizers there.

Since I was working as a reporter at the *Dayton Daily News* at the time, I also arranged an editorial meeting for Stokely and Ivanhoe with Jim Fain, my managing editor, and another senior editor. They had a very long talk. I'm sure the two editors expected Stokely to confirm the media's depiction of him as the young rabble-rouser behind the "Black Power Menace," but, always aware of how to connect with his listeners, Stokely was able to win them over as well.

After Stokely and Ivanhoe left us, I decided to do everything possible to support the young people in SNCC who were "down South" fighting to make a difference. I started doing fundraising for SNCC to support their work.

We eventually did drop our picketing at the white housing projects after our friend Ruth Turner, the regional CORE representative in Cleveland, shared that she thought it was a counterproductive idea. We eventually succeeded in getting a Negro on the public housing board, though not a progressive one, as it turned out. We also stopped our work at the white public housing because we saw the wisdom and logic of Stokely's new direction and ultimately decided to fully embrace the concept of Black Power—which seemed like a logical next step to propel the forward momentum of a movement that seemed to be reaching a plateau.

After spending time with the young leaders from SNCC and being introduced to the workings of their group, I had a feeling I would be able to raise quite a lot of money for them through our Dayton contacts within the Black business and professional classes. Though it might seem today that many people were on board with Movement activity, the fact is that few middle-class Blacks in the Dayton area were truly invested in doing the leg work of the Civil Rights Movement. Many, however, were supportive and believed in the mission, even if they didn't want to do the work. Those were the folks I arranged meetings with and lobbied for support.

Charles was still working his way up the ladder at Gentile Air Force Base and knew all the engineers and other military service professionals. I was still friendly with the women of the Alpha Wives. We had various other connections to the middle-class Black community in the area.

I remember calling a doctor friend one day who was active in organizing a monthly brunch held by the Black medical professionals in Dayton. After exchanging formalities, I immediately launched into my pitch. "Alex, I'm working with Stokely Carmichael and SNCC to help raise funds for their direct-action, voting-rights, and protest work in the South. They're attacking our kids on all fronts, beating them, throwing them into jail at the drop of a hat, and sometimes worse. They need money for food, travel, bail, lawyers. Can you get me into your brunch next month to talk to all your doctor friends? You know this is important. We may not be down there in the thick of it getting our behinds kicked, but we're still part of this," I reminded him.

"Florence," he equivocated, "let me talk to them and see what they…"

"Alex," I interrupted him, "This is urgent! They're locking our kids up, beating their heads in. They need legal representation, and that takes money."

My friend acquiesced. A week-and-a-half later, I was before twelve to fifteen doctors from the Dayton area, plying them for money as they ate their eggs and sausages. I outlined the work SNCC was doing in the South, enumerating the costs of travel, food, and the most expensive item of all: bail.

By the time I finished my impassioned pitch, the doctors were reaching for their wallets and cash was being stuffed in envelopes. When all was said and done, I raised well over ten thousand dollars, which was an enormous sum for those days. I called the SNCC headquarters in New York, where I'd been instructed to share any fundraising news, and told them what I'd raised. The young people on the other end of the phone were ecstatic and wanted me to bring the money personally to New York rather than send it by wire or mail. So, I went to the New York SNCC office to make this delivery, and there met Jim Forman and others, including a young Mae Jackson— activist, poet, and former treasurer and office manager of the New York SNCC office—who would become a lifelong friend. Although I was to discover that the FBI had taken a special interest in my dealings with Stokely over the years, he was only one of any number of young people I opened my house to during those years.

Mae Jackson, one of many young people from various national SNCC offices who came through Dayton during those years, recalls how she ended up at my house after an uncomfortable interaction with a New York Black Panther member when the two organizations were sharing office space in the late-60s:

Mae Jackson: *I needed a place to hide out for a while, and Julius Lester told me that he wanted me to go stay with Mrs. Tate in Ohio. Everybody used to go to Mrs. Tate's house to rest, so that wasn't unusual. When I look back now it seems very odd because people don't open up their homes today in the way that they did at that time. And all you had to do was call Mrs. Tate and tell her you were going to come, and that was it. It was wonderful because it was a beautiful home, and it was a family. I would stay for a couple of months and I would leave, and then I would just show up again. I'd just say, "I'm going to Dayton," and it never occurred to me that you have to call and let someone know that you're coming to Dayton. It just never occurred to me that you did that with Mrs. Tate. You just showed up and said, 'Oh, I'm at the bus station, or the train station, or at the airport'.*

It was anybody who was coming through town.... All that Mrs. Tate needed to know was if you were in the Movement and what you were doing, and you could go to her house. You could stay, you could eat.... She had a family that she was raising, and she opened up her door.

I met many SNCC people upon traveling to the organization's headquarters in Atlanta: Charlie Cobb, Karen Edmonds (who later became Karen Spellman), Freddie Biddle, Jennifer Lawson, Cleve Sellers, and Courtland Cox, among them. They all became and remain a part of my life.

Charlie Cobb: *Florence took a kind of big sisterly interest in me. That's what I remember feeling. And at least part of her mission, it seemed to me, was to relieve—if you will—and help me ease out from under the stresses and strains of the work in the South. So, I'd get these phone calls from Florence: "How are you doing?" and "You need to come up here to Dayton, Charlie, and relax and have a good meal." And I'd go up. She'd put me up in her sons' room—Greg and Brian were little boys then—and we would all sprawl on the bed reading Marvel Comic books, and Florence would cook. It was like being in a real home as opposed to the life we were living in Mississippi in the South.*

And Florence was proud to introduce us, to introduce me and other people who came regularly, like Stokely and Ivanhoe. And she was proud to introduce us to her network, these young SNCC people that she was providing R&R for in Dayton, Ohio.

We became very close. So, in relationship to me, and I suppose also Stokely and Ivanhoe, she had two missions: one, she felt that after a while we just needed to get out of the South and come up and sit at her kitchen table… and two, she wanted people in Dayton to know about SNCC and the southern movement.

I think now that perhaps my own chaotic and transitive childhood not only prepared me to be more flexible in life—because I had to adapt to so many different personalities, and I couldn't get locked into one way of doing things—but was also probably responsible for my inclination toward opening my home to a variety of young people over the years. It put a soft spot in my heart for youth in search of a better life for themselves and others.

I came to realize what our house represented to those kids in the Movement many years later in DC, when Charlie was having a New Year's Eve party. A young man approached me, obviously knowing me, although I didn't recognize him. "Oh, Mrs. Tate! This is Mrs. Tate!" he gestured excitedly to his wife. "You remember I told you how, when we would leave the South on our way to wherever, we would think: 'We just got to get to Mrs. Tate's house! If we could just get to Mrs. Tate's house!' It was like the Underground Railroad. If you could just to get to Mrs. Tate's house, then you'd plot your way from there!"

During the mid-1960s in Dayton and after we moved to Washington, DC, in 1969, our home became an unofficial rooming house for many students, activists, and wandering souls. We always had an extra bedroom because by that time our eldest, Geri, had left to go to college. And, of course, there was always the basement or one of the couches, so it was never a problem for somebody to stay for days, weeks, months, and, in some cases, years.

During those years, I also worked as a SNCC "campus advisor" to Antioch, Wilberforce, and Central State colleges, which were all within a thirty-mile radius of Dayton. I would help to spread SNCC's message during my campus visits with these young people.

One of the young men I met would end up becoming a lifelong friend: Michael Tarif Warren, now a distinguished civil rights attorney in New York. At the time, Mike was attending Central State University in Wilberforce, Ohio. Not long after we met, he was involved in a major incident at Central State. The students were bringing Black Power to the campus and doing whatever they could to increase its reach. Mike was a fiery young man and had given a speech that landed him in some hot water.

Michael Tarif Warren: *The general statement was, if the revolution occurred at this very moment, then, in essence, all Toms would have to suffer the consequences. And a couple of days later, I was brought before the dean at my university, Central State, and I was denied all manners of due process. I wasn't allowed to call any witnesses, wasn't given any advance notice to prepare a case, but simply told to leave the campus and never come back. And I was escorted off.*

And, of course, because we had developed a relationship and Florence knew SNCC people—she was part of SNCC... and we had developed that relationship with them already before this situation developed—... we called down to Atlanta and had some SNCC people come up, and we organized our own core of students between Antioch and Central... and I returned to campus that following Monday. I was escorted off on Friday, and I returned that Monday.

The college was closed down, automatically, for about two weeks. The students were abruptly sent home because the president had ordered it to be closed. The students had taken over the campus, and they had battled. They got engaged in a battle with the state police and the National Guard, and there were casualties on both sides, so the students were politicized as a result of that.

But Florence and Charles were always there.... There was sort of a symposium on the issue of how the school could return to some level of—for lack of a better word—equilibrium. And I remember Florence's real and only demand, and she made this clearly known, was Mike Warren has to be readmitted. I had to be readmitted. That was her only demand at that time, at least her foremost demand.

On the day of the symposium (mentioned by Mike above), I'd called off from work at the *Dayton Daily News* to go over to the campus to be with him that afternoon. I worked for the evening edition of the paper, which meant I should have been out covering a story during that time. Little did I know there was a reporter there from the morning edition taking pictures. He got a picture of me with Mike in the audience that went into the next day's morning edition. There I was: not at work, not at home, and caught on camera—"rabble-rousing"!

My FBI file contains their version of the events:

From the FBI FILES of FLORENCE L. TATE
CONFIDENTIAL

The "Journal Herald," a daily newspaper of general circulation in the Dayton, Ohio area carried the article in the November 28, 1967 edition, stating that MICHAEL WARREN, controversial Central State senior, expelled earlier this month, made a surprise return to the campus on November 27, 1967, when the school reopened and declared publicly, "if the revolution were on at this moment, I would have to kill all (Uncle) Toms."

It was allegedly similar to the statement he made on November 1 to Dr. REMBERT STOKES, President of nearby Wilberforce University. The remark led to WARREN'S expulsion, and subsequent banning from campus.

Asked by reporters if he planned on re-applying for re-admission, he stated, "I can't answer any question because I don't trust you." WARREN was seated in the front row next to Mrs. CHARLES TATE of Dayton, a Black Power advocate. Asked if she was instrumental in bringing WARREN on campus she said she could not comment on the situation.

It is worth noting that, upon reading this excerpt, Mike told me that it was not only misleading but actually got some of the facts wrong regarding the timeline the FBI claimed to be establishing. I have no doubt that his misgivings are valid because, as we well know, truthfulness and "getting the story right" have never been the FBI's prime agenda.

In any case, I was determined that Mike was going to get back into school. The president knew me as a *Dayton Daily News* reporter and as an "upstanding member of the community." I went and delivered my passionate appeal on Mike's behalf and told him what a wonderful young man Mike was. Famed attorney William Kunstler ended up filing a lawsuit on his behalf and, in the end, Mike got back into school.

Some time later, after finishing undergrad, Mike wanted to go to law school but was torn between going back to school and continuing to work on behalf of Black folks, raising consciousness around Black Power.

"Mike," I advised him, "go on to law school, honey. Go get your degree because this stuff that we're fighting for will still be out here when you get through with your degree." And sure enough, he got his degree and went into civil rights law, becoming a lawyer for the legal defense fund as well as moving into private practice.

I take great pride in Mike's accomplishments, and there have been many. He's a highly regarded civil rights lawyer who has dealt with several famous civil rights cases. He's represented high-profile cases for political prisoners including Dr. Mutulu Shakur, Tupac's stepfather, a former member of the Black Liberation Army; and death row inmate Mumia Abu-Jamal. He also represented the young men who eventually came to be called "the Central Park Five" in the infamous "Central Park Jogger" case[4] and pursued the subsequent civil suit against the city of New York for their false conviction.

The FBI obviously felt it was worth their time to stay abreast of my whereabouts during this period as well, as evidenced by excerpts from my files. Also, there was a new project on the horizon which, I'm sure, especially irked them: the establishment of the Black Umoja

---

4   Editor's note: The five men — Kevin Richardson, Antron Mccray, Raymond Santana Jr., Korey Wise, and Yusef Salaam — are now known as "The Exonerated Five."

Society women's group and the Afro-American Cultural Center—the first of its kind in Dayton.

From the FBI FILES of FLORENCE L. TATE

IDENTITIES OF ORGANIZATIONS INVOLVED IN LOCAL RACIAL SITUATIONS; IDENTITIES OF LEADERS AND INDIVIDUALS INVOLVED

Black Umoja Society (BUS)

A "Black power" women's group, the Black Umoja Society, has been formally organized in Dayton, according to the January 13th, 1967 issue of the "Journal Herald," a daily Dayton newspaper. The word "umoja" means "unity" in the Swahili language, according to Mrs. Charles Tate, who, as a volunteer for the Student Non-Violent Coordinating Committee, organized the new group of 26 women.

She said its purpose "is to foster the concept of Black consciousness in the community and to lend tangible assistance to other groups working on projects in the Black community."

"The group plans to open a thrift shop... and a Black arts and culture center here. Its members will also work on telephone committees of local civil rights groups trying to raise funds through special projects." Mrs. Tate said that the group is racially exclusive—"open to all Black women."

The Black Umoja Society was established after my return from a trip to the Atlanta SNCC office sometime in 1967. While I was there, I became very impressed with one of the regular gathering spots that a couple of the young people in SNCC had set up. It had a kind of "cultural coffeehouse" feel. This particular spot had a creative and unorthodox vibe evident in the decor, which included empty telephone company cable spools that functioned as tables. I decided that Dayton could sorely use such a space and headed back determined to create one.

It tickles me now to read the FBI's interpretation of the Black Umoja Society—a group of friends I brought together to help me establish the Dayton Afro-American Cultural Center, the name I chose for our "cultural coffeehouse." It was a perfectly logical occurrence to me, however. I wanted to create a comprehensive community space, and I knew that in order to make such a time-consuming and laborious project happen, I needed to gather a group of Black women together to get the job done.

Some of the women were in DARE, but some were just friends that I brought in to help out. As time went on, most Black people who were able wanted to do something to assist the Movement, even if they weren't at its forefront picketing or marching. Pulling together the cultural center was something that everybody could do, so I got some of my middle-class friends who were not otherwise involved in any Black empowerment activities to help set up the center.

The founding mothers of the Black Umoja Society and the Afro-American Cultural Center were myself, VerDree Harris, Minnie Johnson, Janet Edwards, Nancy Egler, Joyce Herring, Martha Grinner, Jackie Brown (who was brought in by Minnie), Lelia Austin, and the young wife of the United Church of Christ minister assigned to Dayton, whose name I don't remember. Along the way, other younger friends joined, and under my direction we set about finding a place to establish the center.

There was a white pastor in east Dayton, where the poorer white folks lived, who owned a house in west Dayton, where the poor and middle-class Black folks lived. This included us, although Charles and I lived about a fifteen-minute drive from where the pastor's house was located, in a more economically advantaged area of west Dayton. This particular pastor had been mentioned in the news for his pro-Civil Rights activities, so we arranged to meet him at an interracial, interfaith event and successfully convinced him to rent the house to us at minimal cost. We opened the cultural center in the house soon after.

We held poetry readings, art exhibits, and concerts. We invited speakers, musicians, and artists such as Leroi Jones (soon to become Amiri Baraka), Gaston Neal, Phineas Newborn, Charlie Cobb, Bing Davis, Dick Jackson, Archie Shepp, and Pharaoh Saunders. I remember that Pharaoh Sanders or one of his musicians (Charles remembers it being Leon Thomas) was overheard voicing some apprehension about coming through Dayton, grumbling, "Man, this sure is rig city" as they were on the way to the airport after a show at the center. I later learned that "rig" was short for rigor mortis!

We also held dinners for African students from surrounding colleges; offered tutorial programs, literacy classes, and work-preparedness courses for adults; and sponsored musical talent shows for neighborhood kids. We even offered Swahili classes taught by Jonathan Cathumba, a student I'd met while doing my SNCC campus advisor work. And we held one of the first Malcolm X celebrations after his death, with his wife Betty Shabazz in attendance. Soon we began to do all of our political work out of the center as well, and the building soon became the headquarters for DARE.

We had an old mimeograph machine we used to reproduce propaganda leaflets for distribution throughout the neighborhood, and we printed flyers to stick under the windshield wipers of cars in church parking lots during Sunday service. One of our DARE members, George Ducker, was adamant that no one touch the mimeograph machine but him. "If you don't know how to oil it, don't touch it!" was George's constant refrain.

I decided to open a thrift store in the center, where families could purchase low-cost, mostly donated, but still very usable items. We kept everything affordable; fifteen or twenty cents at most for any given item. People who weren't part of the organization but admired what we were doing were happy to support us in any way that they could. Some gave us some very nice things to sell. All earnings and proceeds from the store went back to the center and helped support our community programming.

Eventually, we were able to recruit some people from the neighborhood to work for the organization. I remember one particular woman, Miss Robinson, a single mother who had seven or eight children. On paper she appeared to be a stereotypical "welfare mother," but Miss Robinson came to the meetings and became highly politicized. Eventually, she worked with my husband Charles to help establish a chapter of the National Welfare Rights Organization (NWRO) in Dayton. She also organized other mothers to agitate for continued welfare programs in the community. She and Charles often went to county board meetings to deliver their demands—what they wanted and what they were not going to tolerate—to the county commissioner in person. Years later, she became a local city leader.

I remember a comical incident that happened during Miss Robinson's tenure with the Dayton Moms (D-Moms), one of the organizations she helped to run. One day, Miss Robinson and several D-Moms members marched right into the county commissioner's office. Apparently, they made quite an impressive sight, as many of the D-Moms were "big-boned" women who wore "big wigs," as we used to call them. What made the headlines was when Miss Robinson got into a disagreement with the board members. Tense words were exchanged, and offensive insinuations were made about the so-called "welfare mothers" and their demands. Reportedly, one board member went too far, making a rude comment that was apparently perceived as a threat by Miss Robinson, who then reached into her coat, pulled out a gun, and slammed it down on the table before the stunned board.

"When I get up in the morning, the first thing I puts on is my drawers—and then I puts on my pistol," she growled. That broke the meeting up right there.

Other of our activities at the center were supported by the community to varying degrees. Sometimes community members came out en masse to our events while other events drew almost no one at all. Sometimes we held our events in a local park. On occasion, a church would donate space—a rare occasion indeed—because most Black churches didn't want to be bothered with Civil Rights Movement stuff. But when we needed a place to hold a big meeting or a rally,

I knew I could call on Reverend Flanagan, a sympathetic-to-the-Movement Black minister who would open up his church to us.

Pursuing relationships with various organizations and networking with my middle-class contacts on behalf of the center demanded ongoing community outreach. I was constantly on the lookout for the people, organizations, and/or institutions we could go to if we were holding an event and needed advertising for the program. I also sought out those who could make financial donations or provide gifts in kind. Eventually, fundraising for the center became my primary passion, so I decided to quit my job at the *Dayton Daily News* so I could run the center full-time.

The Black Umoja Society and the Afro-American Cultural Center grew out of my desire to create an authentic pro-Black Power community in west Dayton. The center was still open when we left Dayton to move to DC in 1969, and it continued to operate until 1971.

It's obvious from the FBI file that the creation of a community of Black women marshaled together to create a base of support, education, self-awareness, and pride for Black families was considered a revolutionary act to those who were threatened by any show of Black strength, Black self-reliance, or Black power.

For me, starting the Black Umoja Society and opening the cultural center were successful community and political-action strategies. These activities also provided me with a powerful way to find, keep, and build family and community, which has been a driving impulse throughout my life.

CHAPTER 8

DEPRESSION, COINTELPRO, DADDY DIES

For those of us working in the Movement around the country, 1967 through 1969 were filled with lots of grassroots activism and ground-breaking progress in the political arena. Charles and I traveled to many different conferences, meetings, and events. Across the nation, "Negroes" were becoming "Blacks," and there were countless national meetings and conferences organized to discuss and support a pro-Black Power agenda in cities including New York, Chicago, Cleveland, Columbus, Los Angeles, Detroit, and Washington, DC.

In 1967, Charles went to DC to take part in a special training at the Department of Defense. I joined him there with the children for the summer and stayed in a rental on 11th and M streets. I took a temporary position working with the SNCC office on U Street NW across from the Lincoln Theatre. Lester McKinney was the SNCC director for DC. During this period, I met Marion Barry for the first time, his wife Mary Treadwell, and Marshall Brown, a political strategist.

Summer ended, and we returned to Dayton. It was a busy fall. During Labor Day weekend 1967, we attended the National Conference for a New Politics at the Palmer House Hotel in Chicago. It was a large gathering of post-Civil Rights Movement radicals from all over the country whose mission was to chart a "Where do we go from here?" strategy. I don't remember much strategy coming out of it, but I do remember that Charles, myself, and a handful of other activists ended up "rebelling" against what we felt was the less-than-progressive vision of the conference's organizers.

CHARLES TATE: *During the conference, we'd go to meetings with different integrationists—so-called liberal white people—and they'd talk about creating some kind of coalition with Blacks. Florence and I got together with some of the other people who'd* *come, and said, "Look, we're wasting our time, this isn't about us at all. We should go set up our own convention on the south side of Chicago in a Black church"—which we did! The chairman of our convention was H. Rap Brown, and we had various other people of that standing who gave speeches. We had community people who presented models. We just turned that into a Black event for three days talking about Black nationalism, Black development.*

It seemed to be a time of great possibilities. While my psycho-emotional, "six-months-on" period was drawing to a close in the fall of 1967, with the spectre of depression laying waiting in the wings, my FBI file reveals that I remained the subject of constant scrutiny for my political activities. The file included many surveillance reports such as these:

MISCELLANEOUS ACTIVITIES

Florence Tate attended a Black Unity Conference at Cleveland, Ohio, on October 6-8, 1967.
The goal of the conference was to eliminate the confusion and misunderstanding of the Black people and to define their position.
According to literature distributed at a later date, the conference "was overwhelmingly successful in bridging the gap between the so called 'extremists' and the so called 'responsible' members of the Black community.".

Although Stokely stepped down from his leadership position at SNCC and was once again a field organizer, he continued working with the organization's DC chapter. Of course, he was still under the dogged eye of the FBI's COINTELPRO. According to entries in my FBI file, whenever he traveled to Dayton and met with us, those activities were noted.

FEDERAL BUREAU OF INVESTIGATION
Cincinnati, Ohio
February 12, 1968

On February 7, 1968, Special Agents of the Federal Bureau of Investigation (SAs of the FBI) observed at approximately 11:30 P.M., Stokely Carmichael and William Hall arrive at Cox Municipal Airport, Dayton, Ohio, aboard Jet Flight #442. This flight departed Washington International Airport, Washington, DC 9:30 P.M., with one stop in Columbus, Ohio.

Carmichael and Hall were met at the airport by Charles (Florence) Tate and others and from there drove directly to the residence of Charles and Florence Tate, Westwood Drive, Dayton, Ohio.

Stokely Carmichael, on April 29, 1967, while in Cincinnati, Ohio, stated that Florence Tate is the SNCC representative in Dayton, Ohio, and plans are already formulated to give her assistance in organizing SNCC in Dayton during the summer of 1967.

It is noted that the 'Daily News,', a daily newspaper of general circulation in the Dayton, Ohio area, carried an article titled "Carmichael Visits SNCC Here," on page two of the February 8, 1968 edition.

According to the article the news learned that Carmichael and Ware were in Dayton on February 7, 1968, to help map future activities of the SNCC in Dayton. Mrs. Charles (Florence)

Tate, when contacted by the news, refused to confirm the visit, but commented that, "Black people all over this country are coming together, making plans for their survival."

According to the article, Tate declared that whites "are becoming more and more irrelevant to us." Tate further stated, "We mean to survive by whatever means necessary."

The FBI's methods of operation were both underhanded and petty. They went so far as trying to create discord in my marriage, according to COINTELPRO documents:

SAC, Cincinnati
2/29/68
Director, FBI
COUNTERINTELLIGENCE PROGRAM
BLACK NATIONALIST — HATE GROUPS
RACIAL INTELLIGENCE
(STOKELY CARMICHAEL)

Reference is made to Cincinnati airtel 2/12/68 captioned "Stokely Carmichael, IS — Miscellaneous, Sedition," and attached LHM.

This communication indicated that Stokely Carmichael visited Dayton, Ohio, to help unite the Student Nonviolent Coordination Committee (SNCC) and a group headed by Charles Tate of Dayton. It was also noted that Florence Tate, the wife of Charles Tate, is a particular friend of Carmichael.

You should analyze this situation to determine if it might be possible to hamper

this unification by causing trouble between
Charles Tate and Carmichael. This might be
done through an anonymous letter to Tate
alleging that Carmichael was far too friendly
with Tate's wife.

Furnish the Bureau your observation
concerning this matter and any
recommendations for counterintelligence
action. No counterintelligence action should be
taken without Bureau authority.

Note: During this visit to Dayton, Ohio,
Carmichael made extremely inflammatory
statement saying that the system of government
in the U.S. must be destroyed and this must be
accomplished by violence. Tate is apparently
fully in sympathy and anxious to help
Carmichael in the Dayton, Ohio, area.

Stokely's marriage to Miriam Makeba apparently put the *kibosh*
on that "operation":

Director, FBI
DATE: 5/14/68
SAC CINCINATTI
COUNTERINTELLIGENCE PROGRAM
BLACK NATIONALIST — HATE GROUPS
RACIAL INTELLIGENCE
(STOKELY CARMICHAEL)
Re Bureau let, 2/29/68 captioned as above,
and CI airtel, 2/12/68 captioned, "STOKELY
CARMICHAEL, IS - Miscellaneous, Sedition," and
attached LHM.

Counter intelligence measure to hamper the
formation of the Dayton, Ohio, "SNCC" groups by
causing distrust and discord between CHARLES
and FLORENCE TATE and STOKELY CARMICHAEL was
under consideration, particularly in view of
the fact it was reported that FLORENCE TATE
was a particular friend of CARMICHAEL'S.

However, CARMICHAEL's recent announcement
of his pending marriage to MIRIAM MAKEBA,
South African singing star, and his infrequent
contacts with the TATES has all but eliminated
this possibility.

Cincinnati office has
XXXXXXXXXXXXXXXXXXXXX and any opportunity
to disrupt this group will be utilized and
capitalized upon if the situation arises.
However, as instructed, no counter intelligence
action will be taken without Bureau authority.

During the winter of 1967 through 1968, I fell into a significant
depressive period, one that would continue to deepen throughout
the year. While it was normal for me to become depressed during the
latter part of fall and remain that way through late spring, personal and
family issues would derail my "on" periods for the next two to three
years. The illness of my father leading up to his death the following
year would trigger many painful memories for me. During that time,
I experienced an avalanche of depressive states.

Through the course of those years, however, even during the difficult
months, there was still much work to do, and for a time I was somehow
able to stir myself to do the organizational work necessary. The FBI's
surveillance of our actions and their methods of infiltrating our lives
and relationships continued as well, which was infuriating enough;
but it truly gives me pause when considering that COINTELPRO's
ongoing reports concerning me—a virtual nobody—continued even
on the heels of the death of Martin Luther King Jr. in April.

I, like most Blacks, was grief-stricken by King's death. An article I wrote upon his death was also recorded in my FBI files:

"The Dayton Express,", a weekly Negro newspaper of limited circulation printed and published in Dayton, Ohio, carried an article entitled "The Meaning of Martin Luther King's Life and Death To a Black Revolutionary" by Florence Tate on page 20 of the April 11, 1968, edition.

This article in its entirety is set out as follows:

"Martin Luther King was a great and good man.

Measured by the standards of anyone regardless of their religious, philosophic or political beliefs. Dr. King was a heroic figure, struggling with sincerity and dedication in the way he thought best for the liberation of his people.

Unlike some of his latter-day disciples, he practiced what he preached. He loved ALL people, including Black people. He was censored, cursed, abused, stoned, watered, clubbed, jailed and finally murdered— — for his belief that love and non-violence were the way to gain freedom and equality for Black people on this blood soil of the United States of America.

In the words of the Rev. Jesse Jackson, Dr. King's Chicago aide, "White People lost the best friend they ever had."

This was not said and is not being repeated here to disparage the gains he caused to be made for great numbers of Black people. It is simply a true assessment of Dr. Kings' role

as buffer between white America and young
Black people who are convinced that the
U.S.A. must fall before Black people here and
oppressed people around the world can unleash
themselves from the tentacles of the giant
octopus called America.

As Stokely Carmichael, architect of the
Black revolution in the U.S.A. said upon Dr.
King's death, "They have killed all reasonable
hope that America could peacefully work out
its race problem. They killed love."

If Dr. King's life and death are to have
any real meaning for the masses of the Black
people, it must finally teach us the lesson
that we are dealing with an insane monster
without parallel in human history,' that the
only language he truly understands and will
respond to is the language of violence, upon
which this country was founded, grown, and
flourished.

For nearly 15 years Martin Luther King
walked this land singing, praying, marching
and loving.

During that time came the still unsolved
murders of the four little Birmingham girls;
the murder of Medgar Evers;' the murder of
Malcolm X; the murder of Chaney, the murder
of Sammy Young; the Orangeburg and Alcorn
massacres; and of countless other Black
people— — some engaged in the struggle
to make America livable for Black people,
— others simply going about their normal
pursuits but simply being Black (like Robert
Barbee and Lester Mitchell) in an alien white
country.

Make no mistake about it; they were

murdered by the evil forces of whiteness in America.

And not only the overt acts of murder, but the systematic starvation of children and adults in Mississippi and other portions of the North and South; the high incidence of slum-related diseases leading to early deaths; the often fatal medical experimentation in grant medical clinics always conveniently located adjacent to the ghetto; the unauthorized sterilization of Black women in hospitals across this land; the disproportionate number of Black youth being sent to kill and be killed in Vietnam — these are but a few of the ways America is committing genocide (the killing of a whole race of people) against Black people.

She has in her giant arsenals of destruction in the cities, a vast array of terrible weapons to be used in the ghettoes of the North and South this summer to attempt to annihilate and exterminate Black people.

She also has 34 concentration camps read to be "pacification" centers for anyone even suspected of wanting liberation at any price.

How much more rape and plundering of lives, how many more murders, how much napalm can we endure before we say to this monster, "Stop! I will not take anymore! I will do whatever is necessary to survive—even if it means destroying you, White America!"

Many people say that nobody will win in such a confrontation. That is possibly true, although I don't believe with 87 per cent of the world's population being colored that some Black people won't survive.

You see if Black America would really,

finally and seriously revolt on this alien soil, then the rest of the world would get a chance to breathe.

This country would have to call back its troops from foreign soil to defend its own soil.

Then the Asian, African, and Latin American countries could more easily recover access to their gold, diamonds, tin, oil, tungsten, copper, and other natural resources that this country is systematically robbing them of.

Black and other colored peoples of the world are now realizing that we're all victims of western "civilization's" greed; and that we must act in concert to rid ourselves of our oppressor.

But for the sake of argument let us accept the uninformed opinion that we can't win.

I submit that it is better to die fighting for our humanity than to continue to live forever under the tyranny imposed on Black people by this racist society.

The utter chaos that could result would be a decided improvement over the spoiled lives of millions of Blacks now living in this country.

We must be like Dr. King, prepared to die for Black people's humanity. It is absurd to think that we can all live. Some of us must die so that our race can live in dignity and peace.

I maintain that Dr. King will be judged in history as not only the architect of the Negro revolution, but [also as] one of the greatest heroes of the Black revolution.

I think that when he "went to the mountain," he saw that his actions in Memphis would lead to his violent death. His violent death would lead to the unleashing of Black violence in this country that would precipitate the bloody revolution which finally must come before Black people can be liberated.

He could not in life say this, but his almost chosen death speaks it more eloquently than even he could have.

"The King is dead! Long live the King!"

MRS. FLORENCE TATE

Along with continual FBI surveillance, Charles and my political activities brought grimmer experiences to our door. We were receiving hate mail and phone calls at home. Letters from the Ku Klux Klan threatening us "niggers" and calls from organizations like the National States Rights Party—a white supremacist group—were common.

Geri's memories of that time illustrate the degree to which the Movement became a part of our family life:

Geri Tate Augusto: *I remember when my father started to get all those Klan letters... they're supposed to be anonymous; bad English, hand-written mess... or letters made from newspaper clippings with stuff pasted in.*

We used to have a bulletin board in the living room where Mom and Dad would put up pins from the Movement, these little badges and pins... but they would also occasionally stick up a threatening letter... just post it up there in the living room. I think it was by the door. So, it's a bulletin board, a cork bulletin board, and one of the letters said something like this: "We know where your daughter goes to school. We know the way she walks home." By then, I was in high school, and it was quite a walk. In those days, your parents didn't drop you off in high school; you walked. And it was a good half-hour walk to the school. I would walk down the main street most of the time because there was a drug store to stop in and have an ice cream soda.

> But sometimes I would walk a shorter cut that took me par-
> allel to the main street, maybe about four blocks in—very little
> traffic, the sides of people's homes, not the front doors. And they
> knew, as they intimated in the little letter: "We know how your
> daughter walks home. Be careful, nigger, don't run for office" or
> some mess like that.
>
> And I remember seeing the letter and asking my father, and
> he said, "Geri, fear is contagious. If you're going to work with
> people for freedom, you will be afraid—but don't ever show your
> fear while you're doing the work. Do what you need to do, and
> then you can go home and collapse in fear... or tears. But don't
> be afraid while you're around other people and you're doing
> freedom work."
>
> I never forgot that. And I think that's the only conversation
> I ever remember about fear or danger at all.

Our children—Geri, Greg, and Brian—were there when the many activists and intellectuals from all over the country stayed with us. They were in the room while we held political meetings at our house attended by folks like George Ware, Bill Mahoney, Myrtle Glascoe, Floyd McKissick, H. Rap Brown, Willie Ricks, Ethiopian scholar Dess Rahmato, Owusu Sadaukai (aka Howard Fuller), and Cleve Sellers. They met the various musicians, writers, poets, and performers who appeared at the Afro-American Cultural Center including Pharaoh Saunders, Gaston Neal, Amiri Baraka, Mae Jackson, and Julius Lester. They helped make the signs, draw the posters, and even sang the freedom songs along with us.

And sometimes, they saw our movement guests as heroes and role models. A somewhat humorous example of this was the impression H. Rap Brown made on our youngest, Brian. Rap—born Hubert Gerold Brown—had been elected SNCC's chairman when Stokely stepped down. His fiery language and revolutionary cries had led him to become branded as a radical who promoted violence. The circumstances surrounding a visit Rap made to Dayton in the summer of 1967 would result in his being charged with "advocating criminal syndicalism," although he was not indicted.[5] But as Rap's reputation and prominence grew, so did the respect our youngest son had for him.

Brian's esteem for Rap had grown to the point where the surest way to get him to do anything during that time was to tell him, "This is what Rap did" or "This is what Rap ate" or "This is what Rap would like." We learned to keep all the matches out of Brian's reach after he grew to love lighting them whenever he could. He was found more than once, nearly setting something on fire—lisping, lighting, and misquoting Rap: "*If America don't come around, we gonna burn tha' thucka down!*"

Brian's antics aside, sometime later I would go to New York City for one of Rap's trial appearances, during which he was represented by William Kunstler for a case that spanned several states and included different charges. At some point, I was able to get a call from him while he was in jail. I just remember his replying to my inquiry about his well-being by stating, "Dancing on glass, just to stay fast!" Rap was always a rapper—that's how he had acquired the moniker—but he would release this name as well when he became Jamil Al-Amin in 1971.

Notwithstanding threats by the Klan, being tailed by the feds, and police and white supremacist violence on our people, those years were also full of absorbing, gratifying, and often amusing episodes. I remember once being engaged on a phone call of some importance when the operator interrupted (something that actually occurred in those days). "I have a phone call for Mrs. Florence Tate from General Chui," the operator stated. The party on the line was distinctly impressed as I excused myself from our conversation and accepted the call, but only I knew that "General Chui" was an assumed name taken by a Wright-Patterson Air Force Base engineer. He was one of many self-styled paramilitary leaders of Black Power persuasion, who had started his own cadre of approximately ten brothers to protect the center. Since it was his "army," he had appointed himself General. Why wouldn't he?

I also remember years later having a good chuckle over one of General Chui's "colonels": Ulysses X Garth. Those of us on the "inside"

---

5   Dayton History Books Online, "The Inception of Dayton Police Crisis Intervention Teams (1967-1980)," https://www.daytonhistorybooks.com/daytonhostageparttwo.html.

knew that Ulysses X had a white wife. At that time, this was a deep, big "no-no" for a Black Muslim, so he told everyone that he had married his wife before he became a Muslim. He added that she was "near death" and that because she was the mother of his children, he couldn't leave her. Alas, twenty years along, those of us who remembered his tale of woe would often quip drolly to each other how remarkable it was that Mrs. Ulysses X Garth was still very much alive "after the army was long dead."

During 1967 and 1968, I also worked as director of community relations for the Concentrated Employment Program (CEP), a U.S. Department of Labor-sponsored job training program. Basically, this was President Johnson's attempt to get the Negroes off the streets after the riots or "urban rebellions," as we called them.

Looking back, no actual job training was going on at CEP because there weren't many jobs available, even if the attendees stayed through to the end of the program. Occasionally, we would place somebody, but it was really about keeping Black youth off the street by giving them something to do all day and paying them a little money so they wouldn't riot again.

I was responsible for acquainting the local community with the aims and objectives of CEP. I represented the program at community meetings, on panel discussions, and in seminars and meetings with representatives of business and industry. I was also called a "coach" for the participants. I was supposed to be helping them to solve their problems; but really, it was about listening to them talk about their realities and giving them a check every Friday. I especially befriended two participants—Knuckles and Billy— and recruited them into the Movement. From these young brothers I learned what prisons were really like for Black convicted youth and what they endured while incarcerated. Knuckles was a good-looking, bright, and likable fella who, for some reason, absolutely adored me. Billy was an even better-looking brother who, as he often stated, adored fast cars and fast women.

"Worst part of it's the hole," Billy would say, referring to solitary confinement, the dreaded punishment for sometimes even minor infractions depending on the guard or warden. "Lots of cats make it through either becoming a 'wife' or taking a wife," Knuckles added. He also detailed how dope was traded back and forth and painted various depictions of prison culture in general.

Knuckles and Billy became part of DARE's security team, tasked with warning us about suspicious-looking types (who were probably FBI investigators) lingering around our meeting locations or a police presence on its way to the various marches and protests we organized. They took their jobs very seriously and both probably got a big kick out of the experience.

Billy was later killed while trying to escape re-arrest. While trying to evade a police tail, he crashed into a concrete wall. I am still haunted by the fact that he was driving a car Charles and I had sold him. The last time I saw Knuckles was at my mother's funeral. We had long since moved to DC but had returned to Dayton for the service. The night of the viewing, I looked up and saw Knuckles standing there. "I read about your mother dying in the paper, Mrs. Tate," he explained. "I knew you'd be here…came to pay my respect." I hadn't seen him in so many years, so it was really good to see him there. I never saw him again.

During this time, my father's health was failing. We visited him once in Memphis where he was in the hospital during his illness with cancer. He was just a skeleton of his old robust self—shrunken up like a bony, yellow pigmy. Seeing my father that way was a frightful sight, but I was too depressed at that point to do more than register it.

Lucille Knowles: *He was involved in an automobile accident that broke his neck. He was coming home from somewhere and there was a Greyhound Bus that parked on the side of a two-lane highway. And he tried to pull around it, and a state trooper ran into him, spun the car around, and broke his neck.… He didn't know his neck was broken until two or three days later. He went in the hospital, and it was an old-fashioned way of healing broken necks at the time… they put these pins in his head with weights on them. That would have been '68. He was supposed to be in the hospital for six or twelve weeks, but the week before the pins were supposed to come out of his head, his doc-*

tor went on vacation. Somehow, at some point, the pins slipped and re-fractured his neck, and he had to be in the hospital for another six weeks. While he was in the hospital, he started experiencing nausea... and [it was discovered] that he already had inoperable cancer. So, his last year... it was a bad time. Father died in May of 1969.

Even before Father's death and funeral in 1969, things seemed to be closing in on me. In fall 1968, the FBI apparently decided it was time to let me know I was being surveilled. Two agents showed up at my CEP office. Files show that the actual interview occurred almost ten months after an agent had requested permission to conduct the interview. Much of the following account of this interview was redacted:

```
DIRECTOR, FBI
DATE: 9/18/68
SAC, CINCINNATI
FLORENCE LOUISE TATE
RM
Remyairtel and LHM 5/17/68.
Re LHM contains all pertinent and up to date
background information concerning subject.
```

```
        Subject continues to reside at 333 Westwood
Drive, Dayton,Ohio, with her her husband,
CHARLES. Subject recently became employed as
a consultant for the Concentrated Employment
Program (CEP), Dayton, Ohio, which is funded by
the city of Dayton.
        In view of the fact subject is a SNCC
representative in Dayton and a close friend
of STOKELY CARMICHAEL, Bureau permission is
requested to interview subject.
```

Interview will be handled in accordance
with Bureau policy as Section 87D, Manual of
Instructions and Bureau letter dated 6/20/68
concerning interviews with Black extremists.

Florence Louise Tate, a 38-year-old Negro
female who resides with her husband in
Dayton, is employed as a consultant with the
Concentrated Employment Program at Dayton.
She is a representative of the Black extremist
SNCC in Dayton and is a close friend of
Stokely Carmichael. She is included on the
Agitator Index.

SAC Cincinatti
10-9-68
Director, FBI
FLORENCE LOUISE TATE

Reurlet 9-18-68 requesting Bureau authority
to interview the subject.

Authority granted. Conduct your interview
in accordance with existing Bureau
instructions and submit the results of the
interview in a form suitable for dissemination
with appropriate recommendation as to the
necessity for additional investigation and/or
interview. In the future, submit your request
to interview security subjects in accordance
with the instruction set out in Section 87D of
the Manual of Instructions, page 40.

Bufile contain no pertinent identifiable
information on the subject not already in your
possession.

CONFIDENTIAL
Date 5/28/69

FLORENCE LOUISE TATE was interviewed at
1129 West Third Street, Dayton, Ohio, and advised
as follows:

At the outset of the interview, TATE stated
that she was surprised that the FBI had an
interest in her. She stated that she has not
been involved in any criminal activities and
she is not now a member of any organization
which advocates violence, revolution, or the
overthrow of the United States Government by
force.

TATE stated that she has been affiliated
with Student Non-Violent Coordinating
Committee (SNCC) members in the past, but her
primary connections with SNCC members and
the SNCC organization was strictly social. In
the past she has associated with such SNCC
officials as STOKELY CARMICHAEL and H. RAP
BROWN, but this was only on a social basis.

TATE stated that her primary purpose for
affiliating with SNCC was to raise funds for
their organization.

Tate stated that to the best of her
knowledge the Student Non-Violent Coordinating
Committee is slowly becoming defunct and it
currently has only approximately 60 active
members, none of which are currently in the
Dayton, Ohio area.

TATE stated that the Negro has been
suppressed over the years and although
attempts have been made to alleviate this

condition during the past few years, very
little has been accomplished by the United
States Government. She stated that under the
present policy by officials of the United
States, it appears that the only solution to
the Negro problem is a revolution. She stated
that she believes that revolution is the
only means the Negro has to improve himself;
however, she does not know how this will come
about since Negroes are in the minority and
militant groups are not powerful enough to
overthrow the United States Government.

Tate stated that for approximately the
past twelve months, she has been primarily
occupied as a consultant with the Concentrated
Employment Program (CEP) in Dayton, Ohio.

At this time TATE requested that the
interview be terminated.

The interrogations by the FBI were the absolute last straw and all
I needed to convince me it was time to get out of Dayton for good.
Since the day I'd first set foot in Dayton, I'd wanted to get out of
Dayton, especially before I got involved in my civil rights and political
work. The place simply had nothing to recommend itself to me. I told
Charles at the beginning of our marriage: "Charles, please, let's go
somewhere else! I want to be in a city where things are happening,
where there's culture and some kind of intellectual life—and Dayton
ain't it!"

Charles always responded, "This is where my job is, Florence," to
which my reply was always, "But you can work anywhere! Let's decide
where we want to live, and then you can get a job there!" My pleas
fell on deaf ears. Thank goodness, Charles has always been sober,
responsible, dependable, and prudent. He had a good job, and in his
mind, that was that. Periodically, I'd get on my "let's get out of Dayton"
kick, but to no avail.

Ironically, sometime during the years after Brian's birth but prior to my father's death, my mother decided to follow us to Dayton. She had been living in Louisville but had visited us in Dayton after Greg was born. From the time Charles and I had married and Greg was born, Mother had begun to try to "make up" with me. To me, however, it felt as if she wanted to be around to do for her grandchildren what she hadn't done for me.

Of course, when she told me of her plans to relocate, I complained to Charles: "Why in the world would she move to Dayton?" I didn't want her there. But she came anyway, and immediately started coming around and helping with the children. She tried to be "maternal" in any way she could including buying me clothes and lavishing things on the children. She would take them to stay with her and out to do this, that, or the other. When Charles and I traveled, she would take care of the children and buy things for our house.

Later on, Charles would always say, "She tried so hard to make up to you, and you wouldn't let her." And that's the truth. I just wouldn't. I remember telling my friend Josie, who knew exactly what had happened with Mother during those years, "Josie, she wants to buy me things, and I don't need her to buy me things anymore! When I needed her to buy me things, she didn't buy me things. Now, she wants to buy me shoes. Well, I don't need shoes from her! I can buy shoes for myself!" And that's just the way I felt for a long time. In fact, I was extremely cold toward and angry with Mother.

Besides, I had long since set my heart on some day being able to move to DC. The summer of 1964 was the first time we were financially able to take a nice vacation, and we wanted to take the kids to the World's Fair in New York. Charles planned to drive. I never have driven on the road, partly because I don't want to, but mainly because Charles likes to have the car under his control if he's in it.

We went to New York and the nation's capital. While in DC, we stayed at what later became known as the "Booker T. Washington Hilton" because the Black Caucus's conventions were held there. DC was a city full of political activity and Black folks! During our time with DARE, we would return to DC for various movement conferences. I loved every minute of our time there, and after the summer spent there while Charles was training at the Department of Defense in 1967, I was convinced that Washington, DC, was the place that I wanted to be.

In 1969, former CORE leaders and old friends Ruth and Tony Perot moved there. Tony went to work at the newly formed Urban Institute as a senior research associate and project director. The Urban Institute had been created by President Johnson's administration in 1968 in part to find solutions to America's growing racial problems, injustices, and economic inequalities—challenges that were highlighted by the Kerner Commission that same year. As the head of a special program at the Institute designed to attract Black activist leaders, Tony invited Charles to take a position at the Institute. And that's how we finally moved to Washington.

I was still suffering from one of my depressive spells as we prepared for the move to DC; and after experiencing my father's death, the move from Dayton proved to be extremely draining and very hard on the children and me. Yet, career-wise, the move to DC was pivotal. More than ready to discover what the capital city had in store for me, I bore up under whatever discomfort I was feeling. Perhaps having survived so many moves and transitions in my life as a basically "homeless" child, I had been prepared to survive even the most unstable periods of my life.

After making sure the Afro-American Cultural Center was in good hands, bidding adieu to our extended DARE family members, and making sure that old friends and press folk like Jim Fain knew where to reach me, I resigned from CEP and the Tate family headed east to a new life in "Chocolate City." This time, *I* would be the one leaving my *mother* behind.

Florence at March on Washington, 1963

Florence and Jesse Jackson 1983

CHAPTER 9

DC, THE JOINT CENTER, OEO, ELECTROCONVULSIVE THERAPY

The move to Washington, DC, in the fall of 1969 was a difficult one. I was in the deepest depression I had ever experienced. By 1969, my "six-months-off" period had already lasted for more than two years without the corresponding "six-months-on" period of relief.

Geri was already attending Howard University in DC, entering her senior year, and working at the Center for Black Education (CBE) and Drum and Spear Bookstore, so she wasn't affected by the move. Brian was young enough to "go with the flow," but moving to a new city was a great hardship on my second child, Greg, who was not happy about our relocation. He let his displeasure clearly be known to us all. Greg had always been "adventurous." These days he would likely be called "hyperactive" and probably given Ritalin. The boy was busy from sunup to sundown, swirling, twirling, jumping, hopping, mixing, stirring, breaking, banging, and taking stuff apart. He was a deconstructionist before his time. Once, he "ran away from home" by climbing the backyard fence. When I realized he was missing from the backyard and was nowhere to be found in the house, we scoured the neighborhood streets, but no Greg. I finally called the police, who found him down a back alley, playing with a German shepherd! He was intensely curious and very self-contained and, at that time, never liked to leave the familiar. In those days, parents spanked their children for misconduct, and I kept a leather belt we called "cow hide" in the hall closet for that purpose. Charles and I would use it to bargain with Greg to discontinue certain behavior; if that failed, we would threaten to get the cow hide.

By the time we were getting ready to move to DC, Greg had finally found a neighborhood friend in Dayton. Gary was the same age as Greg, and they were both into music. We could often find Greg at Gary's house listening to records and comparing notes. Greg had also been befriended by Derek, a teenaged musician who lived across the street. Derek would later achieve some prominence as an R&B singer and musical conductor for the infamous televangelist Jim Bakker.[6] Music was revealing itself to be of deep importance to my second child, but since he could not stay behind, he mournfully and grudgingly accepted his fate. The move would be accomplished with me hanging on psychologically by the skin of my teeth.

By October 1969, we had finally settled on a house we found in upper-northwest Washington. We decided to lease for a couple of years to see how we liked DC before selling our house in Dayton. As soon as I could, I began searching for a good doctor. Severely depressed, my early days in DC were spent in the house or going to meet different doctors—and then back in the house.

Meanwhile, it seemed that as soon as we set foot in DC, the FBI got down to the business of wasting the taxpayers' money again. As intimated by reports filed soon after our arrival, informants began sitting across the street from our home spying on my non-activities, twiddling their thumbs, and waiting for who-knows-what.

```
TO DIRECTOR, FBI
DATE: 11/28/69
SUBJECT: FLORENCE LOUISE TATE


     Re FD 128 from Cincinnati to the Bureau,
11/19/69, designating WFO as office of origin.
```

---

6 Florence's son Greg clarifies this passage with the following: "That would be Derrick Floyd, who lived across the street and who played drums and piano and introduced me to his good living-room jam buddy, Junie Morrison of The Ohio Players and later Parliament-Funkadelic. Junie wrote "One Nation Under a Groove" and wee Derrick also had a serious Marvel Comics collection, which he kept in airtight plastic bags, and erotic zodiac-themed Black-light posters. The other friend in the 'hood who was also into music and Marvel Comics was Gary Young, who later became a successful graphic artist in 1980s New York City."

Captioned subject recently moved to WDC. Her residence has been verified by WFO.

Confidential sources of WFO familiar with certain aspects of Black nationalist activity in the WDC area report no activity on the part of the subject since her arrival[al]in WDC.

XXXXXXXREDACTEDXXXXXXXXXXXXX

WFO is maintaining this case in a pending status until the employment of the subject is determined.

TO DIRECTOR, FBI
DATE: 1/29/70
SUBJECT: FLORENCE LOUISE TATE

XXXXXXXXXXXREDACTEDXXXXXXXXXXXXXXXXX

The records of the Metropolitan Police Department, WDC, and the U.S. Park Police were searched during December 1969 and no record for captioned subject was found.

The records of XXXXXXXXXXXREDACTEDXXXXXXXXXXX disclose that TATE resides at 727 Whittier St, N.W., with her husband, CHARLES EDWARD TATE. Mr. TATE'S employment is shown as the Urban Institute, WDC. There was no indication of present employment for Mrs. TATE.

WFO will continue attempts to determine subject's employment.

This kind of activity continued throughout 1970:

```
TO DIRECTOR, FBI
DATE: 4/31/70
SUBJECT: FLORENCE LOUISE TATE
Re: WFOlet 1/29/70
```

Captioned subject is included in the
Agitator Index of WFO. She moved to WDC with
her husband and family in September 1969.
XXXXXXXXXXXXXXXXXXXXXXXXREDACTEDXXXXXXXXXXXX
Available information to date indicates that
the subject is not currently employed other
than as a housewife. Discrete surveillance of
the TATE residence, 727 Whittier Street, has
determined that Mrs. TATE is regularly at home
during the daytime hours.

XXXXXXXXXXXXXXXXXREDACTEDXXXXXXXXXXXXXXXXXXX
In view of the foregoing, this case is
being closed by WFO. It will be reopened and
investigation conducted in accordance with
instructions concerning the investigation of
Agitator Index subjects.

```
FLORENCE LOUISE TATE
```

A representative of the FBI reviewed the records at XXXXX REDACTEDXXXXX, on July 15, 1970. The record reflected that Tate resides at 727 Whittier Street, N.W. Washington, DC Her husband was listed as Charles Edward Tate who is employed at the Urban Institute, Washington, DC

Their former address was show as 333 Westwood Avenue, Dayton, Ohio. She listed her former employment as the 'Dayton Daily News.'

On July 15, 1970, Charles Edward Tate was contacted by representatives of the FBI at his place of employment, the Urban Institute, 2100 M Street, N. W. Washington, DC

Tate stated that he has just recently moved to Washington, DC with his family and is presently employed on the Research Staff of the Urban Institute, Washington, DC He stated that he no longer considers himself, nor his wife, to be militant in their racial outlook, since "the Black man" has other options at the present time. Tate advised that by options he means education or by the Black community joining together and using their votes to elect individuals aware of their problems.

Tate further stated that both he and his wife still keep in contact with many of their friends in SNCC but will take no active part in any racial protests.

Tate advised that his wife at present is a housewife and not connected with any racial organizations.

While Hoover and his goons were engaged in this useless surveillance of absolutely nothing, my family was trying to adjust to our new life in DC. The boys were enrolled in school. Brian did well—initially, at least—but Greg had an awful time. I later learned that he was often beat up for his lunch money and generally mistreated at Paul Junior High. When I became well enough to understand the depth of his pain, we enrolled him in the private Barrie Day School, where he was much happier.

Once Brian entered middle school at Paul, it seemed that he was coping with the new, more urban environment of DC very well. In fact, he was coping too well: he was becoming used to the chaos and a little too friendly with two troublesome buddies, "Tank" and "Mo." Charles and I were regularly regaled with tales of children locking the teacher in the closet, and even some stories about middle schoolers spied "shooting up" in the halls! We pulled him from public school and sent him to private Sidwell Friends School in the ninth grade.

In the meantime, I was suffering brutally. The bout of depression that had started the year before Daddy died had been going on for two years without abating. During my periods of depression, I was always acutely aware that my whole personality changed. Ordinarily, I was generous with my time, but my depression was a very selfish disease, a totally self-centered kind of thing. I just became a different person. I didn't want to interact with people, and I shut myself off. I wasn't sure what I thought about anything, didn't trust my judgment, didn't have any initiative, and didn't care about much—except the way I was feeling. The depression was intense and all-consuming.

But it wasn't as if I was off in "la-la land," unaware of the changing people and places around me. I knew what was happening, was aware of how I was feeling, and knew I had no logical reason to feel the way I felt. "Ain't nothing bad happening to me or happening with me or around me; I'm not sad that so-and-so died or so-and-so is sick.... It's just in my head," I'd tell myself.

It was just me and my feelings and thoughts, and my thoughts were all negative. Positive thoughts never seemed to emerge. Whatever was going on in my life, I would zero in on its worst aspect, ruminating endlessly on the horrible things I'd done and the disastrous decisions

I'd made. "Oh, why did I do this?" "I'm such a bad person!" "I shouldn't have done that!" "This was wrong!" or "That was sinful." I didn't think about anything good I had done. The good was always eclipsed in my mind by what a terrible person I was.

And doing anything took immense effort. Like taking a shower; normally, if you're going to take a shower, you just say to yourself, "I'm going in here to take a shower." But when you're depressed, at least the way my depression functioned, everything seemed to be broken down into pieces, and every single step was precipitated by some awful dread. The simple act of showering became, "Oh boy... now I've *got* to take this shower. I've got to get the soap... Where is the soap? And now, I've got to get the face cloth...oh, no! Where is my face cloth? Oh, Jesus, now I've got to turn on this water! How hot? Too hot! No, too cold..."

Accomplishing even one of those steps took all my willpower and perseverance. It would seem as if hours passed before I even stepped under the water. And heaven forbid I needed to shampoo my hair! That was another one-hundred unbearable steps. "Now I have to find the shampoo... Don't let the shampoo get in your eyes! Watch your eyes! And what about conditioner? Do I have to use conditioner? Then I have to dry myself off... And then, I've got to get back to the bedroom... Then I have to find some clothes to put on..."

Every step was entirely too difficult, too confusing, too disconnected from whatever came before or after it; and none of those actions made sense individually. Nor could I, in my depressed state, see them adding up to any meaningful or discernable end result. Everything was disintegrated. I was disintegrated.

Usually my exhaustion came more from thinking than from actually doing anything because I wasn't really doing that much. Yet, by the time I got through thinking about doing what it was I wanted or needed to do, I was so exhausted that the act itself was overwhelming. It was like I was working double-duty on everything. If by some small miracle I managed to do whatever it was I had to do, a new sense of dread arose: "Well, I've done it... But now you mean I've got to do this all over again tomorrow?"

Although I came to understand this pattern after a while and know that everything was colored by my depression—that it wasn't real, and that what I was thinking wasn't real—it was still, "God, I've got to wake up in the morning and make it through this day, but then there's tomorrow... How am I going to get through tomorrow?" Then I'd start thinking about time and how it passed so slowly, and how I desperately wished to exist outside of it.

There were many days when I wanted to die. I can't count how many times I said to myself, "I can't live another day." "Death would be the ultimate relief," I'd think. But, of course, suicide was out of the picture. My fear of hell was ever-present, and besides that, I frequently thought about the consequences of leaving my children behind. If I ever did anything to myself, they'd never get over it, I fretted. It would just haunt them and would forever linger, echoing, "My mother committed suicide."

So, because I couldn't do that—wouldn't do that—the next best thing was sleep. I just wanted to sleep. And if, for whatever reason I couldn't sleep—which happened often because I couldn't turn my mind off—then I would begin to despair: "I can't get away from this thing; it's just on me, and I have to suffer through it."

Thinking back now on those years of severe depression when the children were so young, I often wonder how my little children got through that. Of course, when I ask them, they pretend it didn't matter. But it undoubtedly had a significant impact on their lives—especially for Brian, who was just a baby—and played a role in how they would go on to understand life. Because when your mother withdraws, when you're sitting around but she's not interacting with you or anything, you have to just viscerally feel that something is wrong. I often feared that as little children they might have wondered, "What did I do? Did I do something wrong?" Whether or not they consciously thought about it that way, I worried that the children felt it, deep inside, nonetheless.

Perhaps I also feared it because I knew how real that abandonment business was. It never totally goes away. You can go to therapy and talk. You can understand fully what happened, why it happened, and how it happened, but it's still there. And I wondered if living with a mother with depression would affect my children in the same way the physical abandonment I experienced with my own parents affected me. Always having that feeling that there's something missing, that there's something about you that isn't quite right because if there wasn't something wrong with you (or so the logic goes), then your mother wouldn't leave you…wouldn't abandon you.

It wasn't rational thinking, but it was the way that I felt and the way I feared my children might feel.

Geri Tate Augusto: *From the time I was eleven years old [up] to today, my mother has suffered from clinical depression. And what that meant was that she was absent half the year. I used to think of it as six months on, six months off. For a long time, that's what it was…. It was cyclical. Later, I figured out that it was also seasonal. So, through the fall and the winter, for the most part, this would happen; whereas as in the spring/summer/early fall, it wouldn't. But it was basically six months on, six months off. As Mom herself often said, at those times I was the mother, the person who took care of the house and especially who took care of my brothers. I took care of her as best I could… but what I did, frankly, was take care of the house. I did the cooking, and I did the grocery shopping…. My father kind of turned stuff over to me, and I learned how to do stuff because he was working. I think the kinds of hospitals she would be in didn't let children come, so he would stop off after work or do as much as he could going to the hospital, which meant that I was at home.*

And I guess a child's view of depression is that the person is sad, is in the bedroom most of the time, is not eating properly. My family is a family that loves sartorial splendor of various types, but when she was depressed, I remember the kind of shapeless housedresses. She would just sit and be sad or lie in bed and be sad, facing the wall.

Much of this was happening when I was at school, so I'd be gone in the day and rush home at 4:00, where there would be some kind of babysitter. At that time, you could get nice Black ladies who would babysit, who would take care of Greg and Brian, and they would leave when I got home. They would leave, and I'd take over, which meant preparing the dinner, bathing the kids, making sure they were alright.... And I remember always running in to check on my mom.

And I can't remember if this was something my dad told me or not... the memory I have is rushing up to her room. And she would of course be sad and not saying anything, but she would have these medicines—pills—arrayed on the dresser. So, I would rush home from school every day to check and see how she was doing and to make sure that those pills, those bottles, were there.

One of the effects of that is that I won't take medicine. I mean, I have to be lying down in the throes of deep malaria where they'll say, "The malaria is not going to leave you unless you take this medicine." I don't take aspirin, I don't take ibuprofen, I don't take anything for pain, and to take an antibiotic you have to wrestle me down.

My enduring memory of pills and medicine was that she had all these things that she was supposed to take which didn't seem to do much good, as far as I could tell. But she had them, and I knew that if she took too many of them, she could die or get really, really, sick. And I would rush home every day and check those bottles.

But mainly it was that six months she was gone, and six months she was there. When she was there, she was the most wonderful mother that one could imagine. I just got used to that cycle, because it was the cycle throughout the rest of our childhood.

By early 1970, I finally found a psychiatrist whom I felt comfortable with. Dr. Charles Prudhomme was a very elegant, tall, silver-haired man, a top-notch Howard University professor, renowned as having worked on the *Brown v. Board of Education* case.

Dr. Prudhomme was fascinating. An intellectual with vast knowledge and experience, he had worked with the Tuskegee Airmen at the Veterans Hospital in Alabama and in 1962 was the first Black person ever appointed to the Washington, DC, Mental Health Commission. During the time I was seeing him, he was also the vice president of the American Psychiatric Association, the first Black person to gain such high office in that organization.

I learned all kinds of things from Dr. Prudhomme. At times, he shared stories of a Washington, DC, under President Wilson that were as harsh and racially nasty as they could get. At other times he shared research and facts from his studies in the medical field. I learned from him that Coca Cola was first made with cocaine and that cocoa leaves were fed to native populations in South America so they could work all day and night without getting tired.

Dr. Prudhomme seemed to find me interesting as well. I remember he would literally be waiting in the door for me to arrive sometimes. We shared thoughts on the civil rights struggle and its different leading figures and compared ideas about Johnson's "War on Poverty" and the ever-growing list of "poverty pimps" that had risen in its shadow.

It was, simply put, a pleasure to go and talk to Dr. Prudhomme, and I so enjoyed our conversations. I would go to him for regular appointments whether I was depressed or not. When I was feeling well, I loved to go to his large, four-story, brick home to meet with him in his English basement office at 17th and R streets in northwest Washington.

With Dr. Prudhomme's analytical support, I felt ready to accept a position as associate director for reporting and evaluation on a three-month pilot project for the Black Child Development Center. I was responsible for contacting organizations, professionals, and activists in childcare and development and for informing them about the project's existence, goals, and objectives as well as publicizing federal plans, actions, and proposed legislation through a weekly newsletter called *The Black Child Development Dispatch*. I also participated in a national planning conference sponsored by the U.S. Office of Child Development (OCD), and the Department of Health, Education, and Welfare. At the end of the conference, I designed, wrote, edited, and supervised the publication of a book on the conference's deliberations. At the request of other workshop participants, I also drafted a proposal for the OCD on the need for quality daycare programs for minority children.

During this time, my moods were still up and down. Juadine Henderson, one of my young mentees who eventually became a close friend, met me during this particularly long-lasting period of depression.

Juadine Henderson: *I met Florence and Charles at Drum and Spear Bookstore, where I worked, in 1969, right after they moved to DC. I didn't know then that she was in depression mode. I just knew she was Florence Tate from Dayton and that she had been very active in the Movement there. But she didn't talk... she was very quiet, so I didn't get to get a sense of who she was until I went to work for her at the Black Child Development Group in 1970, which was my first real job. Florence made sure I kept a job. That was one of the things she did. She was like a mom or a big sister type. She could call up and say, "Juadine, what are you doing?" because I would quit a job in a minute. And I would leave and I guess somebody would tell her, and she would call up, and say, "What are you doing?" And I would say, "I just left...," and she would say, "OK, come to work with me tomorrow."*

In early 1971, I went to work at the Joint Center for Political Studies (JCPS or, simply, "The Joint Center") under Dr. Frank Reeves. This offered me my first "inside look" at how Blacks in elected leadership were faring in the new political climate that had arisen after the Civil Rights and Black Power Movements had begun to shape the national conversation.

The Joint Center had been established the year before as a joint research venture between Howard University and the Metropolitan Applied Research Center, specifically to aid and train the booming ranks of Black politicians who were being elected across the country. Between 1965 and 1970, the number of Black elected officials across the country had jumped from 300 to nearly 1,500. The Joint Center was there to answer questions for and offer guidance to these new leaders, most of whom were the first Black political officials ever elected in their communities. They often had little-to-no preparation— or finances in their city coffers—to deal with the problems in their long-disenfranchised neighborhoods.

As a consultant writer and public relations assistant, I worked on their monthly newsletter (later called *FOCUS*) and wrote several speeches for Dr. Reeves. I had never written a speech before he assigned me the task of drafting one for him to deliver at the national YWCA conference on racism that year.

"Florence, I need to get the word out that it is our ability to use our power to succeed in the political arena that will improve our conditions as a people," Frank stressed. Though I wasn't certain that was completely true, I was excited about the prospect of speechwriting, a daunting new challenge. We chatted briefly about content, and then I began researching the topic. I referred to the extensive list of books on racism in America up through the contemporary moment. I spent time at the Library of Congress and the U.S. Office of Civil Rights reading speeches on related topics, and I tapped into my own personal reservoirs of knowledge and experience.

I delivered the speech—"Using Our Political Power to Change Institutions" — to Frank a week ahead of time. "It's good, Florence, very good," he nodded, apparently pleased with the outcome. I was proud of myself, and from then on considered myself a speechwriter as well as a journalist and publicist. I wrote several other speeches for him on various political issues and wrote speeches for other organizations including the American Federation of State, County, and Municipal Employees, and the Coalition of Black Trade Unions.

It was at the Joint Center that I was to meet my dear friend Hedi Butler, who went on to become the senior writer at Black Radio Exclusive as well as operate her own marketing communications firm, Hed-Lines International.

Hedi Butler: *I had been hired at JCPS as a staff writer. It was the first think tank funded initially by the Ford Foundation to document and assist the burgeoning National roster of Black elected officials. While they were very pleased with my work as a writer, my inability to fit into the corporate structure was a problem.*

Enter Florence Tate, my replacement. Even in the most awkward of circumstances, I was immediately struck by her attractive demeanor, warmth, intelligence, and subtle humor, all of which emerged during our initial encounter. We clicked, became friends, and developed a lifelong respect for each other's special talents and skill sets. And yes, JCPS kept both of us.

While at JCPS, our friendship became a close bond. She was more than ten years older than me, but we shared much. Among the many commonalities was depression. It wasn't long before we became confidantes.

Florence would have longer, more debilitating bouts, while mine continued as a constant dysthymia, which would flare up from time to time and affect my functioning.

While we talked over lunches and sometimes in the office we shared, it was Florence's written notes—an epistolary genius that would mark her response to anything she felt deeply about— that underscored her wisdom and understanding, tempered by the life-honed commonsense she developed growing up in the country outside Memphis. I often called her "The Wizard of Eads."

While Florence's groundbreaking career with the Dayton Daily News pre-dated our friendship, I could see that she maintained the discipline of a working journalist. At JCPS, she brought that same factual, deadline sensitivity. Whether in subsequent work with the Urban Coalition or other political posts, passion was Florence's calling card. She was a sincere and effective advocate for her clients, whether they were organizations or individuals.

During that year, I also took on a project with John Wilson, a former SNCC member and then head of the National Sharecroppers Fund. He was leading a national group of locally based poverty programs that was organizing against an effort under Nixon's administration to abolish the Office of Economic Opportunity (OEO). The OEO was responsible for allocating funds for various community action agencies that were outgrowths of President Johnson's War on Poverty. At the time, it employed over 3,000 people in programs and projects across the country. With Nixon in office and ready to put OEO and its programs on the auction block, John set about arranging a Washington office and staff to do the organizing around saving the agency. He contacted me about taking care of the communications work.

John also brought in a young woman named LaVerne McCain (later McCain Gill), who had worked on the Hill, to act as director. I enlisted the services of my friend Juadine and, along with one or two others, we organized the Community Action Strategy Team (CAST) in an office across from Woody's—or, more formally, Woodward & Lothrop, a department store in downtown DC. In the flurry of intense work required to stave off OEO's demise, LaVerne and I became lifelong friends. She always answered the office phone with "CAST, McCain"—which became my nickname for her for a long time afterward.

LaVerne McCain Gill: *Florence and I met when I was at an impressionable age. I was twenty-four.... I remember Florence told me that, "after twenty-five you turn fifty!" I had just finished working on the Hill with Senator Cranston. Johnny Wilson asked me if I would work with him on a lobby for Congress against dismantlement. Even though I was in charge, he hired the staff. Florence actually named the organization Community Action Strategy Team (CAST). Wiley Branton, a very significant figure in the Civil Rights Movement, was also head of the Alliance for Labor Action, which funded CAST.*

So, we went about the business of establishing a lobby. We lobbied the senators, and we went on television, and we tried to save OEO. During that experience, Florence and I became really good friends.

More important than the work that we did was the fact that Florence represented the kind of Black woman that I had never seen before. She was fashionable, she was witty, she could write, and she was politically a nationalist. She introduced me to a way of thinking and being that I still, to this day, harbor because I knew how sincere she was, and I knew how hard she worked, and I knew how much she believed in what she was doing. And that made an impression on me, and it shaped who I am as a woman today.

This was the interesting part about Florence: other nationalist types that I knew were not supremely middle-class. Florence was supremely middle-class, but she was still a nationalist. So, she was one of the few middle-class nationalists that I knew—people who didn't dress like hoboes and didn't dress like bums—who actually went out and bought expensive clothes. I admired the fact that she had style and class and was still nationalist. For me that fit with what I was about 'cause I wasn't going backwards. I wanted to go forward and still maintain my integrity.

So you can imagine what kind of role model she was for me because I'm thinking, "Well, that makes a whole lot of sense... you can maintain who you are and be who you want to be, and you can still participate in the greatness of capitalism!" Because at that time you weren't offered a lot of alternatives. You were either totally Black and into the people or you were bourgeois and out of the loop. And so how do you get to the point where you actually can be who you are and be who you want to be? In Florence, I saw there was a freedom there that existed for me as a Black woman.

I was forty-something, and LaVerne was in her early twenties. Just as she regarded me as an older and more sophisticated female role model, I developed a kind of maternal feeling for LaVerne. She, like many other smart, on-the-ball, young women I'd met, was somebody I wanted to include in my circle of family and friends.

LaVerne wouldn't be the only friend to talk about what she saw as my style sensibility and my being what she termed a "middle-class nationalist." Hedi would also enjoy and share my love of stylish and well-designed fashions. And both she and LaVerne would be there as I experimented in the world of buying and selling fashions and setting up my own in-home boutique, which I called "The Caravan."

Hedi Butler: *Any serious effort to recapture the richness and fullness of the life of Florence Tate must include her distinctive sense of personal style. It was an evolution that spanned the decades from her southern-girl-white-gloves era in her native Memphis to her role as a working mother and trailblazing journalist...*

Her natural beauty—copper-kissed skin and hazel-green eyes framed by the soft halo of her Afro—was soon complemented by an emerging [and] eclectic fashion presentation. It incorporated both Diasporan cultural influences and her growing interest in haute couture. Florence's keen eye embraced top-tier designers such as Missoni, a line whose bright colors and graphics echoed traditional African textiles. Yet this seasoned shopper could find sensational fashion buys anywhere and dramatically transform the most classic looks with an artful addition from her unique collection of globally themed accessories including her signature scarfs and hats.

With a wide, multigenerational circle of creative friends and exquisite curator-level taste in selecting interesting and unusual pieces, Florence assembled show-stopping outfits that dazzled.... Florence the Fighter was also Florence the Fashionista, and she wore both personas exceptionally well.

Later on, I would support young and up and coming fashion designers and artists, including the jewelry designer Omo Misha, whose work was truly fabulous.

Omo Misha Mcglown: *In the mid-90s, I used to be in a band with Greg. We were running around doing our gigs, and we had done a gig in DC, so we all jumped in somebody's van and we stayed there, at the Tate's, for the weekend. We stayed at their house, and I made jewelry — when I wasn't running around with Greg's band, that was my profession. And we really just connected over the jewelry. The relationship just grew from there we stayed in touch. I used to visit DC, because I have friends there, so we just continued to talk and visit, and she was so excited about the jewelry, and because she was so excited she got everyone around her excited about it.*

We definitely made a deep personal connection. I know she really loved and appreciated the jewelry on its own, for its aesthetic and I know that she was not purchasing and wearing the jewelry just to support my effort. But I think that just seeing that I was a young single mother and creative, doing something, and her definitely wanting to be a part of pushing that — helping to push that to another level, was a big part of it. In addition to really authentically loving the work.

I liked to say we were two girls who connected over clips and baubles. And I never could have imagined, from that first meeting going to DC with Greg's band, that a lifelong relationship was going to unfold.

Thinking about my penchant for style and for being a *fashionista* brings back a funny memory: I had been the first Black woman in Dayton, Ohio, to wear my hair natural. I decided to do so in 1964 after Charles and I had been on a vacation with the boys, traveling to DC and New York. While in New York, I'd made it a point to visit certain stores, and Macy's was on the list. I remember seeing a cashier at Macy's who had a natural, and I just thought it was so pretty. I had seen Cicely Tyson sporting an Afro, but up until that point the cashier was the only person I had actually seen wearing her hair natural. So, I asked her, "How did you get your hair to look like that?" Her answer: "Honey, you just wash yours."

When I got back to Dayton, I couldn't wait to wash my hair. I decided to enlist the help of Mother, who had at one time worked as a barber. She had been staying with Geri, who suffered from carsickness and was unable to ride with us on the long trip. Once we were all unpacked and settled in, I pulled Mother aside and announced, "Mother, I want you to cut all my hair off 'cause I'm going to wear my hair natural!"

A look of horror came over my mother's face. "What? Louise, have you lost your mind? I'm not going to do any such thing!"

"Well, if you don't cut it, I'm going to get somebody else to cut it," I retorted, my mind made up. Knowing that if I said it, then I meant to do it, she shrugged. "Oh, Jesus, Louise...fine! I'll cut it!" she sighed, shaking her head remorsefully—imagining herself, I'm sure, as party to a horrible crime and bemoaning her inability to stand in my way.

And cut it she did, but she cried while doing it. She literally cut my hair and cried. Later, when I started working for the *Dayton Daily News*, she protested: "You're not going to go down there and let those white folks see your hair looking like that, are you?"

Mother's old-fashioned sensibilities aside, the truth was that, at the time, wearing one's hair natural was a big thing—a political statement, not just a style. If you were sporting a natural you were speaking your political beliefs, and you were saying something.

But back to LaVerne. Years later, she got into communications, producing a radio show and then some television. She eventually wrote a book, *African American Women in Congress: Forming and Transforming History*. LaVerne was always entrepreneurial, original, creative, and "doing stuff." At some point, she published a newspaper. When she asked if I would write for it, my response was, "Oh yeah, I want to write for your newspaper!" I had only been a reporter at the *Dayton Daily News*, but with LaVerne's paper—first the *Metro Chronicle*, later re-named the *National Chronicle*—I could have a column and could espouse my views regularly and at length.

Even as my life and professional engagement in DC began to gain momentum, at some point while seeing Dr. Prudhomme I decided that I was "talked out"…but still very depressed. I pleaded with him: "Dr. Prudhomme, please—I know that shock treatment works. It will help me."

Looking back, it seems that about every seven years after my first series of electroconvulsive therapy sessions in Dayton, my depression would get so deep and so bad that, although I didn't want to do the electroconvulsive or shock treatment (ECT) over, I would become so desperate and despairing that I would have to succumb to it. I never wanted to do it because although it would provide me with blessed relief from my depression, there were after-effects—confusion, a complete blank-slate feeling, then losing my memory for weeks afterward.

Most of the time, my memories would gradually come back, although I'm sure there were things of value that I still don't remember. I wouldn't forget relatives or things that were really important to me. I never forgot Charles or the children or the house, but I might have seen a movie or been to a play or party that I couldn't remember at all. Sometimes, people would say, "Remember when we did this-or-that?" and I wouldn't recall anything about it.

In one instance, I managed to forget someone whom I knew fairly well. I was at a party, and the girl came up to me and said, "You don't remember me, Mrs. Tate? I'm so-and-so." And I looked at her and said, "No, I don't remember." Disbelieving, she insisted, "I can't believe you don't remember me!" I responded, "I'm sorry, but I don't." Later, the host of the party told me the bewildered young lady told her, "Florence said she doesn't remember me. Why would she say that?"

To this day, there are many movies I simply cannot recall seeing. "Well, we saw that one, Florence. Don't you remember?" Charles will ask. I'll insist. "No, I didn't see that!" and Charles will hammer back, "Yes, you did!" He still doesn't quite understand.

In any case, after repeatedly asking Dr. Prudhomme, who was firmly against the kind of remedy I thought I needed, he finally acquiesced to my pleading. "Well, Florence, you know I don't do shock treatment, but I can refer you to someone who does," he told me. He sent me to a young Jamaican doctor whose practice was located in a small office building in DC. The difference between this doctor and Dr. Prudhomme was obvious from the start.

I was used to going to Dr. Prudhomme's office in the basement level of his great big house on Dupont Circle. That office was comfortably furnished, with all kinds of books. The office of the doctor he referred me to wasn't inviting in the least. No books, not even a bookshelf—just nothing. You couldn't be comfortable there at all, but that doctor did administer shock treatment in a hospital.

Several people have asked me to describe what it was like to have shock therapy. The fact is, it's often hard for me to recall much about it, probably because for a time after you have it, your memory is either poor or nonexistent. I do remember being taken from my hospital room into the treatment room and being laid on the bed. I remember there were always a couple of people in the room: the doctor, a nurse, and an anesthesiologist, I assumed. Within seconds after the anesthesia was administered, a feeling would start in my toes and roll up my body. It was a feeling of total relaxation, almost euphoria. I remember once telling a doctor in the room, "This is the best feeling," and I remember him responding, "Yeah, that's what I hear."

Yes, they do place electrodes on each side of your head, and they put something in your mouth to keep you from biting your tongue. They also strap your legs to the table so you can't kick anyone, because you will have convulsions—which, of course, you won't be aware of because, by that time, you're under.

The Jamaican doctor stands out in my memory because, for some reason, during one of those series of ECT treatments, I remember feeling what I could only assume was the electrical current going through me. I panicked for a moment, thinking, "Oh, my God, I'm not under yet!" Of course, moments later, I was under. When I mentioned it to the doctor some time during the next few weeks of my treatment sessions, he shrugged it off. "You think that's bad—at least you had anesthesia! I remember the days when we used to just plug the patient into the wall and turn on the power!" I reported this cavalier and inappropriate comment to Dr. Prudhomme, who was incensed and who, I'm sure, let that younger doctor have it!

When I first started my treatments, I would often ask whatever doctor was in the room, "Well, how does it work?" and their response was always the same: "We don't know how it works, we just know that it does work." The last time I had ECT was probably around 1998. I decided to stop submitting myself to it because of the effect on my memory. I swore from that point on to weather the agony unaided by the memory-stealing therapy.

After Dr. Prudhomme, I was lucky enough to find Dr. Frances Cress Welsing, another fine Black doctor, who later also became a dear friend. Depression was still an ever-present specter in my life and in my career. Whether it was during my tenure at the *Dayton Daily News*, my Civil Rights Movement activity, my forays into Black politics, or my African liberation support work…or whether my sickness was accommodated by an understanding employer or a seasonal schedule…my involvement was always at the mercy of an inevitable descent.

It was amazing that I could accomplish anything at all. After realizing the pattern and cycle of the paralysis that gripped me for almost half the year, my mission seemed to be to cram as much as possible into the periods when I felt "normal." I made every effort to let my prospective employers know that although I could go a mile a minute when things were good, circumstances could soon come to a point where doing anything would be impossible.

When interviewing for a job with M. Carl Holman, President of the National Urban League, I simply told him, "Mr. Holman, there will be times when I just can't function, can't deliver. But I'll make up for it when I can." I had precedent for believing Holman would be compassionate. Before I began working for the *Dayton Daily News*— realizing that Jim Fain was giving me an extraordinary opportunity for that time and that place and wanting to represent myself as honestly as I could—it was important for me to tell him about my condition before I began my career as a reporter.

Jim was especially sensitive to my condition, having lost his first wife to her own battle with mental illness. At a time well before telecommuting became part of the culture, he arranged for assignments that allowed me to be at home during my roughest patches. It was during one of my very bad winters that Jim gave me the assignment in Crown Point. Since it was an investigative piece that I could research over a period of weeks, I didn't have to go into the office. I spent much of that winter either in the slums of Crown Point or at home in the depths of my depression. But Jim was very pleased when I'd finished the assignment and submitted the exposé. He later told me that, had he been able, he would have submitted the story for a Pulitzer Prize, but at the time, the award wasn't given to journalists.

The winter has always been the hardest time for me. For a long time, my depression would occur regularly from October to April. As it turned out, it was a major blessing that the most demanding work required in my political jobs usually occurred during my six-months-on periods. The campaigns and the periods immediately preceding the fall election season took place when I was at my peak in terms of performance. Then, just as the whole political circus began to wind down, amid either the thrill of victory or the agony of defeat, my good days for the year drew to a close.

Both my dear friend and comrade Joan Thornell, who worked with me at the National Urban Coalition, and my longtime confidante Juadine Henderson, saw my ups and downs over the course of many years.

Joan Thornell: *Florence was one of the most interesting people I had ever met in my life. Even in the worst times, when she had to be hospitalized, she was still one of the funniest people on the planet and one of the most incisive as well. So, through thick and thin, our friendship grew and grew. She was like my sister.*

Sometimes, she wasn't able to do the other stuff—the work, the politics... sometimes, she was so ill that she was just stopped in her tracks. When she was deeply, deeply, deeply sad, depressed, and withdrawn, the change in her personality and her feeling of hopelessness was very dramatic because when she was firing on all cylinders, she was something else. But when she was depressed, she was like, just sitting there and sometimes very weepy and sometimes feeling like, "How can I go on? This is impossible!"

Juadine Henderson: [Before Florence] I had never seen depression that way or [had it] explained. Florence would come to my apartment in about September to say goodbye because she knew depression was going to hit her about October, and she was like a completely different person then. The first time I saw that I didn't know what to do. She was quiet, she didn't talk.... Charles took care of her. She was gone. The Florence that you knew, that was vibrant, that had lots of energy to do all kinds of things, didn't exist during those winter months. And you knew that when spring hit that Florence would be back and would never sleep, wouldn't need to sleep. She had energy galore and was doing all kinds of things. That [way of being] I had never seen or heard of before. It was a painful thing to watch. And she didn't hide it. She talked about it.

And I think when she found lithium—she was doing research on depression, and she found out about lithium—they were using it in Europe or someplace, and she went off looking for a doctor who would give it to her...

We talked and laughed about it. We made jokes about it because she was going to a counselor, a psychiatrist named Dr. Prudhomme.... She told me, "I told Dr. Prudhomme I can't come back until I get some more stories to tell him. I've run out of stories to tell him now." And she was looking for somebody to administer this lithium, and she found a young Jewish doctor, I think, who agreed to give it to her. But he was going to have to do blood tests to make sure that it wasn't poisoning her system or something.

And she didn't go through the same kind of depression after she kept taking the stuff. And her comment to me about that was, "I miss the highs." The depression was terrible, but then she no longer had the burst of energy she got in the spring after she started taking the lithium.

When I began serious treatment with Dr. Welsing, I remember crying out, "Frances, tell me: *What in the world is wrong with me?*" We talked into the night, starting again at the point of my stroke. For the first time, however, she heard me recount overhearing my obstetrician, Dr. Daniels, say, "She'd be better off dead" while I lay paralyzed in semiconsciousness.

Bells rang and light bulbs popped on in her head. "Florence!" she exclaimed, "That's it! That's the key: *'better off dead'*!" Frances believed that when I heard Dr. Daniel's comment while unable to speak, respond, or even really comprehend what he was saying, it triggered an anxiety, terror, hopelessness, and helplessness that was embedded into my subconscious. She also believed that, combined with a probable genetic predisposition, my chaotic and emotionally abusive childhood, and the stress of the stroke, the *'better off dead'* message could have been the straw that broke the camel's back. It seemed to Francis entirely possible that somehow my damaged psyche was causing me to replay that message over and over, creating a kind of "script" that I was playing out during the darkest, coldest, and least-hospitable period of the year—from late fall through early spring.

It made sense to me and gave me a better perspective on why, during my bleakest periods, I'd spent so many months of so many years focused on death. A large part of my eventual reconciliation with and forgiveness of my mother came with the help I received from Frances. She helped me come to terms with who my mother was and the realities that caused her to make the choices she did. With Frances's assistance, I came to realize that there were many positive things about my mother that I had never acknowledged or appreciated.

Thus, by the last decade of Mother's life, I was finally able to tell her that I loved her. On returning to DC from Dayton after she died in 1982, one of the first things I did was to call Frances and tell her how much I appreciated the way she'd helped me come to terms with Mother. "Frances, it would have been horrible if my mother had died without my having forgiven her or having tried to understand her, and you helped me to do that. That's a huge thing. Huge, huge, huge!" I shared with her.

Frances helped me to understand the dynamics of abandonment and how it affected and continues to affect my life; how it caused me to do—or not do—certain things; how it affected my relationships with people and even informed what I expected from them. Frances helped me understand the effects I couldn't get over and the emotions I would have to learn to deal with and somehow put in their place. I learned to say to myself, "OK, I'm feeling like this because of so and so, but it isn't really like that at all." She also ultimately helped me understand the relationship between my childhood and its possible impact on my lifelong depression.

During my years of seeing psychiatrists and psychotherapists in DC, there also came a point when I could also finally mourn my father, who had died while I was so depressed in 1969. And it was later still when I began holding him responsible for things that had or had not happened during my childhood. Suddenly, one day it just hit me: *I blamed my mother for everything, but I had a father too. Where was he?* While all the stuff with my mother was happening, why wasn't he around? After he left Junior and me with Mama Annie and Papa Elvin on the farm, I didn't remember him ever sending or bringing me or my brother anything. And he never sent me anything later on when I lived in Memphis, not even for birthdays or Christmas. The fact is, my father was often neglectful, and even negligent, during my childhood.

It was at that point I got so mad at Daddy that I didn't know what to do. Furious with him, I sat down and wrote his widow a letter, basically accusing her of enabling him. "How did you stay with him knowing that he had a child and he didn't do anything for this child? And he didn't leave me a thing, not even a teaspoon!" I railed in the letter. It was unfair, but at that point, with him already gone, I had no one else to let it out on. I'd always held my father in such high esteem, always believing I was clearly more his child than my mother's and heavily influenced by him, even in his absence.

Lucille Knowles: *I think because our father was a principal, there were a lot of people who knew us both in the country and the city, and they would always talk about how smart our family was. And so, there were always high expectations about us in* *school, and doing our best, and always being sort of ahead of the curve in terms of advocacy and stuff like that.*

Our dad was one of the founders of the Shelby County Democratic Club—which was one of the first African American movements in politics in Shelby County—along with a guy named Jesse Turner... I think he was an attorney... and Russell Sugarman... and also Benjamin Hooks, who went on to become the head of the national NAACP. But they quietly started the Shelby County Democratic Club, probably when I was around nine or ten. Florence would have been in her twenties. So, the family was always active politically. There was just an expectation.

Although I experienced much pain during the early years of our lives in DC, the revelations I gained in therapy were truly transformative in relation to my gaining a sense of peace despite long-held childhood traumas.

Depression aside, the 1970s would find me involved with some of the most exciting, challenging, and powerful activities of my life up to that point. My professional experiences during these years also greatly affirmed my sense of capability as I worked in the various communications jobs I held. My years working at the *Dayton Daily News* prepared me well for my later work at the National Black News Service (NBNS) in Washington, DC.

I was to later learn from my FBI files that during this time the government would put me back on their so-called "Rabble-Rouser Index"—label me as a "subversive," "Black nationalist," "Black extremist," "potentially dangerous" "racial agitator," and a "national security threat."

But my most thrilling adventure was yet to come because the farmgirl from Eads was about to help gather the largest assemblage of Black Power proponents on the steps of the nation's capital—and, not long after, become an international freedom fighter. Despair aside, I was about to have the best time of my life.

CHAPTER 10

AFRICAN LIBERATION 101

The year 1972 was one of worldwide upheaval, war, protest, and terrorism–state-sanctioned and otherwise. English soldiers killed dozens of civilians protesting in Northern Ireland against the stranglehold of the British Empire. Hundreds of thousands of people around the world continued protesting the escalation of the Vietnam War. A Palestinian group named Black September kidnapped and killed eleven Israeli athletes during the summer Olympics. A break-in at the Democratic National Committee's campaign offices at the Watergate Hotel led to the unraveling of Washington, DC's high-level machinations and shady maneuvering, pointing the way to Nixon's demise. People were struggling for freedom around the globe.

For those of us working for the freedom of Black folks around the planet, it turned out to be a banner year, with many firsts and several watershed events. It was the year that Shirley Chisholm, our first Black congresswoman, would announce her candidacy for president as Andrew Young and Barbara Jordan became the first Blacks to gain seats in the House of Representatives since Reconstruction. Angela Davis, political prisoner and intellectual, would finally be freed and found innocent of the trumped-up charges against her while, at the same time, Pan-Africanism was igniting the souls of Black folk worldwide, and liberation movements all over Africa were gaining full speed.

Despite the lingering ups and downs of my depression, it was an exciting and productive period during which I was called on to bring all my combined skills to the table. I was apparently becoming *the* "go-to" person for activist organizations, events, and people working in the sphere of Black political and social causes. My reputation from the years I'd spent working for SNCC, the *Dayton Daily News*, DARE, CORE, the Dayton Afro-American Cultural Center, and the Black

Umoja Society had gradually spread along the activist circuit. I was immediately recommended to any persons or organizations working to spread Black liberation and who might need a press or publicity coordinator, communications director, or journalist/reporter. Friends and cohorts began to joke that the word on the ground, generally, was *"Get Florence!"*

I was meeting a variety of influential and inspiring Black folks working for our national—and international—empowerment. Situated in DC and able to get my hands into a variety of pots readily, I was right in the middle of it all. Despite ongoing doubts and fears about my health, I was loving every minute of it.

Many of us working in Movement politics and strategies were beginning to feel that we should formally organize a third political force in the U.S. In March 1972, we gathered to manifest this intention during the historic, first National Black Political Convention (NBPC) in Gary, Indiana. On the second weekend of March, Charles and I joined upward of 8,000 (some sources have reported as many as 10,000) Black activists, political figures, nationalists, and community advocates there in Gary. Church leaders and congregations, educators, students, and interested everyday people, all were excited about taking part in the convention. A direct result of the Congress of Afrikan People (CAP) Conference led by Imamu Amiri Baraka in 1970, the NBPC was a groundbreaking event that eventually led to the election of many more Blacks to political office.

Gary had recently elected Richard Hatcher as its first Black mayor, making him the first Black elected mayor of a U.S. city larger than 100,000 people. Hatcher was a very vocal advocate for Black folks, and he had arranged for the convention to be held at Westside High, the state's largest high school, erected only a few years earlier to integrate the city's school system. Hatcher and Baraka were joined on the convention's steering committee by Civil Rights Movement activist and Michigan House Representative Charles Diggs.

It was a widely heralded event, supported by many Black nationalist activists and organizations. Progressive Black elected officials, including California Congressman Ron Dellums, were there as well as many local Civil Rights and Black Nationalist leaders. Among those

I recall seeing were Ron Daniels, leader of the Youngstown, Ohio, organization, Freedom Inc; Third World Press of Chicago's publisher and poet Haki Madhubuti (then still Don L. Lee); Jitu Weusi of the National Black United Front; and Black Panther Elaine Brown. SNCC folks also participated, including Ivanhoe Donaldson and Judy Richardson as well as representatives from other student groups like the Student Organization for Black Unity (SOBU). These were only a handful of the many national organizational leaders who attended from around the country, all of whom agreed that "now was the time."

The convention was organized similar to the major political party conventions—with voting delegates and platforms and planks on the various issues confronting Black people at that time (which are, sadly, many of the same ones confronting us today). Everyone was there with their signs, whether they were Black nationalists, integrationists, socialists, congregants, clergy, or community activists. They all came with their various position papers, prepared to present their ideas to be discussed and ultimately voted on.

Baraka masterfully ran the conference on the organizing principle of "Unity without Uniformity," and it was extraordinarily impressive and absolutely empowering just to see the thousands, representing segments from every part of the national Black community, who attended that beautiful weekend. Most memorable for me was the session during which Baraka had to bring to heel on the convention floor the out-of-order head of the New York delegation, Roy Innis, with a roaring cry of "*SIT DOWN, NEW YORK!*"

Looking back, it was a grand time, really, when we Black people from everywhere and from different perspectives came together to discuss our issues and concerns. Despite seeing those matters from different angles and adopting various and differing positions, it was nonetheless a national conversation *by us, for us, and about us.*

I have to add a blunt aside: virtually no white people were allowed. Some white reporters were there including William Greider, whom I met at the convention and who went on to write for Rolling Stone. They could be found hanging around the hotels trying to get a lead on the proceedings, so it was possible to talk to them after convention sessions. But otherwise, no white folks were involved. The convention was not about the foolishness of talking with white people about race. (Besides, as I believed then and now, when it comes to white people and race, ain't nothing to talk about. Ain't nothing to talk about to white people *about* race, either. They all just need to read Nell Irvin Painter's book, *The History of White People* (published in 2010). If you read her book, then you got it! Ain't nothing new—what we need now is to be talking *to each other* about how we deal with this mess!)

My sister-in-arms and dear friend Joan Thornell, who worked as special assistant to Baraka, Diggs, and Hatcher, the three main forces behind the event, had this to say about the NBPC:

> **Joan Thornell:** *I was the general all-around special assistant for the co-chairs and part of the group in Washington planning the convention before actually going to Gary. That convention was called by three very disparate but interesting people: Dick Hatcher, the mayor of Gary, Indiana; Congressman Charles Diggs from Detroit; and [Imamu] Amiri Baraka.*
>
> *Amiri was an outstanding person who held the whole thing together when it was in full swing.... [As] you can imagine, there were so many different and contentious people there that in order to pull off what finally took place—which was the National Black Agenda—if it hadn't been for Baraka wielding a wonderful gavel and keeping order, it would have been mayhem. It was accomplished through his handling of the many, many, many factions that attended because when the call went out that there was going to be such a thing, people from every aspect of Black life showed up in Gary. I'm talking about every aspect! It was incredible. It was really something.*
>
> *And my hope was that there would be the formation of a Black political party. But good-old Charlie Diggs, who was representing the Democratic Party and specifically tasked with not letting that happen—even though he was someone that I knew and had some respect for—he threw a monkey wrench in the possibility of a national Black political party. It could have happened then if it weren't for the muscle of the Democratic Party, which was not going to let that happen. Because guess what would have happened if there had been formed in '72 a Black political party*

taking all the votes away from the Democrats? You can imagine what would have happened!

And so, alas, all the great intentions, hard work, negotiating, debating, politicking, and praying could not overcome the reluctance of some of the elected officials to break their allegiance to the Democratic Party. Although we had decided that Ron Dellums, a much respected and popular congressman, would be our presidential nominee in the next election, Ron ultimately decided that he would not bear the mantle. And never again since that event have so many Black groups with such great potential power been able to come together to exercise that kind of coalition-building on a unified meeting ground.

Not long after the convention, I was visited by a very intense young man named Mark Smith, one of the leaders of the very active Student Organization for Black Unity or SOBU (later YOBU, Youth Organization for Black Unity). Those young leaders had decided to organize the first African Unity Day demonstration, and Mark had dropped out of Harvard to do organizing full-time. He recently had spent quite a bit of time with Stokely in the South educating people on African freedom movements and Pan-Africanism—the belief in the connected destiny of our people throughout Africa and around the world (the Diaspora). Pan-Africanism was gaining more and more traction as the liberation struggle in African nations intensified. I'm sure it was Stokely who advised Mark to seek my assistance in organizing the event, which was meant to engage Black Americans in the political and economic struggles of these new African nations.

African Liberation Day (ALD) was to be a large-scale event happening in multiple locations over a period of time. Although Geri had made a first visit to Tanzania and was already familiar with the country, I had not yet begun my work with African Liberation on the Continent and had become resigned to the possibility that my political organizing was behind me.

Mark brilliantly and passionately convinced me of the historic worthiness of his cause and of my ability to make a significant contribution to its manifestation. It seemed that my reputation had preceded me, and he would not take "no" for an answer.

Mark Smith: *Florence had been very much associated with Stokely, and when we were looking around, thinking, "Who is it that can handle this information role and dealing with the press?" she came to mind.*

At that time, Florence was about what—forty?—so she was considerably older than most of the folks working on this thing. Most of us were in our twenties, for sure. She was the person who was knowledgeable about the press. I was twenty-one; I didn't know how to write a press release, I didn't know any reporters, and I was a novice about trying to get the word out. If you know anything about ALD, we had buses that came from all up and down the east coast and even as far away as the Midwest. So, a lot of it was how to do that kind of "information spreading" back at a time when there were no cell phones and no one had even dreamt of the internet or social media.

So, you're sitting in an office in Washington, DC... how do you find people in Atlanta who want to come to this demonstration? How do you publicize it, how do you organize their communication, how do you charter buses, all that kind of stuff? So those were the kinds of things we were working on, and Florence's job was in large part to deal with the media. But it wasn't so much the New York Times *or the* Washington Post *as it was Black press and the communication circles in the Movement, which is how we got the word out about the demonstration.*

The thing that I remember most about her was her energy. She was just constantly on the go. She had been a reporter, so she had both those reporter skills and vocabulary and credibility, but she'd also been a long-time activist in Dayton, so she knew a lot of people in the Movement as well. And so, she was just a dynamo of activity. She was the veteran in the whole thing. She was the voice of stability and maturity who had been in the Movement for a long time, so I had great respect for her.

I threw myself into the work of coordinating and disseminating information among the members of the ad hoc committee formed to organize the event, the African Liberation Day Coordinating Committee (ALDCC). I also communicated with the various activist networks and participants around the country as well as in in Europe, the Caribbean, and Africa.

Owusu Sadaukai (née Howard Fuller) was the guiding light behind this effort. He was a brilliant organizer and speaker who had established Malcolm X Liberation University in Greensboro, North Carolina. He had recently returned to the United States after spending time with revolutionaries in Angola, Mozambique, and Guinea-Bissau. He'd returned with the goal of raising political awareness about and aid for those African countries' struggles.

Owusu was a charismatic organizer and a natural leader. He would always say, "I'm not doing this forever.... Y'all think I'm gonna be doing this forever? When I get through with this, I'm going back to teaching!" We would laugh, not believing him, because he could really fire up the crowd. But as it turned out, when organizing and Black Power faded as a mode of change, he did, in fact, go right back to teaching.

Dr. Howard Fuller (Owusu Sadaukai): *I met Florence through Cleve Sellers, via Kwame Ture [Stokely Carmichael]. When we started planning for the demonstration, she was recommended to be the person to handle the press as information secretary. Florence was really connected in DC to all kinds of different people. I depended totally on her for all of the press stuff leading up to the demonstration because, even though it turned out there were like 35 or 40,000 people that came when we started organizing, very few people thought it was going to be the success that it was. Kwame Ture was in Africa at the time. He was in Guinea and he sent me a letter saying that we shouldn't have the demonstration, that it wasn't going to be successful.*

Plus, I wasn't really known and didn't have any standing particularly with all of the "holders of the truth" on Pan-Africanism. We just did the organizer work and made it happen.

Florence was invaluable—both in terms of connecting us to people, but also advice and counsel—and was involved with the formation of the African Liberation Support Committee, which was the ongoing entity that got created after the first demonstration. I was not engaged with the ones after '73, but

Florence and I remained friends. I had created an organization called the Black Alliance for Educational Options, and I was so pleased that she came to one of the symposiums, probably around 2000.

[In terms of her depression,] I do remember being in their house a couple of times where she was non-communicative, and that was kind of hard to deal with because when she was communicating, as you know, it was... it was a surge. So, to see her in a state where she couldn't really communicate was kind of difficult.

Florence was an example of — at least, this is my view of the world — of how, as I try to tell my kids today at our school, you can do well and do good. Because there are clearly people who live a comfortable life, but they're still committed to advancement. And then we have people who, once they get to a certain point in life, don't give a damn about what's gonna happen to poor Black people. Florence was one of those people who remained committed to trying to advance the cause of Black people. But she didn't have to; she did it in spite of illness, whatever it was. She didn't have to do that, but she did. So, I had a lot of respect for, such respect and love for, Florence.

Owusu traveled around the country, as well as the Caribbean and Canada, organizing and gaining support, while those of us in the office at 14th and U streets in northwest DC handled the communications, logistics, and local strategizing. Staff included Mark Smith as director of operations; ex-SNCC activist Cleveland Sellers as field coordinator; my dear friend Juadine Henderson as secretary and treasurer; Mwanafunzi Hekima, one of Imamu Baraka's disciples as logistics coordinator; and myself as information coordinator.

Juadine Henderson: *One of the things about the support committee was that everybody had a person in the office, and Baraka's person was named was Hekima. But when you talked to [Baraka's people] they had a response that was dictated from Baraka. They literally had a book. I remember laughing* *about it with somebody who asked Hekima a question, "Watch him get his book so he can answer you." It was very crazy, and people were pushing each other over for power. It was political egotism all over the place. I ignored a lot of the politics of the ALDCC on purpose. If you were going to do the work, you had to ignore the politics of the Movement or else you couldn't do it. There was a lot of ego-tripping going on. Florence seemed to have stayed above all of it. I don't know how she did it.*

The membership of ALD's National Steering Committee read like a "who's who" list of Civil Rights and Black Power activist notables, along with prominent religious and political figures, representatives from related coalitions and networks, scholars, and student activists.

Much of my prior experience culling and creating media contacts, developing networks of strategically placed individuals in communication and publicity, and doing the feet-on-the-groundwork of grassroots organizing was brought to bear while working on the event. I doubt there could have been a more opportune moment for me to use my skills and engage my passion for the liberation of Black people. Together, we arranged the largest demonstration ever held in the United States on behalf of African liberation. Anywhere from 25,000 to 30,000 people from all over the country attended; simultaneous demonstrations were held in Europe and the Caribbean. It was an outstanding accomplishment of which we all felt justifiably proud.

Mark Smith: *Absolutely, ALD was a success. It was part of the very beginning stages of building support for the South African movement and for the guerilla movements against the Portuguese that began to build in the late 80s [in support of] the divestiture movement all over college campuses, which was picked up by the labor movement. If you read or heard Mr. Mandela speak, from his standpoint, it was support in the West that was a critical factor in the eventual reversal of [these specific conditions Africans were struggling with]. Obviously, the overthrow of the dictatorship in Portugal was part of it,* *but it was clearly the support of people in the West in various ways that was a key part of the end of the settler colonies. And I feel that ALD was a very beginning, early part of the building of that movement and the broader consciousness about those colonies. So yes, we thought that we did good.*

It was also during this time that I was to become aware of UNITA—the National Union for the Total Independence of Angola.

Part of my function as ALD's national information coordinator was to recruit Pan-Africanists and African Liberation Movement supporters from all over the Diaspora. In this pursuit, I met Chenhamo ("Chen") Chimutengwende, a Zimbabwean originally exiled in London, who ultimately ended up serving as a member of the Zimbabwean Parliament for 23 years. In London, Chen led a group of Pan-Africanists, writers, activists, and speakers, and he agreed to come to Washington and speak at the demonstration. He was extremely well informed about the intricacies of the various liberation movements, their compositions, international governmental and private support, their ideological leanings, tendencies and affiliations, and the personalities of their leaders.

One of my responsibilities was to commission signs for the demonstration. While visiting the ALDCC's office prior to the demonstration, Chen saw the placards listing all the liberation movements: PAIGC, FRELEMO, ZANU, ZAPU, FLORISI, MPLA, FLMA, SWAPO. "Where is UNITA?" he asked, turning to me. That particular acronym stood for the National Union for the Total Independence of Angola "Where is UNITA?" he repeated.

I shrugged. No doubt parroting something I'd heard somewhere, I responded: "Well, Chen, reportedly UNITA is nothing but a puppet for the Portuguese, maybe even just a figment of their imaginations."

"Excuse me, but you can't know anything about UNITA, in reality," Chen replied, "because all you hear is what the European Marxists will tell you in the press." "These same European writers, who are the source of much of the information you receive about African liberation movements and leaders, also engage in disinformation campaigns about organizations like UNITA because many of these same people are Soviet-supported or -connected," Chan continued. "And because UNITA has received backing and ideological support and training in China, they are 'out of favor' in Europe. Do not believe everything you hear!"

From that point on, Chen, who himself who was Maoist ZANU (Zimbabwe African National Union) supporter, proceeded to give me a schooling on the political ideologies of the various movements. Feeling quite chastened, I added UNITA's name to our demonstration literature, and later convinced the ALDCC to make a donation to UNITA from the funds allocated to the various liberation movement groups. Armed with Chen's information and my underdog mentality, I was primed to become UNITA's biggest U.S. supporter. This would ultimately become a position that would cause me much alienation and pain but would also result in experiences that were available to only a few American activists of the period.

After the unprecedented success of African Liberation Day came the sticky part: *how would the huge, multi-ideological instrument we created be able to move forward on a common agenda for a cause we all believed in and supported?* First, we decided to make the ALD coordinating committee permanent by changing its name to the African Liberation Support Committee (ALSC). We had several meetings around the country—in Atlanta, DC, Greensboro, and the final, fatal meeting in Frogmore, South Carolina. Unfortunately, by that final meeting, it had become abundantly clear to me that the Marxist-Nationalist controversy was going to destroy the organization. And it did, but not before a lot of acrimonious arguments and out-of-control ego warfare took place.

I was asked to comment on the issue in the Chicago journal, *Afrika Must Unite – A Journal of Current Afrikan Affairs*, Edited by Ruwa Chiri, in 1973.

```
The masses are very intelligent. If you're
going where they want to go, they'll follow
you. They don't follow you because you're going
somewhere you want to go. They follow you
```

because you've led them to believe you can take them where they have themselves decided they want to go. Afrikan Liberation Day 1972 is a perfect example.

I hope there are none among us who believe that a few of us were able to, within three months' time, convince 25,000 people in 1972 that they should support Afrika. No, that consciousness-raising had taken place and taken root and been nourished by many, many organizations and individuals long before the ALSC and the current "movement" organizations came along.

I cite all this to point out that we should be mindful that [just] because 25,000 people followed us when they thought our primary concern was Afrika, does not mean they'll follow us off toward some common meeting ground with the white left in its march to a "workers of the world unite" utopia. When ALSC looks around for its followers, they'll be standing still, as the masses will do, until they find someone or something or some program headed in the direction their consciousness dictates they go.

Later, poet, scholar and activist Kalamu Ya Salaam would use this quote in an article he wrote for *Black World* magazine in 1974. "Tell No Lies, Claim No Easy Victories; African Liberation Day, an Assessment."

Kalamu Ya Salaam: *In Florence's quote you have, in political terms, the Nationalist versus the Marxist. And our people, the masses of our people, have never been Marxist. Nationalism appeals to people because, particularly coming out of Jim Crow, we wanted something of our own. ALSC (the African Liberation*

Support Committee) was the pivotal organization for those of us who thought ourselves progressives, not to mention revolutionary. There were actually three major forces that were going on: Owusu Sadaukai (or Howard Fuller) and the faction around Owusu, which included Nelson Johnson from SOBU and YOBU; you had the faction... around Abdul Alkalimat (Gerald McWorter), and that faction was Marxist-oriented. Around Owusu, I would say they were fellow travelers of Marxism, but they ended up being more nationalist. Then Baraka became a Marxist, but not because of his involvement, directly but because of his overall popularity—not because of his involvement with FRELIMO, MPLA, or any of the others. And it gets really twisted up by then.

Florence had, I think, one of the better grasps of what this meant in the moment—that it didn't have overall impact. In many ways, we were insular. We didn't want to be part of the United States establishment, and so we didn't pay a lot of attention to what was going on with that. We knew but we were not involved in detail with establishment politics. At the same time, we had organizations that were community-based and very active, and we visited each other and had long discussions trying to figure this out. But the independent Black movement failed to come about.

Florence had an ability to work with a lot of different people, and she had done that kind of work, and she'd worked with some of the more radical and progressive organizations. So, she knew people individually, and she did not let that get in the way of what she thought was important to do. And that's often hard to do. When you know about people's real personal life, it's sometimes hard to keep that in check when you're doing political work with them.

Florence was deep with experience. She knew people. And I learned a lot from her about working with people, and how you move beyond personality and personal traits to get to the larger political issues that had to be dealt with. She was good at that.

It was good while it lasted, the saying goes, but the ALSC couldn't find a way to sustain itself past the egos and philosophical arguments.

Of course, I later learned that it was during this time that the FBI re-opened their file on me—closed since 1970—recording my lapse into depression and my life as a simple "housewife," according to their notes.

UNITED STATES GOVERNMENT
Memorandum
ACTING DIRECTOR, FBI

FLORENCE LOUISE TATE
ReBulet to WFO, dated 3/29/72.

XXXXXXXXX have identified FLORENCE
TATE, Information Coordinator of the African
Liberation Day Demonstration and member
of the African Liberation Day Coordinating
Committee (ALDCC), as being identical with the
FLORENCE TATE who moved to WDC from Dayton,
Ohio in 1969.

TATE's activity in connection with the
demonstration on 5/27/72 is being closely
followed xxxxxxxxxxxxxxxxx. After conclusion
of the demonstration, and depending on its
nature, WFO will submit information in a
form suitable for dissemination concerning
TATE, along with recommendations regarding
her interview and possible inclusion in the
Administrative Index.

```
UNITED STATES DEPARTMENT OF JUSTICE
FEDERAL BUREAU OF INVESTIGATION
Washington, DC 20535
April 7, 1972
```

```
     On March 20, 1972
XXXXXXXXXXXXXXXXXXXXXXXXX African
Liberation Day Coordinating Committee (ALDCC)
held a press conference on that date at their
office, 2207 14th Street, N.W., DC (WDC). The
conference started at approximately 10:15 a.m.
and concluded at approximately 11:10 a.m. and
was attended by an estimated fifty to sixty
individuals.
     XXXXXXXXXXXXXXXXXXXXXXX Florence Tate,
Communications Coordinator, ALDCC, opened
the conference and introduced members of the
National Steering Committee of the ALDCC who
were present.
```

Various other entries like these were noted during this time period, but being part of the ALDCC and the event in such a meaningful way was an exciting and memorable experience for me.

The year held other opportunities for me to increase my network of contacts and people sympathetic to the Movement. I became a stringer at the National Black News Service (NBNS), which gave me another chance to immerse myself in the world of journalism. The NBNS was a DC-based subscription news organization that provided national and internationals news of interest to Black readers. Established and run by Paul H. Wyche Jr., it used four or five reporters and three wire services to feed approximately 150 weekly newspapers in the U.S. and the Virgin Islands.

As a writer-editor at NBNS for nine months between 1972 and 1973, I had to be alert to pertinent issues primarily in the U.S., Africa, and the Caribbean and make sure that something was written on all the major issues affecting Black people in those regions in a given week. After helping to gather the news, I wrote stories and assisted in their editing and distribution to weeklies around the country.

As a reporter, I covered as many congressional hearings as possible and gathered other information from various federal agencies. I also interviewed government officials as well as national civil rights, social welfare organizations, and other Black leaders and activists. My growing Pan-Africanist activism also afforded me good contacts among the various African embassies, at the United Nations, and among African Liberation Movement leaders and representatives as well as Pan-Africanist political figures in the U.S. and Caribbean.

Dozens of my articles appeared with and without my byline. Sometimes "NBNS" replaced the organization's writers' names in widely distributed stories. Unlike at the *Dayton Daily News*, I was reporting solely on issues that had to do with Black people, and my writing appeared in newspapers across the country with titles like, "Blacks Fare Poorly In 92nd Congress" (*The Medium,* Seattle/ Tacoma, Washington, November 2, 1972); "Congressional Voting Shows Decrease of Concern for Blacks" (*The Delaware Spectator*, November 15, 1972); "Two Hundred Students to Plan Future of Black Community" (*Louisville Defender*, November 16, 1972); "Humphrey Helps McGovern Woo National Black Vote" (*The Baltimore Afro, October 24, 1972).* It was an exciting position that allowed me to deploy my instinctive skill at ferreting out information critical to the wellbeing of Black people around the globe, and it felt good to be back in the field.

In March 1973, I returned to the area of public affairs when I was hired as a public affairs/public relations writer in the communications division of the National Urban Coalition (NUC) under M. Carl Holman. Holman was a wise, learned, funny, and wonderful man; a published poet with an MFA from Yale. (His most famous poem, "Mr. Z," is still taught in English and creative writing classes.) He had previously been the deputy staff director of the United States

Commission on Civil Rights. When I found out that a position had become available at NUC and my name had been highly recommended, I was happy to accept the offer to work under such a brilliant mind.

The NUC was created after the Kerner Commission released its study on the causes behind the race riots that came to a head in Detroit in 1967. By the next year, it, the National Conference of Mayors, and the National League of Cities had joined to devise a way to attack the myriad issues that were still rampant and destructive for the nation's poorest citizens. The NUC was designed to funnel resources and funding from the government to communities struggling against the insidiousness of poverty, to address the issues of jobs, wages, housing, and crime.

When I joined the NUC staff, plans were underway for its first national conference, but little or no effort had been made to publicize it. I immediately started a press campaign by sending preliminary releases to national and local urban affairs reporters and systematically informed them of the progress of our plans for the conference.

Among the conference's many speakers, panelists, discussion leaders, and participants were labor leaders, corporate presidents and board chairmen, civil rights and social welfare organization leaders, heads of national church organizations, Black political leaders, representatives of ethnic minorities, university presidents, feminist organization leaders, and other educators. I prepared biographical sketches and other pertinent background materials on these individuals, disseminated them to the press, and arranged media interviews for figures such as Vernon Jordan, Julian Bond, Leonard Woodcock, Dorothy Height, Msgr. Geno Baroni, Shirley Chisholm and David Rockefeller.

My hard work paid off. The conference was well-publicized and well-attended. But what came next was altogether unexpected.

"Florence, your work on this project in such a short time was impressive," Mr. Holman began, after asking me into his office. "I need the kind of energy and results you displayed. We have too much to do, and no time to waste. I want you to take over as director of the Communications Division—immediately. Are you interested?"

I was taken aback, and to be honest, uncomfortable with the idea of replacing the person who initially hired me. But in no way did I want to disappoint Mr. Holman, so I accepted and took over the position.

The new job meant that I had primary responsibility for the development and implementation of public relations and publications policy and practice for NUC and its thirty-odd local affiliates. Supported by a staff of ten, I was responsible for the writing, editing, and publishing the organization's monthly magazine, *NETWORK*, and all brochures, pamphlets, annual reports (including the president's report and annual program budget reports), and other written materials for NUC's housing, health, and education divisions. These publications were designed to provide information about the activities and functions of the organization to the more than 7,000 representatives of labor, business, religion, civic and social welfare, and professional and civil rights organizations that comprised NUC's national constituency.

Additionally, I handled all speechwriting for President Holman and press relations for the entire executive staff (him and three vice presidents). In that capacity, I also supervised or prepared and edited all of Holman's frequent congressional testimony in addition to NUC position papers and press statements on urban issues. I maintained liaison with other national organizations and established and coordinated the work of the NUC's Media Advisory Council, composed of top-level advertising, public relations, and communications professionals who assisted and advised the organization in its nationwide communications efforts. I did all this while supervising and controlling the division's annual budget of several hundred thousand dollars.

My responsibilities and duties also included using both local and national broadcast and print media to publicize and promote events sponsored by NUC and its more than thirty local affiliates. These events ranged from local and national seminars and conferences on urban problems to star-studded entertainment fundraisers, awards dinners, and benefits. Still other duties included writing publicity copy for posters, newspaper ads, and even designing souvenir programs and award certificates.

Of course, there were all sorts of folks who supported Carl Holman and those who worked with him in various ways. This was also my first close contact with the Hispanic and Asian community members with whom the NUC worked in various capacities.

As NUC's communications director, I traveled more than I ever had before. I traveled to Los Angeles, Oakland, and San Francisco; became acquainted with Bloomingdales, Bergdorf's, and Bendel's on a board trip to New York; and traveled to locales in Boston, Philadelphia, Newark, and as far off as Puerto Rico for NUC meetings, conferences, and conventions. I got to stay in the best hotels, enjoy wonderful restaurants, and even brought young friends like Juadine to work with me. My friend Joan Thornell (who had known Carl from working on the staff of a previous White House conference) also worked with the NUC and traveled with us. But even this period couldn't compete with what was coming next. My life was soon to take another turn.

> **Joan Thornell:** *Florence was very much interested in the liberation movements, and the Urban Coalition was not progressive enough in its dealings. It was an attempt to meld corporate interests and government interests and private organization interests. It had a lot of money to do things, but getting things done was difficult. It was an attempt after the height of the Civil Rights Movements. With the cities burning and all kinds of craziness happening, the feds called upon corporate leaders to buy into doing programs to benefit people in the city. Those programs were never enough, and they were never reaching the people who needed the help most.*

While working at NUC, I remained involved with the ALSC and, through it, 1974 would bring me my first opportunity to travel to the African continent and provide the catalyst for me to develop yet another persona: that of international freedom fighter.

Years later, my dear friend Stokely Carmichael, by then known as Kwame Ture, would solemnly warn me: "Florence, whatever you do, be careful. You don't want to get involved with African politics." His words carried a wisdom and experience I lacked at the time, yet my philosophy and opinions and heart and soul were where they always were and still are: with what I perceive as the advancement of Black people.

Little did I know how the next period of time would land me smack in the middle of both literal and figurative minefields. By the end of the 1970s, my dealings with African liberation movements would result in questions about my intentions, attempts to malign my reputation, and efforts to put my very life in peril. Still, the journey from Eads to Angola would be exhilarating, inspiring, and transformational. My time in the homeland would fill me up with sights, sensations, emotions, and revelations that are still with me today and still informing my visions for the freedom of Africans around the globe.

CHAPTER 11

THE CONTINENT, 6PAC, AFRICAN SERVICES BUREAU, UNITA

I finally landed on the soil of "the Continent" in Dar es Salaam, Tanzania, in June 1974. I was traveling as a guest observer to the Sixth Pan-African Congress (6PAC). As I viewed the city's white stucco structures and palm trees and observed what appeared to be a peaceful co-existence between the rural and the metropolitan, I thought giddily to myself: *"You did it, Florence! You're really home! Africa!"* It was all I could do not to hug one of my weary fellow travelers as they bustled past me in the airport terminal.

I was especially thrilled that I'd get to see my daughter Geri. She had graduated from Howard University and after several years of working with the Center for Black Education and Drum and Spear in Washington, she moved to Dar es Salaam to work with the International Secretariat for 6PAC. She also served as information officer and liaison to the various African liberation groups with offices throughout the city. Geri would later come to reside and work on the continent for nearly two decades, and raise her three sons there. But by 1974, I was already pining for her and bemoaning the distance between us. Years later, a friend astutely observed that my brilliant, learned, and world-traveling daughter had indeed inherited a streak from my mother, her grandmother. "Florence, Eads wasn't big enough to hold Callie, so she left that little town for the city," the friend observed. "Tennessee wasn't big enough to hold you," she continued., "so you left the South to go North. America wasn't big enough to hold Geri, so she left the country for the Continent." It made a lot of sense when I looked at it that way!

"FLORENCE TATE" read the sign held by an old man called *Mzee* (roughly translated as "old man" or "elder"), whom Geri had sent to meet me at the airport. "Welcome to Tanzania!" Mzee shouted, nodding as he directed me toward his vehicle. He expertly packed my suitcases and garment bags into every available space, then helped me settle into the passenger seat.

Taking in every bit of scenery on the forty-five-minute drive to Geri's home, I must have looked like a real tourist—craning my neck from right to left; drinking in the colors and fragrances of the exotic shrubs; eyeing the groups of women wrapped from head to foot in vibrantly colored *kangas,* some with children tied on their back; and observing the men selling fruits and vegetables from market stalls dotted along the road. The giant expanse of the Indian Ocean spread into view as we approached the Oyster Bay neighborhood where Geri and my grandson Samori lived. I was enthralled. Though I had seen both the Atlantic and Pacific oceans in the United States, neither came close to the power evoked by the Indian Ocean off the East African coast.

I stayed with Geri for a week before checking in to the Kunduchi Hotel near the University of Dar es Salaam, where the 6PAC was to be held. On my first evening with Geri, we went to eat at a very nice open-air restaurant. It was there that I was quickly introduced to my own cultural limitations. After ordering and receiving our meals, I decided that I wanted a Coke, and I ordered one from our waiter. It seemed as if an eternity had passed when I realized the man had not returned. By then more than halfway through our meal, I spotted him talking to another waiter. Quite frustrated, I turned to Geri, lips pursed, and asked, "Why doesn't he bring me my Coke? He's just over there running his mouth!"

Geri calmly replied, "Mom, just calm down. Try to remember that you're in Africa now. Here, people are more important than things, and I'm sure he thinks it's more important to converse with his coworker about whatever they're discussing than it is to bring you your soda. He'll bring it when he gets through talking." My reaction to her words likely betrayed my very American sense of indignation, and I responded with something like, "Well, what kind of service is this?!" Without a doubt, I later realized, an acclimation process was required to settle into the culture of the Continent.

Going to the bank was another lesson…in patience. The bank in Dar es Salaam seemed to have not the least bit of automation, not even compared to what little we had in the States in 1974. The tellers would take your currency and begin an unending series of stamping and stamping and stamping and stamping and stamping—each and every official document necessary for the transaction. I quickly learned the locals' expression for the necessarily relaxed way of approaching life that was practiced in the culture: *pole, pole,* which means "slowly, slowly, just slow down." The point was, "Don't be in such a rush!"

I was reminded of the wisdom of this attitude on a daily basis. I remember one day exiting a cab too quickly and knocking my head on the door frame to the driver's immediate exclamation of *"Pole, pole!"* In a matter of weeks thereafter I would adapt to the wisdom of that approach, and by the time I got back to the United States a month or so later, I was so *pole, pole* I could hardly get anything done!

When the first day of 6PAC finally arrived, it was a thrill to see people from the Caribbean, Canada, and every reach of the Continent in attendance at what would be the first Pan-Africanist conference to be held on African soil. Over 200 Black Americans traveled to the Congress, including Imamu Baraka, Owusu Sadaukai, the Republic of New Afrika's "Queen Mother" Audley Moore, poet Don L. Lee (later Haki Madhubuti), and Julianne Malveaux. Additionally, dozens of professors and students from African universities were there as well as representatives from various political and community organizations. It was quite an honor to meet Tanzanian President Julius Nyerere himself, who received us at his estate.

During the conference, I met Tony Fernandes, UNITA's representative in southern Africa. All that Chen Chimutengwende had not told me about UNITA's history and struggle, I found out from Tony. I was impressed with his recitation of how much UNITA members knew about the life and struggles of African Americans and the concern they expressed for us and our wellbeing. This was a different posture from any of the other movement representatives or contacts I had met. Understandably, they were focused on their own wars of liberation, but never had I heard any expression of solidarity with or concern about Blacks in the United States. UNITA's practice in this regard impressed me deeply. While in Dar es Salaam, I also met another UNITA supporter, Malik Chaka, who was to become a lifelong friend and coworker in the struggle.

The following is taken from a personal (and thoroughly opinionated) account I wrote about my 6PAC experience.

A Very Personal Point of View

Some observations, Impressions, Opinions re: the Sixth Pan African Congress—Dar es Salaam University, Tanzania, June 19–27, 1974

First of all, I'd like to emphasize that despite several shortcomings, the Congress was an extremely worthwhile effort in that it allowed—for the first time—Africans from all over the Continent and nearly all parts of the diaspora to come together to discuss firsthand their common problems, unique problems, and various perspectives on the best approaches to solutions.

I cannot overemphasize the importance of leaders representing varying ideologies or "sub-ideologies" communicating directly with each other, rather than relying on the European press interpretation of each other's thoughts, ideas, utterances. To be able to vocally parry back and forth gives a specificity and clarity to one's position that cannot possibly be obtained in a press release or edited press statement. To me, this was the most valuable part of the Congress and in the future, will facilitate the building of some much-needed concrete Pan-Africanist organizations, institutions, armies, or what have you.

In spite of the limited coverage in the European (particularly the American) press, the world has been put on notice that Africans on the Continent, and on the rest of the globe are determined to forge ahead together, and in large measures hold as their ideal socialist government structures.

Even some of the negative aspects of the Congress contributed to the political development of the participants, thereby indirectly amplifying its reach to thousands of other Africans. For example, the exclusion of the Caribbean peoples' movements highlighted the contradictions faced by even independent African countries to the extent that we cannot always do the "correct" thing for the people when it is not also the diplomatically and feasibly "correct" thing for a given government...

Too, it was unconscionable, I think, for UNITA to be given only "special guest" rather than "delegate" status at the Congress. "Special guest" is the same status that even I, who at best am a "part-time revolutionary" was given, when UNITA has actually been fighting and killing Portuguese for many years in a fierce struggle to liberate Angola. While I was honored to be accorded "special guest" status, UNITA by the same token must surely have been insulted!...

Again, on the positive side, the graciousness, warmth, and hospitality which the party, the government and the people extended to Africans from all over the world in itself went a long way in dispelling the doubts that many Africans in the diaspora have about whether or not we "belong in Africa." Tanzania told us that we are indeed "an African People."

When I left Dar es Salaam, I traveled to Lusaka, Zambia. That country was host to a number of African Liberation Movement headquarters including those of the Movimento Popular de Libertacao de Angola (MPLA), African National Congress (ANC) and Pan-Africanist Congress (PAC) of South Africa, Frente de Libertacao de Mocambique (FRELIMO), South West African People's Organisation (SWAPO) of Namibia, and the Zimbabwe African People's Union (ZAPU) and Zimbabwe African National Union (ZANU).[7] I visited several of these organizations' headquarters and also delivered some donations that had been entrusted to me by African Americans who wanted to support some of the movements including Carl Holman, my boss at the National Urban Coalition, who entrusted me with his financial contribution to the MPLA.

While in Zambia, I met Chinosole, a sister from New York who had been teaching in Zambia and later in southern Angola. She later became chair of the Women's Studies Department at San Francisco State University. She was a big UNITA supporter and further convinced me that UNITA—a peasant-based, nationalist-type movement—was the organization that most deserved my support. Chinosole and I formed a deep friendship. We spent many years corresponding as we planned and plotted how best to aid those engaged in the liberation struggle in Angola.

After leaving Zambia, I flew to Gambia, to the home of Charles's and my adopted son, Lamin Jangha, who lived with us when he first came to the United States. Lamin had been one of "Nkrumah's boys"—the band of young men from across Africa whom Ghanaian president Patrice Nkrumah had brought together through his Pan-African Academy—and he had traveled to Guinea with Nkrumah when the latter was ousted from Ghana. While Lamin was preparing to travel to the U.S. for further education, my friend Ethel Minor (whom I had met while working with Stokely and SNCC) was visiting Stokely in Guinea. She met Lamin there and sent me a letter of introduction to let me know he would soon be on his way to our house! Lamin lived with us for a time while he attended Howard University, and Charles and I stood up for him as his parents when he married.

---

7 https://scholarship.law.cornell.edu/cgi/viewcontent.cgi?article=1053&context=zssj

Lamin Jangha: *I met Florence my first day in USA. I was living in Guinea, working for Kwame Nkrumah, the former president of Ghana, and then Stokely Carmichael was there too, so we were all hanging out together. And so when I finished working for Nkrumah, I decided to come to the U.S., so Stokely and Freddie Green and Ethel Minor, who were very close to Florence and Charles, worked it out for me to come to the U.S. and arranged for me to stay with them. And I stayed with them for about three months in DC and then from there I went on my own to the South. But from that point on, they treated me as a son. I was really part and parcel of the family... so everything that I was organizing, Florence and Charles were present, my wedding and everything, the whole nine yards.*

In '72, I came back from the South, back to Washington, DC, and even though I've been traveling around the world since that time, I've always been with them. Whatever events they had at their house, they'd invite me. If ever she was in DC for any function, I'd be there, so I was literally a part of the family. She was like a mother to me in all senses of the word except the biological.

She was always passionate about the struggle. I followed her moves all the time, so I knew what she was doing. She was a real Pan-Africanist. She loved Africans from all over the world. She took herself as African and loved Africans, no matter where they came from. So, as a result, she had friends from all over the Continent, people I didn't even know personally. So that was her. She was a Pan-Africanist in all the senses of the word.

On the flight from Lusaka to Banjul, my seatmate was a white South African on his way to Bamako for business. He was very curious about me, my reason for being in Africa, and particularly my reason for going to The Gambia. He wanted to know which hotel I would be staying in and, as it turned out, when I told him the name of the hotel that Lamin had recommended to me, he was staying there as well.

I was not going straight to the hotel, however; I was going to visit first with Lamin's family. The South African insisted that we take the same cab into town and then on having the cab driver take me to my destination. I gave the cab driver the directions Lamin had given me. When we arrived at the stucco enclosure that surrounded the courtyard of the Jangha home, the South African remarked as he stepped out of the car, "This is very different from the United States, isn't it?" I grimaced without response as he drove off in the cab. It was my first time visiting this sort of native dwelling, and I couldn't deny that my heart sank at what seemed to be the relative poverty of the surroundings. But I was still excited about meeting Lamin's family.

Several small, three-walled huts dotted the circular courtyard, around which a number of other families lived. I entered the courtyard and observed children playing and chickens roaming about. Clothing and linens hung drying on lines that were suspended across the yard. Women and men were scolding each other and laughing together. These scenes of community were immediately familiar. Lamin's brother ran to greet me and take me to the family quarters.

Lamin's mother, who was the first wife, greeted me in English and introduced me to Mr. Jangha and the other wives and children. Mrs. Jangha #1 translated for me as I expressed how happy I was to meet them. I gave them a brief update on what I'd been up to in Dar es Salaam, told them how much we loved having Lamin live with us, and shared greetings from Charles and the children.

I explained that Lamin had arranged for me to stay at the hotel for the three nights I would be visiting, but as Mrs. Jangha #1 translated my words, Lamin's father insisted vociferously in Wolof that I must stay there and that he wouldn't hear of my leaving. I acquiesced and submitted to the adventure of a stay at their home.

As several hours passed, I badly needed to go to the bathroom. I'd been holding it until I would be able to relieve myself at the hotel. Since my plans had changed, I finally got up the nerve to ask Mrs. Jangha #1 where I could use the bathroom. She took me to the nearby outdoor enclosed area that had a hole in the ground for squatting over and a showerhead attached to the wall. I was relieved—in every way.

Soon it was time for dinner, and a large bowl filled with *jollof* rice was placed on the ground right outside the door of Mr. Jangha's bedroom, around which the whole family squatted to eat with both hands. Mrs. Jangha #1 brought a small table, chair, tin plate, and fork to the yard, where she set me up for dinner. I sat on the chair, literally looking down on them eating the family meal. I felt like a complete fool, a colonialist, Queen Victoria…just horrible. At the next meal, I asserted to Lamin's mother, "Oh, no, this will not do," regarding the Queen Victoria setup, and I sat around the bowl with everyone else and dug in. It felt good. I felt at home.

When I first arrived, Lamin's brother had taken my bags and placed them in Mr. Jangha's bedroom since it had been decided that I would sleep there. The room contained a large bed dressed in white linens and covered by white mosquito netting. A naked light bulb hung above the bed, and an electric fan and a transistor radio sat atop a side table. A large chest—on which were placed a vast array of bottled herbs, roots, and tinctures—completed the furnishings. Chickens flew in and out of the room through an open window as goats ambled through the door leading to the courtyard. Despite the animals, Mr. Jangha's room was immaculate, and I realized that I was being especially honored.

When nightfall came and it was time to go to bed, I turned in, shut the unlatched door to the bedroom, and pulled down the window. I wondered if there were any other "honors" attached to the privilege of occupying the old man's bedroom given that I didn't know the customs. In a letter I later wrote to Geri detailing the whole set-up, I admitted to being a bit concerned that I might have to endure a "night visitor," meaning the elder Mr. Jangha. Of course, my fears proved to be no more than the stuff of nonsense, as nothing untoward happened at all.

In the morning, the young ladies from the entire compound were out washing and hanging their laundry on the line. I was struck by their beauty, as they did their chores adorned in gorgeous cloths and *geles* or headwraps. Imagine my surprise when, in the afternoon after they had finished their work and wanted to go downtown, they took off their beautiful African garments and donned western European and American clothes, which struck me as old-fashioned and were probably used. "Oh, your own dress is so pretty; why did you take it off?" I asked a few of them, referring to the traditional clothes they had worn earlier. Though they were English speakers and understood what I'd said, they only laughed in response.

The next day Lamin's brother took me to the market where Mr. Jangha, a silversmith, gifted me with a number of items I had admired in his stall. I soon realized that Lamin's father was giving me anything and everything that captured my eye: a hand-tooled leather briefcase, a sterling silver friendship ring with a large silver nugget in it, a silver-nugget necklace on a silver chain, and some other items. As I ooohed-and-aaaahed through the Janghas' market stall, Lamin's brother made some very sweet Turkish tea in a copper pot for me. It was delightful. He later took me out to the countryside to show me a factory owned by ex-Peace Corps volunteers who had stayed behind to become wealthy by exporting garments made from African fabrics.

On the day I left, Lamin's mother presented me with a used plastic bag full of chicken parts cooked in lime juice and seasonings. My first thought was, "How am I going to eat this on the plane without making a spectacle of myself?" My second thought was the memory of the box of fried chicken I had carried with me on the train from Memphis to Cleveland when I first left the South. The significance of this connection evoked an emotional response; I hugged the woman with all the strength I had in me.

As it turned out, my travel staff and I had to layover in Dakar for one night before the flight back to New York. The airline put us up at the hotel airport, but it gave us no food allowances. I had spent all my African currency down to my last coins, knowing that I would soon be home and unable to use it once back in the States. That night, however, I was hungry as hell. Then I remembered the bag of chicken Lamin's mother had given me. That lime-flavored chicken tasted good when I whipped it out in that hotel room. I can still taste it! Lord, I thought, has the chicken been good to us!

I arrived safely in New York with exactly one quarter in my pocket, which I used to call Charles to tell him I was back and to meet me at the airport. It had been an exhilarating, emotional, and life-changing trip. The warmth of the people, both in Dar es Salaam and in The Gambia, had touched me deeply. My trip to Africa was so inspiring, the experience so exciting, and the trip so moving for me that I later found it very difficult to readjust to life back in the U.S. or to go back to work at the NUC.

After returning from a month in Africa, I experienced a kind of culture shock. I was still functioning under the *pole, pole* way of life. After a few days back in the NUC's offices, I felt like I was trapped in a frenetic bubble. I was so busy with meeting after meeting and making dozens of phone calls to endless lists of people. Most disorienting to me was my perception that everyone kept going along as though Africa and the liberation struggle in the outside world weren't happening.

The routine of rushing about—attending meetings, writing reports, and engaging in the interoffice politicking that I had done in the past—seemed pointless to me. After noticing a great need that I could fill, I decided to create an organization that would facilitate communications between various parties and people in Africa and the United States. It seemed to me the ideal way to further African unity and liberation. I'd gained years of media and press experience and had worked in so many capacities—from journalist and information secretary to director of communications—that I was confident about my ability to create an organization that would truly encourage the ever-growing Pan-African movement in the U.S. Given the contacts I had amassed over the years from my press, radio and television, and community and political work with leaders in the Black world, I was sure I could gain the attention of enough people to create support for my new, Pan-Africanist venture.

I quit my job at the Coalition and, in his letter of support, dated December 18, 1974, M. Carl Holman wrote:

> It was with great regret that I accepted the resignation of Florence Tate, who had served as the Director of [the] Communications Division of the National Urban Coalition. The dedication, creativity, and humanity that Mrs. Tate gave to her job will be hard for us to ever replace.
>
> However, those very same qualities assure me that her new project, the African Services Bureau, will be a successful one. Mrs. Tate's

```
deep concern for the plight of the oppressed
has been evidenced by the strength of her
involvement in the Civil Rights Movement
during its early and most difficult days.
That same concern motivates her to extend her
efforts to work with those struggles in Africa.
     I urge you to support Mrs. Tate and her
program.


Sincerely,
M. Carl Holman
President, The National Urban Coalition
```

I decided to establish a center—the African Services Bureau (ASB)—as a nexus for such communications and proceeded to find funding for the endeavor. After numerous attempts and some bruised feelings, I succeeded in securing seed money from Reverend Charles Cobb at the United Church of Christ's Commission for Racial Justice.

I opened an office for the ASB in downtown DC on the third floor of a building right across from the Mayflower Hotel. I spent the next several months writing letters and making phone calls, contacting representatives in the city and ambassadors from various African countries. I compiled endorsements from dozens of leaders from community organizations, universities, and political and professional organizations. I developed lists of supporters whom I would later need to approach in accomplishing the cross-cultural work I intended to do through the ASB.

I was truly moved and encouraged by the overall level of support I received. One support letter came on official letterhead from Julian Bond, who at the time was the serving in the Georgia State House of Representatives. I knew Julian through the work I'd done in the Civil Rights Movement years earlier. Along with his general letter of support, which I would include with the other endorsements I received, Julian included a more personal letter that touched on several of the issues associated with garnering support from Blacks holding positions of influence in the nation at the time.

```
House of Representatives
Atlanta, Georgia
August 26, 1974


    Dear Florence:
    I'm glad to have your proposal and I
support it fully. Enclosed with this note is a
"to whom it may concern" letter that you may
feel free to use in any way you can. In this
note, I want to urge a special interest of my
own on you.
    What you propose—without specifically
naming it as such—is a coordinating agency
for the various groups interested in Africa
generally, and African American Blacks,
specifically. Since my own interest is the
politicians, let me waste a few lines on that
subject.
    I've tried—using the mailing list and
contacts of the Southern Elections Fund—to
drum up support among Black elected officials
for such issues as the Byrd Amendment repeal
(and several non-African issues as well) with
mixed success.
    The success is mixed because of the historic
reasons why Black Americans are dis-interested
in Africa, and because much of the Pan African
movement exists in an academic vacuum or
views all Black elected official as flunkies
or slaves for white interests. Additionally,
```

general information about Africa—from a
Black perspective—seldom reaches most Black
elected officials, except in an occasional
mailing from the American Committee on Africa
or some other source.

Whatever you can do to remedy this division
between the elected representatives (good and/
or bad) will be appreciated by someone who
believes that these men and women have the
potential to lead Black people in a variety of
ways that they now do not do; if you can help
educate them about African concerns, and can
get them to respond politically with the power
they have, then you will have done a great
deal for Africa and for the Black people they
represent.

Sincerely,
Julian Bond

Vernon Jordan of the National Urban League also sent his support,
writing:

August Thirtieth, 1974

I heartily endorse Florence's proposal to
establish the African Services Bureau as a
vehicle for maintaining and improving the
relationship between Africans and Blacks in
the United States.

Florence is a person who has demonstrated her commitment to the fight for universal justice, and through many years of practical work with a broad spectrum of people, organizations, and institutions, has shown remarkable ability to bring very diverse people and groups together to deal with common problems.

I'm sure that under her direction, an institution such as the one she proposes would be very instrumental in strengthening the ties between Africans and Afro-Americans.

Sincerely,

Vernon E. Jordan, Jr.
Executive Director,
The National Urban League

Other letters of support came on official letterhead from ambassadors of the African countries I communicated with regarding my plans.

EMBASSY OF THE UNITED REPUBLIC OF TANZANIA
Sept 4, 1974

Dear Mrs. Tate,

Thank you very much for your letter of August 8, 1974, together with a copy of a

PROPOSAL FOR THE ESTABLISHMENT OF AN AFRICAN
SERVICES BUREAU.

After having had the pleasure of meeting
and exchanging ideas with you, I personally
believe that the objectives are excellent and
I trust that in the spirit of cooperation and
self-sacrifice you will succeed in establishing
a viable link between our two countries and
our peoples.

Needless to say, I admire your courage and
thoughtfulness in these matters and wish to
pledge my full support for your relentless
endeavors in the realization of these ideals.

Wishing you every success, I remain,

Yours sincerely,
Paul Bomani
AMBASSADOR

EMBASSY OF GHANA
8th November, 1974

Dear Mrs. Tate,

I write to acknowledge your letter of 17th
October, 1974, under cover of which you sent me
a copy of your proposal for the establishment
of an African Services Bureau.

Having read and discussed it with you at
our meeting on 31st October, 1974, I am more than
satisfied that the proposal is commendable

and should indeed be feasible. It would, when implemented, satisfy a long-felt need and contribute immensely towards the achievement of a closer rapport between the Black community in the United States and Africa.

I, therefore, unhesitatingly endorse the proposal and will be happy to lend any support that I can towards its realization.

Yours sincerely,

SAMUEL E. QUARM
AMBASSADOR

EMBASSY OF THE REPUBLIC OF ZAMBIA
January 27, 1975

Dear Mrs. Tate:

I would like to inform you that I have read your proposals for establishing the African Services Bureau with much interest. Your suggestions have my support and I also commend them to all persons and organizations desirous of harmony and better understanding between Americans and Africans.

I agree with the goals and objectives, both long-range and intermediate, which you have ably enunciated in our paper under reference.

I would like to inform you that this Embassy will render any possible assistance in providing literature, visual aids, and material such as film etc. on Zambia and/or Africa

including where possible, the participation
of Embassy officials in seminars which the
proposed A.S.B. may be able to hold from time to
time.

In conclusion, I wish to express my thanks
to you for the courtesy of consulting my mind
on your valuable proposals.

Yours sincerely,

SITEKE G MWALE
AMBASSADOR

Old Civil Rights Movement and Black Power cohorts also sent
me letters of support.

CONGRESS of AFRIKAN PEOPLE
Chairman's Office

To Whom It May Concern:

Florence Tate was an indispensable part in
putting together the first Afrikan Liberation
Day demonstration in Washington, DC, 1972. I'm
sure she is committed to Afrikan struggle, and
an able administrator as well.

Imamu Amiri Baraka
Chairman
To Whom It May Concern:

Florence Tate's idea for the establishment

of an African Services Bureau is one which I
whole heartedly endorse. I know her to be a
hardworking, talented and dedicated person who
will do everything that she can to further the
cause of African liberation, unification and
development.

Owusu Sadaukai

It also was good to get the support of Gary, Indiana, mayor Richard
Hatcher, who had been one of the sponsors and co-chairs of the 1972
National Black Political Convention.

OFFICE OF THE MAYOR
GARY, INDIANA

Dear Mrs. Tate:

Your proposal for the establishment of an
African Services Bureau is excellent. You are
quite correct in asserting that a Pan-African
movement is on the rise in this country.
The African Services Bureau, as you
have outlined it, would be a major step in
increasing the cultural and intellectual ties
between Black Americans and Black Africans.
Be assured that you have my full support
and endorsement in this endeavor

Sincerely,

Richard Gordon Hatcher
Mayor, City of Gary

Of course, it was always vital to reach out to the key Black women whose support I knew I would need to spread the word through their networks and connections, and I did everything in my power to reach out to female leaders of organizations both large and small. One such leader was Inez Smith Reid, executive director of the Black Women's Community Development Foundation (later the Honorable Judge Inez Smith Reid!), who wrote:

```
BLACK WOMEN'S COMMUNITY DEVELOPMENT
FOUNDATION
30 September, 1974

Dear Florence:


    With all the intense work we had to
do on our Sojourner Truth Dinner, I lost
sight of your letter for a while. What you
are trying to do with the African Services
Bureau is extremely important. Since your
proposed agenda does not overlap with that
of some existing organization, it would be
good to touch base with them even though,
philosophically, they may not blend with your
perspective.


Hope all is well.
Sincerely,

Inez Smith Reid, Executive Director
```

Mae C. King, founding member of the National Conference of Black Political Scientists, also sent her support, as did Georgina Thornton of the Universal African Improvement Association.

National Conference of Black Political
Scientists
August 15, 1974

Dear Florence:

I have read with interest and enthusiasm
your proposal for the establishment of an
African Services Bureau. I personally endorse
your effort. I believe that the establishment
of such a Bureau would provide a much needed
service for the national Black community and
continental Africans. May I extend to you my
cooperation and best wishes for success in this
very important endeavor.

Sincerely,
Mae C. King
Membership Secretary

September 24, 1974

TO WHOM IT MAY CONCERN:

This letter is to endorse Florence Tate for financial support in establishing an African Services Bureau. Any assistance given her would be greatly appreciated by the Universal African Improvement Association.

Georgina Thornton
Third Asst. President General, Universal African Improvement Association

In the midst of all these efforts, I established a support organization called Friends of Angola specifically to fundraise for UNITA, one of three Angolan liberation movements, which had heretofore received no support from African American groups in the U.S. It was not a widely known movement and, given its Maoist support in Europe, it was seen as being affiliated with China. The other two Angolan organizations: the *Movimento Popular de Libertação de Angola* (MPLA) was supported by the Soviet Union; and, at that point, the *Frente Nacional de Libertação de Angola* (FNLA) was supported by the United States. Two major activities undertaken by the African Services Bureau and Friends of Angola were the collection of books and supplies for the school-aged children of Angola and a much-needed medical project to send twenty Black doctors and nurses to the country.

Along with holding a variety of fundraisers, I spent the next eighteen months reaching out to religious and political leaders, educators, doctors, pharmacists, and medical personnel to help send a medical team, supplies, and educational materials to Angola. Additionally,

I organized and sponsored consciousness-raising cultural events including film screenings and exhibits on several of the countries involved in the liberation effort as well as informative gatherings, lectures, and talks to further develop a cross-cultural dialogue. One of those films, *Kwacha: The Struggle for Angola*, was produced by a fellow UNITA supporter, Kwadwo Akpan, who would be among a group (including me) caught in a tense and life-threatening position in the Angolan bush during my trip there in 1976.

The work was endless, absorbing, and rewarding. Unfortunately, it was also soon to come to a halt. After Angolan independence was achieved and the civil war broke out among its three liberation groups, UNITA was driven out of Luanda. The U.S. then began supporting UNITA through Zaire and South Africa, which predictably caused all African Americans to denounce UNITA and everybody and everything associated with it.

Kalamu Ya Salaam: *There were three organizations in Angola— UNITA, MPLA, and Holden Roberto's FNLA. The last one was basically a paper organization as far as most of us were concerned, but there was a big ideological battle that happened here. Again, I'm not speaking about what happened on the Continent but here between [supporters of] MPLA and UNITA. UNITA had what we would call a more Pan-African, nationalist orientation; and MPLA had a Marxist orientation. The Marxists won that particular struggle. And part of it was that they were far more educated or had what we call P.E.: political education. They had far more political education than we did. They had international help, and we didn't have the same. And I'm speaking specifically of the Soviet Union. We didn't have significant international support. When I'm talking about "we," I'm talking about basically Pan-African nationalists. In many ways, our commitment was abstract and romantic, and UNITA was an example of that. And I think that's one of the reasons they didn't prevail and MPLA did. It wasn't just what was happening with MPLA as an organization, but that they had global contacts through the Soviet Union that were significant. And we didn't have that level of working relationships.*

Due to my activities in support of UNITA, I was labeled a spy for both entities. I became a *persona non grata* and was denounced, shunned, and Blackballed. Both Friends of Angola and the African Services Bureau were accused of working with the CIA and South Africa, causing an almost overnight cessation of support for both of the organizations for which I had worked so tirelessly for months to establish.

Malik Chaka, whom I'd met at 6PAC in Dar es Salaam, worked alongside me to create the Florence Tate Agency a few years later in 1980. Through that agency, we continued our liberation work on UNITA's behalf. As someone who'd lived in Tanzania since 1971, who was familiar with and had worked in over forty countries, and who still works in the development field on the Continent, Malik was philosophical about my "downfall" among the Black Power/Pan-Africanist/Black American activist circles of the period:

Malik Chaka: *The first time that I ever saw Florence Tate she was in the movie about the first African Liberation Day. And I eventually met her when she came out to [6PAC]. One of the very special and unique things about Florence is that Florence could relate to younger people. I'm 69 years old today, which means that Florence could have been my mother, but she's more modern than I am. Florence was just modern and almost avante garde; the broadness of her intellect—I'm talking about how smart she was—her ability to make an analysis of things. And she had an ability to throw herself into things and generate enthusiasm.... You go back and you look at the leadership of the African Liberation Support Committee.... When she was the communications secretary, she was older than everybody, but I don't think anybody saw her as old. And the bigness of her personality, her enthusiasm about the liberation of Black folk.... To use a term from that period of time, she had an undying love for Black folk.*

There's a book, edited by a guy named Richard Cross, called The God That Failed. It is about the disillusionment of Western intellectuals with communism. At one point in time they grasped communism, and communism was going to be the god that would change the world. But they became disillusioned over a period of time, and then they denounced it. And with Florence you had a similar situation. She was a fervent supporter... and then disillusionment set in.

And while she was a fervent supporter, Florence was a larger-than-life personality. Friendship and connections meant a whole bunch to her. And she was criticized by many people for her association with UNITA. This is particularly after the outbreak of the Angola civil war in 1975, when the Soviets and Cubans came in on the side of the MPLA; the U.S. came in on the side of UNITA, China also; and then South Africa came in on the side of UNITA. So caustic criticism came her way, which came up years afterwards. To give you an example... when she worked for Jesse Jackson, she was working, she was doing a great job, but yet you'd hear some people raise the question of whether Jesse should have her as press secretary because of this whole UNITA thing. And this was very painful and very hurtful to Florence.

You know we live in a world where people don't deal with difference, particularly political differences, very well. I think it was a kind of being politically correct because they could have taken a position which would have been a more appropriate one: "You know I love Florence, but I disagree with her" or "Sister, you wrong there." They didn't go that way; it became scurrilous at certain points in time.

Needless to say, this rupture caused me much pain and isolation from my former civil rights, Black Power, and African liberation support movement colleagues. Yet, I chose to continue to support the people involved with UNITA, even though it was at a high personal cost to me. I believed in them and what they were doing and had tried to do in the anticolonial struggle. In my opinion, they represented the "Black" Black people—those in the southern part of Angola, who were rural, agrarian folks—not the sons and daughters of the Portuguese. They had not been integrated into the elite, educated, mixed class—the *mestiço*. They were just the *Black* people. I identified with them.

I'm sure some of it had to do with the people that I had come to know, but it also stemmed from the UNITA supporters' desire to know more about African Americans. In 1981, I wrote at length about my reasons for continuing to support UNITA in an article titled, "Perspective on Angola: A UNITA Supporter's View."[8]

At some point after the civil war broke out, UNITA leadership asked me to travel to Huambo, Angola, to meet the people I was working to help. I accompanied members of UNITA to the extraordinary Organization of African Unity (OAU) summit in Addis Ababa, Ethiopia, in January 1976 to hear a discussion about, and formal adoption of a resolution on, the situation in Angola. The head of the UNITA liberation movement, Jonas Savimbi, then invited me to travel from Ethiopia to Angola (by way of Zambia) on his plane for that study visit.

My daughter Geri was still living in Tanzania during this period. She, however, had become a supporter of the rival MPLA (*Movimento Popular de Libertacao de Angola*) and had married that organization's representative in Tanzania. She and her husband went back to live in independent Angola in 1979, but because she and I supported two rival groups, we ended up politically estranged for a long time. We weren't hostile, but she became very close to the MPLA's leadership, and I was to become a friend and strong supporter of Jonas Savimbi.

I should note that my support of Savimbi began a long time before he deteriorated into a madman. Though it was the opinion of many that he had always been a madman, I never saw signs of it. In any case, after attending the summit on Angola in January 1976, I returned to Angola to spend several days in the southern part of the country. That area was UNITA's stronghold in terms of support from the largely Ovimbundu population, the ethnic group to which Savimbi's family belonged.

Over the course of a week, I interviewed officials from UNITA and Cuban prisoners of war. I spoke with UNITA soldiers, party intellectuals, and organizers of the party's women's group, *Liga da Mulher Angolana* (LIMA). I also interviewed internationally based journalists who traveled in and out of the country, agricultural workers, Red Cross nurses, hotel and factory workers, peasants and market women, union organizers, and schoolchildren. I visited medical,

---

8   This paper, as well as many of Mrs. Tate's writings, clippings, and historical documents, can be found in the archival collection, "Florence Tate papers, 1960 – 2006," in the David M. Rubenstein Rare Book & Manuscript Library, Duke University.

educational, and social services organizations and wrote extensively about my experiences, including the piece, "The Beginning of UNITA's Path to Socialist Reconstruction in Angola—An Eyewitness View."

Extremely memorable was the time I spent with LIMA, the woman's auxiliary, which was a vital part of the UNITA program. This organization boasted a membership of approximately 10,000 women, many of whom were wives or widows of UNITA soldiers. Originally trained to fight, the women of LIMA were responsible in large part for everything from running the social services and hospitals that cared for the injured and orphaned to staffing local radio programs and holding rallies and educational workshops. I was treated extremely well by the LIMA organizers who spent time with me in the country. They also organized a special reception in my honor.

Some of the women in LIMA included Sister Eunice Sapassa, the organization's director; Judith Chimuma, assistant director of UNITA's Department of Social Services; and Salome Olivera, who spoke five languages and ran the radio station. Being among those women, I couldn't help but think of the work I had done with the Black Umoja Society women back in Dayton during my DARE days.

On one of my visits with the women of LIMA, we went to observe the soldiers during a training session. Watching them sliding along on their bellies to avoid the live fire that was being shot above them terrified me. I was scared I would see someone get killed right before my eyes. But the women of LIMA allayed my fears by explaining how rigorously the men had trained before reaching the level of exercises we watched that day. Thankfully, I witnessed no accidents.

Right before leaving the country, I experienced a frightening moment that could have ended quite differently and dangerously. UNITA officials had been warned that Cuban forces and MPLA troops were headed toward the area I had been visiting, which had become a target within the war zone. Along with several international journalists, filmmaker Kwadwo Akpan and I were scheduled to be picked up by plane on a landing strip in Huambo that was used by small charter planes. Our charter was to fly us to the main airport in Luanda, but the opposition troops were calculated to arrive in our area perilously close to the plane's arrival.

I'll never forget the sensations I felt as we waited for the aircraft to reach us—the initial, nearly imperceptible low hum; the slight tremors followed, with steadily mounting intensity, by the shaking of the earth beneath my feet; then a low, rumbling thunder. "What is going to happen?" I wondered.

The tense conversations around me quickly revealed that the rumblings and tremors were caused by the heavy artillery of the approaching Cuban troops. Panic spread throughout our group as everyone began to express what we all feared. Did they know we were here? Were they coming for us? How far away were they? What if they captured us...or worse?

As we scanned the sky for the plane that should already have arrived to pick us up, I thought about the t-shirt I was wearing with "UNITA" painted in large colors on the back. *I should take this off so I won't be identified as a supporter,* was the thought that ran through my mind. *Maybe then, they'll think I'm just a journalist...*

Suddenly, I felt a cold resolve come over me. Something hardened inside me, and my attitude changed. *No, I won't change...because whatever is coming, is coming,* I thought to myself. *Don't take off the t-shirt. Don't do nothin'!* In that moment, it was as if I was ready to die, to be captured...whatever. Something inside me just refused to change who I was—for anyone or anything!

Someone once asked me, "Were you ever afraid?" They were talking about my work with CORE and DARE, my Black Power years, the protests and pickets and police, and my time in Angola during that nation's civil war. I replied that I never saw any of those situations as being "dangerous." I've always wanted to see what's out there, I continued, explaining that I wanted to see how things work, to be a part of this or that without regard for whether it was dangerous or not.

I'm not sure where that fearlessness comes from. Maybe from everything I went through in childhood. Perhaps the old adage, "Whatever doesn't kill you, makes you stronger," fits me. None of the things I experienced as an often-homeless child killed me, so standing there, with my UNITA shirt on as the rival forces approached, my subconscious attitude was, *what could Cuban troops possibly do to me that I haven't already experienced and lived through?*

Thankfully, our charter arrived before the troops. I was just as quick as everybody else to jump on that plane, shouting, *"Get me the hell out of here!"* All I wanted to do at that point was get on board and get out of Angola.

I returned home to write extensively about my experiences and observations and to launch the Florence Tate Agency to continue the work of presenting UNITA's case to the States, but I eventually became disenchanted with Savimbi. Several tragic events associated with my UNITA experiences have lingered on my heart for many years—specifically, the murder of a young man named Tito Chinguchi, whom I had come to call "my Angolan son," and his family. Tito was UNITA's foreign secretary, and he spent time with me and my family whenever he visited DC. I heard that he, his wife, brother-in-law, and several other family members, including children, were violently killed by soldiers acting under Savimbi's direction.

> **Malik Chaka:** *If one looks at [Florence's] relationship with UNITA, it was also a relationship with people. One of the people that she became close to, and who was almost a son to her, was a guy by the name of Tito Chinguchi. And Tito, in fact, had a falling out with the leadership of UNITA, with Jonas Savimbi, and he ended up being eliminated. He was killed in an inter-party struggle. That's probably the straw that broke the camel's back. [Florence] never embraced MPLA, but the death of Tito, I know, had a profound effect on her.... These inter-party struggles in liberation movements weren't unusual. If you read the history of these things closely, you'll find that such things happen—but you're talking about people who she was close to.*
>
> *Florence was almost legendary in UNITA, particularly among the women in the organization and people like Tito, who had known and worked with her. Once again, [due to the] connections and friendships that [Florence] has with people, her capacity for work, her enthusiasm, the fact that she embraced a cause.... So, "Miss Tate, Miss Tate! Miss Tate!"—that's what you would [have] heard in Huambo. She was someone who was looked up to.*
>
> *Florence took a cause to heart, and it became, in 1975, a very, very, unpopular cause because of the South African involvement.*

She stood by her friends until there was a breaking point. But she saw the trajectory of an organization she had supported wholeheartedly going in a direction which she [abhorred]... especially with the death of Tito and other people... and she broke with them but never in fact denouncing them because, for her, the MPLA was not the epitome of virtue either.

Among political people [her support of UNITA] became an issue. It did make an impression and it [is] probably [still] an issue to some people, despite the fact that Florence broke with UNITA around the question of Tito and other issues. And it was a very painful thing—a very, very, emotional thing for her. What I find very interesting is that today, in 2016, UNITA is a legal political party in Angola. It has seats in Parliament... so I would say this animus is probably more prevalent in the U.S. in the Black community than it is in Angola itself.

Kalamu Ya Salaam: UNITA was a bust, a complete bust. But initially many of us were impressed with UNITA because it spoke in a romantic way towards our belief [of] an African identity. Let me put it that way. I was well-read in terms of Marxist literature, but I was never a Marxist. It just didn't—the one way I could describe it—they could run but they can't dance. They were happening as a political organization, but they just didn't have that flavor that appealed to me. I'm speaking personally, but I also represent some other folks. MPLA was never attached to that kind of view. MPLA, as we would say, was strictly business.

Charlie Cobb: *Well, two things about Florence: one, once Florence made a commitment, to you or your organization—in my case, SNCC—that commitment was absolute, and she's not ever going to abandon it. She'd have to see you doing something so unimaginably wrong before she could [abandon you]. So Florence made a commitment to Jonas Savimbi and UNITA, whom we considered—at least I considered—a puppet of South Afri-*

ca. Florence, I think, was attracted to the way Savimbi articulated a kind of Black nationalism, and she was committed to his organization. For all practical purposes, she was his communications director.

Florence and I had deep, deep differences on this. She introduced me to Savimbi because she was convinced that once I sat down and talked to Savimbi—I was then a young reporter—I would see the error of my ways and the rightness of her... and Savimbi's ways. And I was going to sit down with Savimbi because Florence wanted me to sit down with Savimbi. And, of course, Savimbi didn't change my mind [or] my knowledge... and Florence and I reached a kind of unspoken agreement not to talk or debate about UNITA and Savimbi. But Florence had that kind of absolute kind of commitment once she made it, and that could be political or it could be personal. She had the kind of commitment to me personally and other people she liked in SNCC. That was part of her make-up.

It was a difficult period for her. I mean, think about it: her daughter Geri is married to a high-ranking MPLA official, and MPLA was the bitterest of rivals with UNITA. And people like me, whom she loved, were often in profound, not just disagreement [with] but [also] had profound hostility towards Savimbi and UNITA. So, it had to be an extremely difficult period for her because her political friends and personal friends in many instances were, for the first time, on opposite sides of the fence from her. And nobody that I know of who was in disagreement with Florence wanted to lose either her love or friendship because of this. So, it was an awkward time. And a lot of us just decided we're just not going to engage Florence on this issue.

I was never sorry about the path I took or the choices I made because I know why I made them. They were true to me, and I have no regrets. I do think that my heart was broken over the murder of Tito and his family, and a number of other painful revelations I experienced toward the end of my time working with Savimbi and UNITA. I don't remember how or when, but at some point, I decided that, with well over fifteen years of my life spent on the journey with UNITA, I had

had enough. I was no longer up to the emotional strain, the allegations, and the terrible stories. And perhaps, as my old friend Stokely had warned me early in my induction into the political landscape of the Continent, it was not, any longer, the place for me.

Over the course of time, I had become more fragile than I realized. One day I had to admit that the struggle had taken its toll on me psychologically. I finally decided that it was best to remove myself from it. I didn't announce it, or even plan it, but I closed the agency and withdrew from all my political obligations.

> **Malik Chaka:** *In looking at Florence in terms of this whole thing is, first of all, an undying love for Black people. I think that that's what's key. And anybody who reduces Florence's involvement around Africa stuff to the very, very, strong and close relationship that she had to UNITA—it would be a huge blind spot because it doesn't take into account the African Liberation Support Committee. It doesn't take into account relationships that she developed with somebody like Lamin, who was sent to Charles and her by Kwame Ture, by Stokely Carmichael, and who lived there as her son.*
>
> *For me, Florence's relationship with Africa is bigger than UNITA. It was embracing the cause of Africa's liberation in the same way she embraced the cause of liberation of Black folk here in this country.*

My daughter Geri would live in Angola until 1991 before returning home to live in the United States, bringing with her my wonderful grandsons Samori, Kilamba, and Nzingha. I will never be able to articulate my joy at having my daughter and those boys back home. She had given Africa truly everything she had to give. And I was so glad Africa gave her back to me, finally.

> **Geri Tate Augusto:** *From the time I got to Africa, and throughout the eighteen years there, both my mother and my father were carried inside me—I mean, inside my head.— and especially Mom. She was inside my head when I went into*

political situations. She would be inside my head when I was thinking about how to set up my home. She would be inside my head particularly when I was trying to understand art and culture. I think the reason she was inside my head is because the greatest gift that she gave to me, to Greg, and to Brian, was a way to be intelligent about learning in the world. She's the one who taught us to "read across"... across disciplines, across political ideas. She would read what she agreed with and what she disagreed with. She would read the conservative newspapers and the liberal and most radical newspapers. And when I asked her one time, "Mom, how am I supposed to do all this reading across?" She looked at me and said, "Double up your brain!"

That was a refrain for me throughout my life—"Double up your brain" —because I was living in cultures that were not mine by birth... and I was having to adapt. I was in my twenties and thirties and thrust into all kinds of political situations, and I would ask myself, "How did I get here?" And I was far away, thousands of miles away from home and where I grew up. So, it was the voices inside me of my mother, father—and particularly my mother—that carried me through. And for me, that's a priceless gift from a mother to a daughter.

CHAPTER 12

MARION BARRY

I was determined to continue my Pan-African support work after I returned to DC from Angola, but during those years it seemed as though I was living in virtual isolation. Due to my association with UNITA, I was Blacklisted among activist circles. Frustrated with my constant traveling and UNITA-related activities, Charles had withdrawn emotionally, and we had hit a rough patch in our marriage. Geri was still on the Continent, and Greg and Brian were young men who were busy with their own lives.

My body began rebelling, and I was forced to have emergency gallbladder surgery. As I lay recuperating in the hospital, Charles and I recommitted ourselves to our marriage and agreed to focus on repairing the breach we had suffered. By 1978, after surviving the initial scalding rejection and libelous accusations caused by my work with UNITA and reconciling with Charles, I felt like things were settling into a more even keel again.

In January 1978, Marion Barry, who sat on the DC Council as chair of its Committee on Finance and Revenue, announced that he would be running for mayor. I had known of Marion before we moved to DC. He had attended my alma mater, Lemoyne College, and had headed up its chapter of the NAACP. I knew of his work with the young people who organized the SNCC chapter at Fisk University, including his participation in the Nashville sit-ins while he was working on his master's degree in chemistry.

Marion had been elected SNCC's very first chairman, but he left that position to return to school and pursue a PhD in chemistry. He later dropped out of his doctoral program to work full-time for SNCC. In 1965, he moved to DC to head SNCC operations there.

I also knew that Marion had gained a reputation for being a radical firebrand involved with many causes in the District. He had been involved in the DC transit bus boycott, and the Free DC movement to attain home rule. He had also established an organization, called Pride, Inc., with Mary Treadwell, who later became his first wife.

Pride was a District-funded program that employed undereducated Black youth to clean the streets of DC. The program provided the first paycheck many of those young people had ever earned, and Marion's work with the organization from 1967 to 1974 endeared him to city residents. Decades later, many would proudly claim, "Marion Barry gave me my first job!" The Pride program was one of many accomplishments that earned him the title of "Mayor for Life," a moniker that he would retain among his Black supporters, even after his scandal-ridden activities in the 1990s.

In 1971, Marion was elected to the DC school board and served as its chairman. Then, in 1974, he was elected to the city Council. Four years later—and seemingly unstoppable after surviving a Hanafi Muslim-led shooting attack in the District building in 1977, he was ready to run for mayor.

I found Marion's reputation, particularly for standing up to white folks, rather admirable. I felt that with him as mayor, Black people in the District of Columbia would have a fairer chance to be a part of the city's power structure. Although there were Black people working in the District government, by and large they weren't employed as heads of departments or any in positions of power. I knew Marion would correct that. I had the impression that he was fair-minded across racial groups, but he would also make sure that Black people's rights were respected and protected.

Given his SNCC background and the work I'd done with SNCC years earlier, Marion and I had many friends and colleagues in common. Ivanhoe Donaldson, Marion's campaign manager, had been one of the first SNCC members I met when he stayed at our house with Stokely all those years ago.

I decided I would volunteer to work for Marion's Democratic primary campaign—which, in the District, would be tantamount to the actual mayoral election because, at that point, ninety percent of DC voters were registered as Democrats.

I realized, as did everyone else, that it would be an uphill battle. For one thing, Marion was the first Civil Rights Movement activist to seek office as mayor of a major city. All the other Black mayors had been long-time politicians, firmly entrenched in the politics of their respective cities. Marion would also be running against two other Black men who were diehard "establishment" politicians well-entrenched in the status quo of DC government: Walter Washington and Sterling Tucker.

The history of political leadership in DC was one of white supremacist neglect, if not outright oppression. As the "seat of government," the majority-Black city had been run for nearly a century by an all-white Congress under the control of a series of southern, segregationist senators and inept three-member commissions. Some of those power brokers had included the worst of the worst: Mississippi senators Ross Collins and Theodore Bilbo (who repeatedly referred to Black people as "niggers" on the Senate floor) and later South Carolina's John "Johnny Mac" McMillan.

By 1965, President Lyndon Baines Johnson supported a bill to enact home rule in the District, but it died in the Senate. Not to be deterred, LBJ sent a bill to Congress in 1967 that would establish a DC mayor/commissioner position as a step toward independence. When it was approved, he appointed Walter Washington, who worked under Kennedy and in several other political positions, as DC's first and only mayor-commissioner. In 1974, after expansion of home rule rights for the District, Walter Washington was elected mayor by popular vote. He was well respected, but he was from the era when Black men wore stocking caps to crimp their hair down. He was a lawyer and a well-educated member of the DC Black *bourgeoisie*. He was a good man, but he was a "safe" choice who worked to maintain the city's racial status quo. He was, in short, "Old Washington." His wife Bennetta was the director of the Women's Job Corps, and they were both very influential in the city's Black elite circles.

Sterling Tucker was a former chair of the District Council and executive director of the Washington Urban League. He too was part of the Black "establishment" in Washington.

Marion, a District councilman-at-large, was basically seen as an unsophisticated, naive young boy from "the sticks"—what people in those days called a "bama." He'd come up from the South and made a name for himself within the Civil Rights Movement and consequently was considered a radical and revolutionary. Nobody really believed that he could be victorious over the other two candidates, who had the support of the Black middle class, the white business community, and the conservative white community.

Also at issue was Barry's decision to try and "jump ahead" of Washington and Tucker, who were both senior District politicians. When Marion announced he was running for mayor, many felt that it was simply "not his turn." In DC, the political "stepping-stone" sequence was first to get elected to the school board and then to the Council. The next step was to serve as Council chair; only then, could an aspiring DC politician run for mayor. District Democrats operated methodically: "This one is in line, then it's the next one's turn, and then the next one," and so on down the line. Marion was not "in line" to become the next mayor; he hadn't held the Council's chair. But he wasn't interested in politics as they had been played. He had his own plans.

Known as a champion for "the least of these," Marion was bold. Many of those around him, including his chief strategist Ivanhoe Donaldson, had activist backgrounds and were equally bold. His supporters included liberal white people who had supported the Civil Rights Movement and had followed his work for many years. Ivanhoe had put together a powerful coalition of groups whose interests Marion had represented in the past. This coalition included lower- and working-class Black Washingtonians and members of the District's Latino community, DC's small Asian American population, and the gay community.

Marion was one of the first politicians in the country to support gay rights. As early as 1972, while acting as chairman of the city's school board, he pushed through a resolution to ban discrimination against homosexuals in the school system. During his mayoral campaign, he welcomed gays in, even though some on his staff wondered, "Why are we bringing them in here?" Marion related to gay people in a way that made them feel welcome in his campaign. They would come in to volunteer on his campaign after work, and they were largely the ones who manned the telephones. They were also primarily the ones who would call people to make sure they were registered to vote. Some other volunteers may or may not have shown up regularly, and Marion's campaign could not always depend on them, but the members of the gay community would show up, and stay, and *work*.

Gays were so involved in Marion's mayoral campaign that some people, especially some in the District's Black community, began to question if he was gay. Although Marion loved women, his sexual preference became such an issue during the campaign that he started addressing it in public forums. He'd say, "I hear you think I may be gay, but that's not my *preference*…that's my *politics*." In time, it became a non-issue.

Marion also courted and appealed to the liberal whites of the District's toney Georgetown neighborhood, to young white entrepreneurs, to senior citizens, and to the part of the labor movement that was dominated by Black people. Collectively, these groups gave him strong backing and allowed him to run a competitive campaign.

At some point after I started volunteering for the campaign, Ivanhoe approached me about becoming its press coordinator. He knew I had a journalistic background and had worked in several organizations as either press secretary or director of communications. He also knew that I had connections in the media. I was all for it and began drafting press releases that were reflective of who Marion was: militant, outspoken, and Black Power-oriented.

I had a knack for creating copy that could be blunt, direct, and confrontational, if necessary. I remember one incident in which Walter Washington, Marion, and Sterling were at a radio station preparing to participate in an on-air debate. Prior to the debate, Walter Washington said something very off-putting, even though he delivered in a joking manner. Marion turned to Washington, nodded toward me, said quite matter-of-factly, "You see that woman? She's my press secretary and I'ma put her on you!" Of course, it too was said in humor, but the meaning was clear.

The primary race ended in a very close call. In fact, it was too close to call on election night. The results were so close that Sterling wouldn't concede to Marion without a recount. The final results gave Marion 32,841 votes (34.65 percent), Sterling 31,277 votes (33.00

percent), and Washington 29,881 (31.52 percent). We had done it! We were ecstatic!

Winning the Democratic primary is tantamount to being elected in DC, so we knew we were going to win the election against whoever the Republican Party ran in November. As it turned out, the party found a Black man, Arthur Fletcher, who had served under Nixon. Fletcher's race was no advantage for him in the election, and Marion won the election with seventy percent of the vote. His victory was labeled a "landslide," and when Marion took office in January 1979, he appointed me to serve as his press secretary.

From his earliest days in politics, Marion Barry embodied the term "man of the people." He was no different when he became mayor. The people just loved him, and there were many, many reasons for this sentiment. To begin with, there was the way he related to people. Marion made everyone feel as if they were important. He let you know that he was interested in you and what you were doing. He wanted to know who you were, where you lived, where your people came from, and how many children you had. He could remember the names of a grandmother he had met—and the names of her three grandkids—six months after meeting the family for the first time. That was the way he related to people, and it made everyone feel special and confident that he had their best interests in mind.

Everyone knew that Marion cared about youth and children because of his work with Pride, Inc. He implemented the District's Youth Employment Act of 1979, which assured that every young person in DC could get a job, irrespective of their background, and instituted the Summer Youth Employment Program. He also formed Mayor's Youth Leadership Institute and organized a night basketball league to keep kids off the streets after dark.

Marion was known for taking a special interest in senior citizens. He generally cared about them and did his darndest to make sure their needs were addressed. His support for and among the District's seniors dated back to his days on the Council, when he had championed and helped pass legislation to decrease the amount of property taxes seniors had to pay. He courted them during the campaign and, once in office, he created the DC Commission on Aging and tasked a member of its staff with ensuring that seniors received their Social Security checks on time and that their medical care was in order. He established senior service centers and ensured that housing support was put in place to help the District's elderly. When Marion got into trouble for smoking crack, several elderly, church-going Black women responded to criticisms about his behavior with, "Yeah…*but he's good to the seniors!*"

From the days of his earliest work with SNCC, Marion identified with and worked on behalf of the poorest of the poor. In DC, those were the Black people who, by and large, lived in Anacostia on the east side of the Anacostia River. Marion was a long-time resident of that area. As mayor, he made sure that the people of Anacostia were included in whatever the city-at-large was doing. He brought the attention of the District government and whatever resources he could to the people in Anacostia. They didn't forget that. The residents of Anacostia subsequently helped reelect him to an unprecedented fourth term as mayor, even after he had served time in prison on the trumped-up drug charge.

Marion also embraced the DC arts community. Two of his early supporters, Ann and Gilbert Kinney, were great patrons of the arts. Gilbert was the finance director of the Corcoran Gallery of Art, and Ann sat on boards for several museums and arts projects in the city. I'm sure their influence also motivated Marion to bring the arts community into his campaign and then to city hall.

During his campaign, several members of the arts community hosted a fundraising event for him. Artists completed paintings especially for the silent auction that was conducted as part of the event. All the money from the auction sales was donated to his campaign. I bought a painting by Frank Smith. At the time, I didn't have the money to buy any major art, but Frank, who was a member of the Chicago-based, AfriCOBRA arts collective, hadn't yet become a well-known artist. I had met him when I was coordinating a trip to Angola, and he was part of the group that signed up to go. In any case, I knew who he was and knew how important his work was going to be. Frank's painting was one of the silent auction pieces for sale, and someone had already bid on it. In the end, I placed a slightly higher bid and wound up with the painting. Later, when Marion and his staff moved into the District Building, where the city's mayoral and City Council offices are located, he installed art throughout his offices and common spaces and hosted a reception for the exhibited artists.

Marion had already brought the city's Latino population into the political process, beginning when he first became involved in DC electoral politics. Years earlier, as chairman of the Council's Finance Committee, he'd gotten strong support from the Latino community by working to enforce fair hiring requirements for city contracts and making them more accessible to minorities including Latinos and Asian/ Pacific Islander Americans. As mayor, he established the Office on Latino Affairs and the Commission on Latino Business Development to facilitate outreach to the District's Spanish-speaking community.

Marion was loved and respected by all these different groups of people because he treated everybody with the same honest respect. Whether it was poor Black people, his gay supporters, or those in the arts community, he was always himself—no matter the race, gender, class, or education level of those he came into contact with, from the youngest child to members of what he would comically call the "bid'ness" community—Marion was always Marion.

I must stop here for a humorous aside regarding Marion's early habits of speech. Now mind you, he was college-educated and working on his PhD when he got involved in the Civil Rights Movement, and it didn't take long for anyone to realize how smart—really brilliant—he was. But he was born in Mississippi and raised in a very poor family in a very poor neighborhood, so he said things like, "bid'ness" rather than "business" and "axed" instead of "asked."

Marion's worldview often leaked into the office, quite humorously. I remember once he and I were at a television station for an interview. It was wintertime, and I was wearing gold leather boots I had gotten from my friend Josie, who used to have a dress shop out of which she sold things she'd gotten in Paris. When we got in the elevator, Marion looked at my boots and asked, "Girl, what's that you got on your feet?" I said, "Mr. Mayor, these boots are from Paris!" "Well, you ain't in Paris!" he asserted.

All jokes aside, Marion later acquiesced to taking speech lessons. He was representing the city, he realized, and he needed to be able to speak properly. One day, I heard him on the radio after he had absorbed some of that coaching. He was in the second year of his first term, and I had by then left his administration. He sounded really good, I thought. No more dropped consonants; he used "standard" subject-verb agreement, the whole bit.

Not long afterward, I saw him on the street and I told him, "Mr. Mayor, you sound so good on the radio. You're not saying 'bid'ness' and 'axed' anymore!" He chuckled and said, with highly enunciated and very proper speech, "Yes! Isn't it wonderful?"

The fact was that Marion really was not proud in that way. You could correct him about anything, and he would take the correction to heart. If he came across a word he didn't know, he'd ask, "What does this mean?" And once you told him the definition, he'd use the word perfectly.

My initial months as Marion's press secretary were a thrill. I loved communications and loved working with the media. As a former journalist, I understood how things worked in that field and understood its deadlines. I also understood that the media "had to be fed"—the mayor's office had to be represented in the best possible way—and that I was the one to do it. I made sure that media outlets, both large and small, knew about all important city government events ahead of time so they could plan their coverage. Plus, Marion was always doing something interesting or new and innovative, so it was a fun job for me and an exciting and rewarding time.

My tasks began each morning with making sure that Marion knew what the overnight newspapers were reporting so he wouldn't be blindsided that day. I considered it part of my duty to let him know anything I thought was big or relevant news. Next, I would work with his scheduling secretary to find out where he was going and when. We'd review his invitations and, if necessary, I'd help the secretary decide which ones he should accept, which ones he couldn't afford to accept because of time constraints, and which ones he HAD to accept, no matter what, because the invitation came from a major supporter. I would then usually coordinate with the office of Marion's (second) wife Effie, to ensure she was informed about all the public events she was expected to attend.

Given that my job was to be as informed as I could be, I frequently visited the various city departments or offices such as the city manager's office, the Department of Health, or the Department of Library Services. I wanted to know what was happening all around the administration so as to be able to inform the mayor about anything he should know—as well as anything he might not have heard about through other channels. And, of course, it was also my job to interface with the press every day. City hall newspaper reporters and representatives from radio and television stations were always in the press room covering some program or event or looking to get a statement about some program or policy.

Sometimes, my job was to represent Marion at different programs or events. If there was any event he couldn't attend but at which someone from the mayor's office needed to be present, I was often the person to go. I remember several important events he could not attend for one reason or another. For instance, I once had to represent Marion at an event honoring comedian Bill Cosby that was hosted by an organization or newspaper. I recall thinking that Bill Cosby might be put out because Marion wasn't there to meet and greet him and, sure enough, Cosby gave me a droll message for Marion. "Tell the mayor that I see he has a light-skinned wife like I do, and I know she's hard to get along with," he quipped. I assumed it was supposed to be a joke or perhaps some kind of private message to Marion, so that's exactly what I went back and told him. "He said what?!" Marion balked.

I also met former First Lady Mamie Eisenhower at an event at which I was representing Marion. I can't remember the nature of the event, but I do have a picture.

As mayor, Marion was fully in charge of his decision-making. Ivanhoe was his closest political advisor and undoubtedly the most vital member of his cabinet. It was Ivanhoe who would broach any sensitive or high-level decision-making issue with Marion, but sometimes I would have something to say about various issues or decisions he faced. One such instance involved a decision over whether to schedule a sitting for Marion at the Scurlock photography studio.

The Scurlocks were an old and renowned family of Washington, DC, photographers, whose prominence, reputation, and clientele rivaled that of Harlem's James Van Der Zee. The Scurlocks had taken official portrait photographs of leaders in government, business, philanthropy and other spheres of influence in the District of Columbia for generations. When Marion became mayor, one of the Scurlocks called his office to schedule a sitting for a photographic portrait of him.

Marion didn't know anything about the Scurlocks. "The who?" he grimaced. "Mr. Mayor," I tried to explain, "you have to sit for the Scurlocks. They've taken portraits of everybody, including the former mayor. Marion was not impressed by people or their positions; in his mind, the person calling on behalf of the Scurlocks was just another "somebody." He waved me off, "I don't have time to do that." I realized that he didn't understand who the Scurlocks were — but that, also, it wouldn't do to *not* sit for them. On that occasion I had to do quite a bit of convincing to get him to agree, but I finally managed to do it.

Marion's impact on DC's Black middle class is nonetheless widely acknowledged. Prior to the fight for home rule, Black people had been kept from attaining top-level government jobs and, really, political power of any kind. Even after Walter Washington was elected in 1974, the white faces that represented the power structure in DC government remained basically the same. Few, if any, Blacks had any positions of authority.

When Marion became mayor, he brought in Blacks, Latinos, gays, and women for cabinet-level positions. He brought Black folks into all the departments of local government that they previously had not gained access to because those positions historically had been filled by whites. He also enacted laws which ensured that minority businesses had access to a certain percentage of District government contracts.

No one can deny that Marion Barry expanded the Black middle class in DC; notwithstanding, there remain members of the District's Black middle-class, people who proudly call themselves "native" or "old" Washingtonians, who will tell you how good it was in the District before all these "other" Black people came up from the South. I have heard native-born Washingtonians express the view that they "didn't have all these problems before these Negroes from the South moved up during the war"—meaning World War II. E. Franklin Frazier wrote about this particular set of Washingtonians in his book, *The Black Bourgeoisie*, in which he reveals the racial "dirt" about their strictly held class/color line, intraracial prejudice and colorism, and things like the dreaded "paper bag" test. Some of these middle-class Black "elites" worked or taught at Howard University, which was (and remains) a big, big employer of Blacks in the District. Others were doctors, nurses, or held other positions at Howard's Freedmen's Hospital. Still others were lawyers, businesspeople, morticians, and other professionals.

Before Marion, that was DC's Black middle-class community—but he enabled many, many more Blacks to attain a more equitable income and lifestyle and enter the middle class. Many of the Blacks from the South—some college educated, others who were not—found work in low-level civil service jobs. Ultimately, many, many District residents bought their first house or could afford to send their children to college because of Marion Barry's efforts to make DC government more inclusive and to make it work *for* its Black citizens, not against them.

Of course, white people were suspicious of Marion's background because of his radical activity, and I'm sure they were waiting for it to surface in some way that negatively affected the city. While I was serving as press secretary for his mayoral campaign, a reporter from the *Washington Post* contacted me because his paper wanted to gain access to Marion's FBI file. At the time of that request, Pride, Inc., was under investigation for spending government money in ways that it was not supposed to be spent, even though everyone knew Marion had long ago left that organization, and no discrepancies had ever been alleged under his directorship of it. Still, the reporter who called from the *Post* obviously could not get a copy of Marion's files and he wanted our permission or assistance in getting them.

"No, you cannot have permission to request his file," I answered matter-of-factly, hanging up. (This was the interchange that spurred my curiosity regarding my own files, and very soon after I decided to request them.) When I told Marion I had refused the *Post's* request, he agreed with my decision. Truth was, they were barking up the wrong tree about the money thing. Reporters were always looking for something that might have suggested Marion had embezzled money or otherwise managed it improperly, but money didn't mean a thing to Marion, so there was never anything negative relating to money to find because he literally "spread the wealth around."

By his fourth term (many years after I'd left his administration), Marion had spent so much of the city's treasury by hiring people into city government that Congress felt the need to step back in. They put DC government into a kind of receivership so Marion became just a figurehead and could no longer make independent decisions. A control board, on which served my friend Joyce Ladner and five or six other people—people in responsible positions in the community—made the city's financial policies, taking away a large portion of Marion's mayoral power.

Still, the media never stopped searching for something that could bring Marion down. The *Washington Post* might have endorsed him for more than one of his bids, but they were always trying to get something on him, as was the FBI. In the end, the "powers that be" did figure out how to snare him. Everyone knew his reputation with women; he loved the women and women loved him. In the end, that was used against him.

I believe that no politician should be allowed to serve more than two terms because, after that, in my opinion, they all start "going downhill." I'm sure this is not universally true, and I'm not necessarily saying this is what happened to Marion, but it's easy to see the dangers involved. Once the popular official is voted in for that second term, they begin to lose their "self" and start to become "The Office." Everybody wants to please them, and nobody will tell them anything that will upset them. Add to that, they no longer have to do anything for themselves—everyone is at their beck and call.

I don't know what kind of person one would have to be in order for that to not go to their head or to avoid being affected by it, but once they lose their grip and begin believing they are not themselves anymore, that they are "The Office," they seem to stop thinking in terms of "serving" and begin to think in terms of "ruling."

To be certain, Marion had vices, and they have been recounted *ad nauseum* in other places. I will simply say that, at some point, his vices allowed the forces that wanted him out of office to bait and trap him.

When he said, famously (or infamously), "The bitch set me up"—that's what happened. The FBI and the DC police organized the "sting," and they got an old girlfriend of his to work with them. And that's how he wound up on television, smoking crack in a hotel room.

I had long left the administration by that time. My decision to leave was influenced by many factors, not the least of which was that I was simply tired of the kind of politics that were being practiced in DC government. I also grew angry with Marion because I became aware that I wasn't being included in meetings to which I should have been privy in order to do my job properly. Those meetings would have supplied me with vital information that would have enabled me to make properly prepared presentations to the media. As a result of my exclusion from them, I was caught off-guard on several occasions when members of the press asked me to comment on certain events or decisions. Ultimately, I realized that, outside of Marion's inner circle of advisors, I would never truly be given the tools I needed to do my job effectively. By the end of 1979, I'd had enough, and I let him know it in a letter I wrote to him dated January 30, 1980, and excerpted here:

> From the time you took office, I did everything possible to be included in meetings and discussions dealing with matters and issues involving the business of the city.
>
> From [my] experience... I knew that in order to fulfill the responsibilities and duties of this job, it was imperative that I either be included in such meetings or receive a thorough, detailed briefing following them. As you know, rarely did either thing happen...
>
> To be elementary about it—it is not possible for a press secretary to respond to erroneous press reports unless he/she knows what the true situation is, or was. How could I possibly know if a reporter has made an incorrect assertion unless I have been privy to some

knowledge of the situation in question...?

    How could a press secretary give public relations or media relations advice in a vacuum about how to handle a situation that he/she knows not of...?

Other things transpired that I wasn't happy about as well. In 1980, Marion scheduled a tour of Africa that included a visit to Tanzania. Since the trip was, in part, an official diplomatic visit, he was allowed to take a staff person with him. Geri was living in Luanda, and I had not seen her since 1975. Marion knew that, yet he refused to take me on the trip. In retrospect, it may have made more sense for him to take the staff person who accompanied him on that trip because that person had lived in Tanzania and knew more about African politics than I did at the time. I still felt that I had been slighted and that he could have, if he had wanted to, taken me. I was "put out" with his decision, and it was, as they say, the straw that broke the camel's back.

"Who needs this?" I thought, offended and upset. On that Friday, I strode into his office and announced, "I don't have to take this mess. I have a husband who would just love for me to be at home, and *I'm going*!" And that was it. I left.

I had already planned to resume working with UNITA on a more formal basis under the auspices of my own company, the Florence Tate Agency. I soon released information about my new venture as the "official" justification for my departure from the Barry administration. The papers had a field day with it, however. The *Post's* headline read: "Barry's Press Secretary is Resigning to Represent African Guerrilla Leader."

Marion came to my office at the agency sometime later to see if he could get me to come back. "You ain't the only one with a husband!" he said. "None of these people *have* to work. You talking about you don't have to work 'cause you have a husband!" Ivanhoe also tried to convince me to stay on, but I was through with the job.

I admit I was—and always have been—impetuous, temperamental, and emotional. Marion wasn't the first person I had left like that, and he wouldn't be the last. Not that I'm proud of it, but I'm just saying that it wasn't really all that unusual for me to make a decision to just leave some place in a manner that might seem abrupt.

My sister Lucille had moved to DC in 1978 and had worked with me on Marion's campaign and later within his administrative team.

Lucille Knowles: *One time, Marion came to me and he said to me, "Why are you all so different? Why do you all act so different?" Because for one thing, I was younger than he was. I had met him under different circumstances... so the way I approached him was more like he was a boss and I was an employee. But her relationship with him was entirely different. She was more like an advisor because she would go in and she would just tell him exactly what she thought, and that was that. If there was something he was doing that she didn't think was appropriate, she would tell him. I didn't approach him in that way, and she did, so I think that's one of the reasons that he asked that.*

Between Florence and Marion, number one, she was older than him; and, number two, she had mentored him in a lot of different ways. So, it was more like, you pissed me off, and I'm done. It was just like, this is not what I want to do, this is not how I want to operate.

I am, and forever will be, a supporter of Marion Barry. Of course, when the FBI sting happened, I felt bad for Marion. I also regret expressing my disappointment in him during an interview; however, at that time, crack was raging throughout the Black community, and it was just a complete embarrassment and let down that he would get caught up in such a situation. I guess at the time I was feeling, "Oh, Marion...how could you?" But I didn't stay in that place because I knew how he had been trapped.

As far as I'm concerned, the entire episode, although it was awful, was a blip on the radar of Marion's legacy. I stack it up against all the good things Marion accomplished: his record of support for and participation in the Civil Rights Movement, his work in the various

DC movements, his work on behalf of youth and seniors, his support for minorities and gays, and his concern for the welfare of Black people generally.

That is why, when people from outside DC, my friends from different places, would ask, "How can you keep electing that man?" I just say, "It's a DC thing, you wouldn't understand!" You just can't explain it in a way that people from outside DC could understand or that would make sense to them, and there is just no point in trying.

Of course, the white newspapers will probably always start any story about Marion with "Marion Barry, who served time in prison for..." Sadly, he will always be identified with that scandal. But anybody who wants to memorialize him honestly will have to acknowledge that Marion's legacy is that he was a well-loved man of the people. The people loved him because he was one of them, and he identified with them and with the downtrodden, the poor, and the sick.

In many ways, Marion Barry is a metaphor for Black people in America because he fell, repeatedly—knocked himself out, even—but he always got up and kept going. Just like Black people! You just can't destroy us, and you can't keep us down. You may push us down, but we get back up. You may force us down again, but we'll also rise again. Marion was like that—neither illness, nor bullet, nor drugs kept him down. However low he fell, he just wouldn't stay there. He was gonna get back up and keep movin'...and that's what Black people do.

As fate would have it, Marion actually arranged for my next foray into government politics—an experience that would be, as Charles put it, the ultimate feather in the cap of my communications and press career. To me, however, it would also be the final, bittersweet leg of a journey that had defined the previous two decades of my life. It was the final "hurrah" of my uphill battle from novice Dayton news reporter during the Civil Rights Movement era to communications director for African Liberation Day and later press secretary for the stunning campaign that elected Marion Barry to the office of mayor of Washington, DC. My time working with Jesse Jackson would be the final chapter in my history of press coordination for a Civil Rights Movement champion who would attain a new and higher level of Black power in American politics. Little did I know, however, that it would also see me in the Middle East at the height of the Reagan era—and that I would become a participant in a historic drama with international consequences.

Jesse Jackson, George Wallace and Florence

Jesse Jackson on campaign trail (photo courtesy of Julia Jones)

With Jesse in Syria (photo courtesy of Julia Jones)

Marion Barry, Kwame Ture, Ivanhoe Donaldson, and Florence 1978

Florence and Mayor Richard Hatcher 1975

Florence, Shirley Chisholm, and Carl Holman (1974-75)

Florence and Mamie Eisenhower (1974-75)

Florence as emcee at a prayer breakfast for Marion Barry 1979

Best Wishes to a very dear friend - Florence Tate -

Marion Barry and Florence 1982

GIL PADILLA

IMAMU BARA

Florence, Gil Padilla, Amiri Baraka at the Conference on the Cities

CHAPTER 13

JESSE, SYRIA

Having left Marion Barry's administration, I was still working on behalf of UNITA at the Florence Tate Agency when, in fall 1983, I received a phone call from my former employer. After a few minutes of formalities, the "Mayor for Life" got straight to the point: "Florence, you know Jesse is about to announce he's entering the presidential race," Marion informed me. "He needs a press secretary, and I told him you're the best. Come to the convention center on November fourth. That's when he's going to announce. I've already told him all about you, and we need you to be there." Marion was clearly thrilled about the Reverend Jesse Jackson's bid for the presidency. After he again impressed upon me that my skills would be vital for that campaign and how Jesse needed the support of all of us, I assured him I would be there.

Of course, Marion didn't need to give me the hard sell to convince me. I was as excited about Jesse running as he was. Like everyone else, I had watched the young preacher journey from student activist to becoming one of Dr. Martin Luther King Jr.'s lieutenants. He'd run the Southern Christian Leadership Conference's (SCLC) Operation Breadbasket in Chicago. Young, bold, and telegenic, Reverend Jackson had always stood out in the crowd.

By the time he decided to enter the campaign, Jesse Jackson was well known not only among Movement people and activists but also by Black people all over the country. Since leaving Operation Breadbasket and SCLC to form Operation PUSH (People United to Save (later Serve) Humanity) in 1971, his many activities, programs, and speaking engagements kept him in the news. He had also recently finished a highly successful voter registration drive for Black people throughout the South. Even the media was forced to acknowledge Reverend Jackson's impact as rumors of the possibility of his plan to enter the presidential race began to swell.

Jesse would be only the second Black American to run for president. Shirley Chisolm had launched her historic bid as the first Black American seeking the Democratic Party nomination for president in 1972. Since her campaign was for the most part ignored by Black politicians and apparently abandoned by the women's rights movement, her bid came to stand more as a symbol of her fearless determination to fight for what she believed in and to serve as a voice for those she represented. Jackson's campaign, while not without its detractors, was much more widely supported, making him the first "serious" Black candidate for U.S. president.

I would say that most people thought positively of Jesse, at least most of the Black community-at-large. Of course, there were those who might have been "professionally jealous" of him and what he was doing because he was often in the limelight. Certainly, others had long been "doing the work" in the Movement. but they didn't have his personality, charisma, or energy. It was Jesse's politics, however, that convinced most of us that he would bring issues important to the Black community forward onto the national agenda. That, in and of itself, was a good thing.

Jesse also had the support of the Black arts community due to his work with the Chicago Black Expos. By 1966, Jesse had become the leader of Dr. Martin Luther King Jr.'s and the Chicago chapter of SCLC's Operation Breadbasket. Operation Breadbasket, launched in 1962, focused on increasing the economic fortunes of Blacks throughout the country. It successfully brought about positive changes in hiring and housing practices in the seventeen states in which it operated, mostly through the use of boycotts.[9] One of Operation Breadbasket's projects in Chicago included the annual Black Expos, which Jesse helped organize and which were aimed at bringing Blacks together for a week of workshops on entrepreneurship and business, entertainment events, and political and social forums. The

---

9   Enrico Beltramini, "SCLC Operation Breadbasket: From Economic Civil Rights to Black Economic Power" *Fire!!!*, *Vol. 2, No. 2, Expanding the Narrative: Exploring New Aspects of the Civil Rights Movement Fifty Years Later*, 2013, pp. 5-47. Published by The Association for the Study of African American Life and History, *https://www.jstor.org/ stable/pdf/10.5323/fire.2.2.0005.pdf*

1971 Black Expo drew nearly a million people, but its impact was tainted when questions arose at the SCLC over the handling of a reported $500,000 in receipts. Reverend Ralph David Abernathy, SCLC's leader, subsequently ordered Jesse to move the Black Expo to Atlanta, where SCLC's main office was located, but Jesse refused. SCLC then began an investigation into Jackson's handling of the event's finances. Reportedly, the last straw for Abernathy and the SCLC was learning that Jesse had formed separate nonprofits to sponsor the Expos, without SCLC's knowledge or permission. They gave Jesse a sixty-day suspension of activities, and he quit.[10] By 1972 Jesse had formed Operation PUSH, and he continued to hold the popular Black Expos through his new organization.

One of the highlights of each Expo was its big concert event. Dozens of music-industry celebrities would participate in the concerts, which were attended by hundreds of thousands of people over the years. Quincy Jones and Don Cornelius served as the concerts' executive directors. Isaac Hayes; Barry White; Curtis Mayfield; Nancy Wilson; Al Green; Reverend James Cleveland; the Staple Singers; The Jackson 5; Earth, Wind, and Fire; The O'Jays; Sammy Davis Jr.; Dick Gregory; and Gladys Knight and the Pips were among the notables who performed over the course of the Black Expos. Other renowned musical artists who performed at the Expos included The Main Ingredient, James Brown, Aretha Franklin, Marvin Gaye, Roberta Flack, Stevie Wonder, Bill Withers, The Temptations, B. B. King, The Fifth Dimension, and Cannonball and Nat Adderley. Several of these performers worked on behalf of Jesse's campaign or were frequently consulted during the campaign.

By the time Jesse made his formal announcement, he was entering the race almost a year behind the other candidates. Several prominent Democrats were already in the field including former Vice President and Senator Walter Mondale (Minnesota), Senator John Glenn (Ohio), former Senator George McGovern (South Dakota), Senator Gary Hart (Colorado), Senator Alan Cranston (California), Senator Ernest

---

10 S. King, "Jackson Quits Post at S.C.L.C. in Policy Split with Abernathy, *The New York Times*, December 12, 1971, https://www.nytimes.com/1971/12/12/archives/jackson-quits-post-at-sclc-in-policy-split-with-abernathy-jackson.html

Hollings (South Carolina), and former Governor Reubin Askew (Florida).

When I arrived at the DC convention hall the night of the announcement, the large ballroom was already packed. The atmosphere was charged with anticipation. TV cameras and members of the press added to the frenzy. As Jesse mounted the stage, the chant, "Run, Jesse, Run!" broke out several times. Boos and catcalls could also be heard from a group of detractors I later learned was made up of Jesse's enemies from the Jewish Defense League. After the audience had been calmed and many introductions made, Jesse's speech was met with thunderous approval. The "Jesse for President in '84" movement had formally begun.

Marion had arranged for me to meet Jesse after all the fanfare had died down some. When he entered the room, he greeted me with, "Well, I heard you're going to be my new press secretary!" And that was it. The rapidity of his decision was a harbinger of what was to come. There was no time for an interview or even a quick get-to-know-you chat. He was due at a Democratic National Committee meeting the following day, and he wanted me to accompany him. I went home to get ready to be on the road the very next day. Campaigning with Jesse meant moving at breakneck speed, often without much time for preparation. For most of the time I was with him, we were traveling from one city to the next, with very little down time between stops.

Jesse had already hired Tom Porter to serve as his campaign strategist. Tom had held a range of leadership positions previously including executive director at The Martin Luther King Jr. Center for Social Change in Atlanta; director of The Washington Center of the Graduate School of Education in Washington, DC; and dean of the Center for Afro-American Studies at Ohio University. He was well-versed in everything from overseeing departmental budgets and planning, to economic and program development, and to research and evaluation. He had experience in politics as well.

Tom Porter: *When I started working with the campaign, there were two of us who were actively traveling with Reverend*

Jackson and that was myself and Florence. We were called the Road Team. We traveled on a daily basis with Reverend Jackson, Florence as press secretary and me as chief strategist for Jesse at that time. It was fascinating; it hadn't been done, and Jesse is a character in and of himself. Florence was handling the press stuff and a lot of the strategy as well.

Eric K. Easter was a friend of my son Brian's and a smart young fellow who had just graduated from Howard University when I hired him as my deputy press secretary. Eric would later go on to become an influential media figure, taking positions as chief of digital strategy for Johnson Publishing and editor-in-chief at EbonyJet.com. He also became president and CEO of Black Heritage Network TV as well as an author, filmmaker, and media producer of a variety of projects. I saw all that potential when I gave him his first job out of college as my second-in-command. What a trial-by-fire position it *would* turn out to be! Eric performed the Herculean task of handling the public while I was on the road with Jesse and Tom. He would field the calls and do everything else because we were constantly out of the office, traveling for the campaign.

Tom Porter: *We were the first set of people in the office in DC on 2100 M Street. This was before we had a formal campaign manager, Arnold Pinckney, and then Preston Love, the deputy campaign manager, who came after a couple of months. Florence was the most senior in terms of strategy. She was very much the core person to listen to because, given her varied experience, she had the most direct campaign strategy. A lot of the folks around him were advisors but not necessarily campaign people.*

Reverend Jackson had a lot of contacts from the religious community, not necessarily organizers, so Florence was very helpful bringing those kind of people on. She didn't have the close personal relationship with Jesse... but relatively quickly earned his trust, and was very much responsible for bringing in people who were SNCC-related—folks like Cleve Sellers and others—into the field operation nationwide... folks who were not necessarily involved, but who really knew their ground game from state to state.

Florence was very focused on strategy, very knowledgeable about the kinds of personal relationships that needed to occur from place to place. She may have been a little too professional for their liking sometimes. That campaign did a lot of things in terms of scheduling that were kind of haphazard or came at the last minute. So, a lot of the early battles, a lot of her wins, were over how you actually schedule, what's the process, how you begin to determine what you do, what you don't do, why you need to do certain things with thoughts of the press involved. Without the technology [we have today], there were a lot of things that had to be baked into the schedule to allow the press to operate.

That was the first win, having the campaign slow down. The press was complaining wildly, "Hey, we don't have time to file," "We can't write this story on time because you didn't stop for three days," "We can't clean our underwear because we've been going for a week, and we haven't been in a city long enough to catch the laundry." Florence had to bring that sense of how campaigns work because we really were operating by the seat of our pants. And we had been saying for the first two or three months, "This is not a campaign, this is a movement," to excuse the fact that it was very much just made up—until that sense of professionalism that she brought.

As the campaign gained steam, Black people became more and more excited about Jackson. He had nonstop speaking engagements, and he continued his voter registration efforts whenever possible. I'll never forget marching with Jesse at a voter registration drive in Palm Beach, Florida, one of the many "spontaneous" campaign activities that were neither organized nor planned. Always professionally dressed, I was wearing little heels that day, and the spontaneous march ended up being a couple of miles. Initially, while I was walking and concentrating on what we were doing, our purpose for being there, and where we were going, I wasn't paying any attention to my choice of footwear. My feet weren't hurting—yet. Over the course of the next day or so, however, my feet and legs began to hurt so badly that I had to go to a podiatrist. She told me to massage them every day and soak them in warm water. That episode reminded me about the toll marching could take on your feet if you didn't have on gym sneakers or comfortable shoes! It also made me think about all those who marched that long trail from Selma to Montgomery, and about the Montgomery bus boycott, when people walked to and from work every day. Marching was a big part of the Civil Rights Movement.

Jesse was a sure-enough marcher! He always wore boots when he marched, and he marched so much that he got "bad feet." Back then, he had to go to a podiatrist periodically to have his feet worked on. Once, we were at the Howard Inn in Washington, DC (which I never could stop calling "Harambee House," its original name), and his feet started bleeding. "Florence, I need you to get me a podiatrist or a doctor to come over here and work on my feet," he requested. "Well, Reverend Jackson," I answered, "I do know a podiatrist, but she has an office. You'll probably need to make an appointment to see her; she's not going to come over here." Jesse was not to be deterred, "Florence, you just tell her to come over here! Tell her it's me. Tell her I'm in pain, and my feet are bleeding, and I need her help. Trust me, she'll come!" So, I called the Black female podiatrist I knew, and because it was Jesse Jackson—the presidential candidate—she came.

It was absolutely historic for Jesse to be running, and everyone knew it. It was huge, actually. Everywhere we went, folks would turn out to see and hear him. He always had large crowds at his appearances, and I was usually able to get a lot of writers and journalists to come out.

Tom Porter: *Florence had ongoing relationships with press people and that was extremely important. She knew a lot of the people who were covering us because a lot of those folks were Black, initially. When people thought that Jesse's [campaign] wasn't going anywhere, they were all Black. So, the* New York Times, *the* Washington Post, *the* Atlanta Constitution—*everybody sent their Black reporters.* Newsday, ABC, NBC, *sent Black producers and reporters until he was starting to do well and get some buzz, and then all of a sudden a lot of them became white.*

One of the things that [Florence] did that was super impactful was using radio as "social media"—meaning, how do you keep the Black community, without all of the technology that exists today, how do you keep the community, on a daily basis, knowledgeable [about] what Jesse Jackson is doing when most of the Black papers are [weeklies]? How do you keep people knowing what's happening every day, and keep people enthused and talking about what happened? The only way to really deal with that was radio. At the time, you still had a lot of Black owners of radio stations. You still had excellent deejays and not syndication.

Florence made sure that every morning we were calling two or three radio stations, at six or seven in the morning during drive time. That was the first thing on the schedule. "Let's call Black radio. First thing in the morning, you're going to call Stevie Wonder's radio station, and you're going to talk to Deejay X." We would connect them with Jesse Jackson, put him on the phone... [and] he'd talk directly [and] take calls. Florence also hired two radio people to be with her. They'd record his speeches and then spend all night cutting two or three minutes of it, wrap a story around it, wrap a beginning and an end around it, and send that out to the radio stations so that they could run it the next day. We'd send it to the big Black radio syndication news houses in town, and the people who owned those were big supporters. Eugene Jackson was a big supporter; he ran National Black Network (NBN News), which had maybe 100 or so Black radio stations in syndication. Dick Griffey was another who owned a bunch of radio stations; he used to run Solar Records. Stevie Wonder had a station. Percy Sutton was key to that as well; he owned WLIB and WBLS in New York.

In the South, there were a bunch of stations that were run by churches in New Orleans, Alabama, South Carolina. "Reverend this" and "Reverend that" had radio stations or had three or four newspapers, so if you talked to one, it would appear in ten. So, Florence was really great at engaging and understanding the Black press and making them a part of it so that Black voters could very much be engaged with it.

When we went to places like Vermont, Connecticut, or Maine, the liberal white people who came out to see Jesse were very supportive of him. After he finished speaking, they would get excited and start vying to see who could do what for Jesse the fastest. Sometimes, we'd hit two or three cities the same night, before different groups or crowds of these white folks who just seemed very enamored of and impressed by him. Then we would get back on the plane and head somewhere else. And Jesse—who's a very funny man, and witty—would always say, with a droll expression on his face, "There's something happening out there, y'all!"

Based on my experiences with him, I am certain the appeal Jesse Jackson had among his supporters during the beginning of his campaign was real. Later, when Barack Obama ran for president, it would irk me when I read or heard someone call him the first serious Black presidential candidate. Jesse was dead serious—as were we, his staff—and so were those who supported him. His presidential candidacy was real to us and initially to all his supporters, regardless of their race.

Of course, the big highlight of that campaign was the trip to Syria to obtain the release of Lieutenant Robert Goodman. New Year's Eve in Syria, and [the Black press that was there] had me in a room, and they were saying, "Let's face it, Tom. You guys can't win. You don't have any organizations. Blah blah blah." And I said, "You brothers never covered an international story, so it got all of y'all out of New York!" The fact of it is, at that time, Jesse was number three—and there were seven candidates! And I [reminded them], as Jesse had said before when they asked him that question, "There are at least four candidates who would like to take my place."

So, yes, Jesse had a chance of winning... but then again, he didn't have a chance of winning because the rules of the Democratic Party were stacked against him. From the very beginning, Jesse, as a Black man—a radical Black man—running for President of the United States as a Democrat, [there were many] within the Democratic Party (because it wasn't just the Republicans) who didn't want Jesse to run.

It seemed to me that we were always on planes, whisking into and out of the private, relatively luxurious airport lounges reserved for dignitaries. Everything was quick and easy in terms of travel, but it still took me a while to get used to not having to go through lines to buy a ticket or go through bag check. On some occasions, a celebrity might loan us a private plane. On several occasions, supporters who owned large hotels reserved accommodations for him and his campaign staff at some of the finest hotels I'd ever experienced. There were perks to the job, and it was exciting for me to see and be around some of the celebrities and diplomats who found their way into Jackson's presence during the campaign.

Jesse's popularity, or lack thereof (depending on which side you were on), caused him to attract constant media attention, and not, as I was to discover, necessarily for good reasons. It seemed odd to me that once he announced his candidacy, the television news teams with their cameras always seemed to be there to meet the plane when we arrived at an airport. I had never experienced that before, nor had I heard of that kind of media attention at any of the other candidates' arrivals. I mentioned it offhandedly to one of the other cameramen one day, asking. "How, and why, are you all at the airport so quickly? There's always media already here when we arrive."

The young white cameraman shrugged. "Whenever they find out Reverend Jackson is flying into a location, we're told to be there when he gets off the plane in case he gets shot. They want us to have the live footage." I was taken aback at this response and perhaps a bit disturbed by his nonchalant tone. Of course, this was part of the reality of Jesse Jackson being the "first serious" Black candidate for president. Our office received hundreds of death threats, and because of that, Jesse received Secret Service protection before any of the other candidates.

> **Eric K. Easter:** *I remember getting threats from people claiming to be from the Jewish Defense League. Anything having to do with "Hymie Town" or Farrakhan, we got death threats on an almost daily basis. And before we had the Secret Service...and Secret Service didn't answer the phone anyway...but before they were around, we had no one to field those calls and had*

no knowledge of how to deal with them. So generally, the receptionist would just send them back to me, because I was press, and press meant that you talked to people outside. So, every crazy person, I got.

Most of it, early on, were calls from people claiming to be from the Jewish Defense League. And that was because a couple of years before he ran, there was a picture of Jesse Jackson with Yasser Arafat that immediately floated around when he announced his candidacy, as well as his position on Israel, and his pro-Palestinian stance. So, that was the reason he was being pegged as an anti-Semite from the beginning.

It was my job to get Jesse press coverage, and that I did. The Black press and Black radio were extremely supportive of him.

In early December 1983, a Black U.S. Navy pilot, Lieutenant Robert Goodman, was shot down over Lebanon flying as part of a mission to attack Syrian forces on the ground there. He was being held in a Syrian prison, and there had been little-to-no publicity about it in the media. Reagan was in office, and there didn't seem to be much interest in getting Goodman out; we thought it was because Goodman was Black.

Now it may not have been because of that, but Black people had, and still have, every reason to be suspicious about what the government does or does not do when it comes to us. There was a lot of talk about the situation: "Well, we ought to do something! Is *anybody* trying to get this pilot out?" But if anything had been attempted, it hadn't been publicized; and it seemed as though the government was content to just let Lt. Goodman languish as a prisoner of war.

Jesse was brilliant; he was always on top of things and consistently aware of what was happening in the country and around the world, and Lt. Goodman's plight did not escape him.

It was just before Christmas. Government offices were closed, and all the officials were going home for the holidays. It was a slow time for most of the campaigns. Jesse gathered his team together for what we thought was a regular staff meeting at the Harambee House Hotel, which was where he always stayed when he was in DC. Without preamble, he announced, "We're going to go get Lt. Goodman!"

He always said these big things with a straight face, as if whatever bodacious idea he had was just normal—as if he were telling us to go the store to pick up lunch. Astonished, we looked around the room at each other. We knew Lt. Goodman was in prison in Syria. "So, how we were going to do that?" someone asked.

In his typical fashion, Jesse had decided that he would be the one to try to get the pilot out. He told us his plan, concluding with, "Everybody else, they're going to be off for Christmas, but we're going to be working. We're leaving for Damascus in a few days." We didn't have time to be stunned.

The next few days were a whirlwind of hustle and bustle with very little time to prepare for the trip. Government officials had to be notified and consulted. Initially, the State Department tried to dissuade Jesse from making the trip, but he was determined to travel to Syria and try to get Lt. Goodman released. He called it a "mission of mercy," so, at that point, the State Department had to get behind it. I'm sure that public relations concerns were a big part of their recapitulation; they didn't want to be seen as preventing a prominent Black American from trying and rescue a Black American. Who needed that kind of attention?

The whole episode turned out to be a thrilling and nonstop adventure. A more thorough accounting of this historic journey can be found in Reverend Wyatt Tee Walker's book, *Journey to Damascus*. I will only share some highlights that stand out in my memory.

Before he made any major move, he always gathered the staff in a circle holding hands while he prays. And when I say Jesse prays, I mean, he *prays*. So, before we left the hotel that day, he led us in prayer. His message was something to the effect of, "Heavenly Father, please watch over this mission. Let us remember why we're there when we get there. While there will be lots of attention focused on this mission, aid us in focusing the attention where it belongs: on Lt. Goodman." He also reminded us that while everyone else on the Hill would be off, we were going to work, and we had with a goal: to bring Lt. Goodman home.

Before we left for the airport, Jesse turned suddenly to the young woman I hired as the campaign photographer. She was following us as far as the airport but wasn't traveling with us. "You need to come," he told her. "I need my campaign photographer there." This would be difficult, she had not intended to go with us. She had no luggage, change of clothes or passport. But Jesse was insistent. He turned on his heel and strode on, barking back to me with, "Florence, call somebody and get this girl a passport and whatever else she needs. And get her on the plane with us!" Just like that.

Jesse was like that. If there was something he wanted accomplished, he wouldn't wait for you to lay out all the problems. He just expected you to get it done.

Like I said, it was a different time and, thankfully, by that point the State Department was on board with what we were trying to do. They had no choice, really. Once Jesse had cabled Syrian President Hafez al-Assad's office, and al-Assad himself had cabled back extending Jesse an invitation to come to Syria, it was a go. What could the U.S. do but watch nervously, even though, we had heard, President Reagan would not take Jesse's calls before we left?

Somehow, we got her on the plane, which took us to Kennedy Airport in New York. When we landed there, I called our liaison in the State Department. He knew our delegation would have to lay over in Frankfurt along the way, and he gave me instructions on how to get her a passport when we got to Germany. In Frankfurt, I rushed off to the American consulate. I went to the window the State Department aide directed me to. Not only did they have the passport, they also included a little care package with a toothbrush, a face cloth, and some panties! I remember thinking, "When the government wants to get something done, it sure can get it done!"

Someone in Jesse's camp had contacted Lt. Goodman's mother before we left Washington, and she had arranged to meet us there at Kennedy to see us off. I remember her turning to me and asking, "Are you really going to bring him back?" Of course, I had no way of knowing what the outcome of our mission would be, but I knew I wasn't going to tell her that we were going to go over there and simply try to get him out. Instead, I chose to look her in her eye and squeeze her hand. "Oh, we're *going* to bring Lt. Goodman home," was my firm reply. I needed to convince *myself*.

Jesse had arranged for a cross-section of influential ministers from various churches and denominations to accompany him on the trip. His delegation included Reverend Wyatt Tee Walker, pastor of Canaan Baptist Church of Christ in Harlem, who had served as Dr. Martin Luther King Jr.'s chief of staff and executive director of the SCLC. The delegation also included Dr. Thelma Adair, president of Church Women United; Reverend William Howard of the National Council of Churches; and Reverend Jack Mendelsohn of the Unitarian Universalists.

Staff and associates on the trip included me, Tom Porter, the campaign's policy strategist; Eugene Wheeler, who was in charge of campaign finances and travel, and Ed Theobald, our on-the-road coordinator. Jesse's personal physician, Dr. Andrew Thomas, also joined us, as we would need someone qualified to conduct a physical examination of Lt. Goodman if all went as planned. Jesse brought his sons, Jesse Jackson Jr. and Jonathan Jackson, along as well.

Minister Louis Farrakhan, leader of the Nation of Islam (NOI), was also among those accompanying Jesse to Syria. Minister Farrakhan played a very important role in, and was a very welcome addition to, the delegation. He had been supportive of Jesse when other key leaders were not. He had dispatched the NOI's Fruit of Islam to serve as security before Jesse got Secret Service coverage. Minister Farrakhan had been there throughout the campaign. He and Jesse both had strongholds in Chicago and had worked in the community. It was Farrakhan who, at Jesse's request, opened and closed each session we held with Syrian officials after we arrived with a prayer in fluent Arabic. He was accompanied by his personal assistant, Minister Akbar Muhammed.

The members of the media that accompanied us were very eager to talk to Minister Farrakhan. All the way on the plane to Syria, during our stay there, and on our way back, the press was always on me, "We want to interview Farrakhan." But he wouldn't talk, and he wouldn't deal with the press.

During our long flights to and from Syria, I occasionally sat with him, so we had regular conversations. During one of our conversations, we discussed the role of women in the Nation of Islam. Farrakhan was working to provide more equality for women and to modernize the role and regard for women within the Nation. When I congratulated him for the work he was doing in that regard, he demurred, "No, Sister Florence, we have a lot of work to do," he told me. When I told him about how much the press was interested in speaking with him, he simply shook his head and said, "I'm not ready for that yet. I'm not ready." He stayed out of the limelight in terms of being a part of the delegation, but inside the meetings when Jesse was speaking with Syrian government officials or the religious community, Farrakhan's participation was invaluable.

Several meetings were held with various representatives of Syrian government and religious organizations before Jesse finally met with President al-Assad. The meetings were with people of influence who would undoubtedly contribute to the final decision regarding the release of Lt. Goodman. Beginning with the very first meeting, Jesse asked Minister Farrakhan to open with an Islamic prayer, which he did, in fluent, melodic Arabic. His prayers were very impressive and seemed to immediately strike a positive note with our Syrian hosts.

Jesse had a good name throughout the Arab world because of the public stance he took during an earlier tour he made through the Middle East in 1979. On that trip, he traveled to Israel and Beirut to help allay tensions between Arabs and Jews, but he was clear on his support for the Palestinians. It was then that he took the famous photo with Palestinian Liberation Organization (PLO) chief Yasser Arafat, a very controversial figure, especially in the West, and especially among Jews. Jesse visited Damascus as well on that trip, establishing the contacts that enabled him to even think of traveling to Syria for our mission. No ordinary person would have gone or thought about meeting with the president of Syria to try to get Lt. Goodman out of prison, but Jesse had made those contacts and felt confident that he could do it.

We arrived in Syria on Saturday with a plan to be there for only four days. During the first two days, Jesse met with various officials but not with President al-Assad. We among the staff were beginning to get anxious. The press was getting impatient and wanted to know the reasons behind the delay. We finessed it, and we never let them know that we really had no idea if, or when, Jesse would actually meet with the Syrian president. It was my job to go before the press and say, "Well, we're not going to meet today but possibly tomorrow. We'll be back in touch, and we'll let you know."

In the meantime, Jesse arranged for the delegation to visit a Palestinian refugee camp. While there, I distributed a handful of pictures of Jesse that I'd brought, and eager Palestinian youth grabbed them from my hands and waved them in front of the cameras. On the third day, Jesse finally met with al-Assad, who informed him that he had not yet decided whether to release Lt. Goodman. Later that evening, we received a request from the Syrians to delay our departure. That request led to one of the most memorable "meet-the-press" events I can recall.

I hastily arranged a press conference to inform the reporters traveling with us that our departure would be delayed for a few days at the request of President al-Assad. I also informed them that we didn't have any information to share about Lt. Goodman's release. Suddenly, a small, slender man, possibly German, jumped up and shouted a disrespectful comment, something like, "You're full of it!" In swift response, Brother Akbar Muhammad, Minister Farrakhan's personal assistant/security person—a great big man—jumped in front of me and pointed his finger at the little German. "I will put my foot dead up your ass!" he thundered. That room got quiet, fast! No more yapping. The press conference was over, and that was it.

After that, I would jokingly say, "No wonder Minister Farrakhan can go around with that beatific smile all the time, he has Brother Akbar there to put his foot up your ass if you mess with him!"

One afternoon, as we waited for feedback from the Syrians, Reverend Walker, who was the head of the delegation in terms of protocol and staff, decided that he was going to take the members of our delegation to the *Souk,* a world-renowned Syrian/Arab market. The excursion, though only a few hours, was a welcome relief from the tension. The market was absolutely huge, with all kinds of merchants selling everything from food, spices, clothing, and housewares to diamonds, gold, and rubies. While there, I bought several rings for friends and family.

Every day, the Arab newspapers carried a big, front-page story about "the Reverend Jesse Jackson and Lieutenant Goodman." I still have copies of those papers because the Syrian press person assigned to our mission brought them to me every day. Apparently, back in the U.S., it was just as Jesse predicted: we had the media all to ourselves. I remember calling a friend, asking, "Is there anything about what's going on here in the paper?" "Florence, there's nothing else *in* the paper!" she roared. So, our mission was very well covered, nationally, and internationally.

It was riveting to watch Jesse's persuasive power and eloquence of speech, up close and personal, during his sessions with the Syrians. At one of the assemblies of Syrian council members and clergy, he seemed to take an especially momentous religious "leap," seemingly traveling to a higher spiritual plane. I told Charles about it when I got back home, telling him I literally saw Jesse go "someplace else." The Syrians were likewise transfixed and moved by his words. It was at that moment that I believed we were truly going to accomplish our mission. We were going to bring this boy home!

In the end, al-Assad and his council were convinced. Apparently, they decided the release of the Black pilot and his return to the U.S. with Reverend Jackson and his delegation would foster good international relations. Emotions ran deep among us all when we got the news. Jesse had done what the U.S. government had been unable to do! It was an incredible feat, and we all felt like we had been part of something monumental.

The State Department arranged for a military transport and a delegation of naval officers to pick us up in Syria and escort us back to the U.S. base in Frankfurt. From there, we were picked up by Air Force Two (which is what the U.S. president's plane, Air Force One, is called when the president isn't on it). It was a very luxurious aircraft, and it felt like a pretty big deal to be on the president's plane.

Of course, when we landed, all the major media greeted us. When we disembarked from the plane with Lt. Goodman in tow, we each felt a tremendous sense of victory and accomplishment. The rescue mission greatly increased Jesse's stature. He was no longer just a presidential candidate, he was a national hero. President Reagan—who wouldn't return Jesse's calls before we left—held a reception for the delegation in the Rose Garden.

Before we departed from Syria, Jesse pulled the members of the staff aside for another of his prayer circles. In his deadpan, matter-of-fact manner, he both admonished and gave advance notice to those of us who were Black nationalists in the delegation, with the warning: "And, um, we're going to embrace Lt. Goodman's white wife." "Don't be a fool when you see Lt. Goodman with that white woman," he added, giving us time to internalize it before we got back. I knew that Minister Farrakhan didn't know, so, on the aircraft carrier going back, I wrote him a little note to that effect and, while sitting beside him, I surreptitiously stuck it in his suit pocket. Without missing a beat, Minister Farrakhan calmly retrieved my note from his pocket and read it. When he was finished, he returned it his pocket calmly and gazed off. His expression was unreadable, but knowing as I did the NOI's "white devil" refrain at that time, I didn't want him to feel blindsided when Goodman's wife made her appearance at the Rose Garden press conference.

Another delegation member who wasn't prepared for this in advance was Jesse's doctor, Dr. Thomas, who joined us at the luncheon at the Howard Inn after the White House press conference. He and I were sitting together at a table, and Jesse, Lt. Goodman, and his wife were on the dais when Dr. Thomas leaned toward me and murmured, "Florence, Lt. Goodman's wife looks white." I said, "Dr. Thomas, Lt. Goodman's wife IS white." The physician's look of surprise—perhaps with a tinge of dismay—was almost humorous. Nonetheless, everyone in that room agreed on one thing: our mission of mercy had been a great success.

The day after our victorious return, we headed to the "Motor City" for a rally at the University of Detroit. Detroit's Mayor Coleman Young had already endorsed Walter Mondale. Usually, when we went to cities where there was a Black mayor or Black elected official, Jesse was very well received. We'd be met at the airport by a police escort, along with a mayor or councilman or an official delegation. This time, because Young was supporting Mondale, there was no police escort, and nobody from the government met us at the airport. Minister Farrakhan's people turned out en masse at the rally, however. Over 7,000 NOI supporters and others were there, donating money to Jesse's campaign. Although Minister Farrakhan was soon to become a thorn in the side of the Jackson campaign, my respect for Farrakhan never waned, and no one can ever say he wasn't an important initial figure and supporter of Jesse's 1984 bid.

Unfortunately, the campaign didn't have much time to enjoy the fruits of its successful mission of mercy. Within a few weeks, we were embroiled in the scandal that would become part of the reason I departed from the campaign. [11]

My relationship with the Black press and the manner in which it responded to, and covered, Jesse's campaign was always good, yet relations between the media and the campaign took a negative turn when an incident occurred involving a Black reporter for the "mainstream" white-owned press.

Eric K. Easter: *Florence managed that relationship [with the press] very much and tried to put some controls on Reverend Jackson as well. To [help him] realize that, while these people were all Black, he could not let his guard down and just assume that he could chill because these were Black people. It was very different from the Movement, where Black people who covered it were sort of about the Movement as well. In this case, they were working for mainstream publications and being tested very much by their editors, who said, "Well, the test of whether you are a fair and good journalist is if you can come back with some dirt on Jackson that is not supportive."*

---

11 Not long after Florence left the campaign, Reverend Jackson defended comments Minister Farrakhan made to "enemies of the campaign" when he said, after the controversy over Jesse's use of an offensive word regarding Jews arose: "If you harm this brother, I warn you, in the name of Allah, this will be the last one you harm." This created yet another opportunity for those who repudiated Farrakhan and who blamed Jesse for Florence's relationship with the PLO to continue to label him an anti-Semite. But when Farrakhan reportedly called the creation of Israel an "outlaw act" and called nations supporting Israel "criminals in the sight of Almighty God," Jesse was forced to repudiate Farrakhan, and the incident was to drive a wedge between them. For more on this, see M. Hirschorn, "Jesse and the Jews," *The Harvard Crimson*, March 5, 1984, https://www.thecrimson.com/article/1984/3/5/jesse-and-the-jews-pbtbhis-is/; and F. Joyce, "Jackson Criticizes Remarks Made by Farrakhan ss 'Reprehensible,'" *The New York Times*, June 29, 1984, https://www.nytimes.com/1984/06/29/world/jackson-criticizes-remarks-made-by-farrakhan-as-reprehensible.html.

Florence would get calls saying, "Hey, I need something because I'm getting pressure, because my editors don't think I'm legit. I'm writing good stuff, I'm writing what I see, and they essentially don't believe it." So, she had to manage that. She was sort of godmother to them as well. The odd thing about being a press secretary is that you are working for your candidate, but you're also working for the press. So, you have to advocate for the press to your candidate... while you're also battling with them about how they cover what you're doing. And they're all on the plane with you, so you can never get away from them. She handled that very well.

At the beginning of Jesse's campaign, just a few reporters were following us, and they were mainly Black. The white news establishments would send their Black reporters because they figured this was going to be "just a Black campaign"—that is, just a Black man doing something. But after the Syria incident, we started getting attention from so many national reporters we had to have a separate press plane.

It was after the white reporters started coming that one of the Black reporters with a major new outlet (whose name I won't mention) pulled me aside one day and said, "Florence, tell Reverend Jackson to quit saying 'hymie' because if one of these white reporters hear him, they're going to write a story on it...and then all the editors at our outlets will want to know why we didn't report that he was saying it."

So, when we got off the plane, I said to Jesse, "Reverend Jackson, you need to stop saying 'hymie' because a reporter is going to write it up—and then we'll be in trouble." Jesse nodded, "Got it," and he never said it again, to my knowledge, and certainly not publicly.

That same reporter told me that one day a group of Black reporters were talking about Jesse's use of the term and how he'd had his coattails pulled about it and had stopped using it. Milton Coleman, who had been put on the campaign by the *Washington Post*, was in the circle, and he piped up, saying, "Well, *I'm* going to write a story about it!" My friend from ABC said he told Coleman, "Look, you can't write a story about it 'cause you didn't hear him say it!"—but Milton wouldn't be deterred.

As it turned out, Milton co-wrote his story with a white *Post* reporter, and they included a line about Jesse's use of the "h" word. They wrote that Jesse "had been overheard at an airport saying he was going to 'hymie town,'" or something to that effect. I'm pretty sure Milton was the one responsible for that getting in the paper, and I believe he did it to curry favor with his bosses after getting into hot water over another story.

Tom Porter: *Milton Coleman was apparently picked by the Washington Post to say that he heard Jesse say "hymie." He never heard Jessie say "hymie." I said to Jesse, "Man, quite frankly, you should just deny that you said it." And so, there was a split. Some of the people were saying, "Well, they might have a tape." So, Jesse was coerced into admitting that he said something which he had not said in the way that they were using it.*

They wanted to use the incident against Jesse, but from the very, very beginning there were members of the Jewish community and some Jewish organizations who were simply opposed to his running for President.

Eric K. Easter: *My remembrance of that story is that Milton never was really on the plane up until that point; that, over the course of drinks with the Black crew that was traveling, they got into talking about [how] "Jesse's gotta not be so loose," joking around about him saying "hymietown" and saying other things that were too loose. But they considered themselves to be protective of "boys-on-the-bus" culture.*

I remember a conversation between Florence and Milton. I could only hear Florence's side, but I remember her saying, "Milton, you weren't on the plane. You didn't hear that,"... which he took as "Well, you didn't say he didn't say it, you just said I wasn't there," and him, in talking to Jesse afterwards, essentially saying, "Well, Florence confirmed it by basically saying, 'you weren't on the plane.'" And that became kind of a point of contention between Jesse and Florence over "Did you confirm it?"—that kind of thing.

And then the tone of the apology...there was a lot of conversation around what should be said, what shouldn't be said; whether he should apologize, whether he should not.... It became sort of a huge internal battle of professionals versus people close to him. All along it was a battle for trust and understanding because the press was seen as kind of the enemy. There was a bit of "Whose side are you on, are you advocating for me or are you working for those press people?"—which all press secretaries get because that's the nature of the gig...but because the stakes were so high, Florence battled a lot with that.

And I think the "hymietown" thing, that became a real issue around then. It was into the primary season [and] the apology happened in New Hampshire. Shortly after that, I know there was a bit of a rift because of the [lost] sense of trust. Candidates always blame anything related to the press on the press secretary eventually, and I think that [the question]—"Can I trust you?"—came up. Relatively soon after that, in a matter of weeks or a month, she left.

The whole thing really created a dilemma for the campaign because, after that, everywhere we would go—whether Jesse was making a speech or going to a meeting—when he got off the plane a delegation was there waiting for him to talk about why or whether he had "said it or not." He couldn't talk about anything else. At first, he denied it, but finally, after many denials at different places, he ended up admitting and apologizing for it.

I've been asked many times, "If that bomb hadn't detonated, could Jesse have won?" and my answer is this: I do think that it put a damper on his campaign. It was a blot on his candidacy, and it had to have had an impact. I don't think Jesse would have won, but he did have a number of delegates, and he would have gotten more votes and won more delegates if it had not occurred. Jesse is not a bigot. It was a careless, unthinking, unkind slip up, but it was not malicious. Yet, as far as many whites and Jews were concerned, he was a pariah after that. Black folks, on the other hand, never turned away from him and continued to support him.

Tom Porter: *Jesse had a populist message, and people were ready for his message. On the other hand, Jesse initially told me he wanted to build a movement... and he left the building of a movement, actually really believing he could win when the rules were stacked against him.... And the "hymie" thing, they were never going to let him live that down. But yes, it was exciting. It was clear that he had a shot.*

Eventually I left the campaign, but my support for Jesse did not wane. These days, people who don't know Jesse and his history just see him as someone who shows up for the cameras. I don't believe that is the case. Jesse Jackson today falls into the category of someone who is often invited and depended upon to do something or to lend his name to a different causes. He is relied upon even today to bring attention to problems that would otherwise linger if someone of his stature didn't shed light on them. Of course, Jesse knows that he still attracts attention and publicity, so he often decides to appear at a strike or a demonstration at which Black people are trying to raise awareness about an issue that they would not otherwise get support for. He knows that if he shows up, the action will become a national issue.

I also remind people that when the media vilifies Jesse or Marion or any other Black political personality who has done something "disgraceful," they do so with a certain viciousness that is reserved for Blacks. They don't seem to hold white politicians or personalities to the same standards. Any judgment or castigation meted out against whites for inappropriate speech or conduct is cushioned by layers of protection that basically amount to white privilege. We Blacks have long known we can't afford to do the same things white folks do. We simply aren't afforded any kind of protection from the ire and rancor of the public.

I, for one, say that I continue to hold both Jesse and Marion in high regard. They have paid their debts many times over—if any of us can judge them as having any debts—through their service and commitment to the work of Black liberation in the United States and, especially in Jesse's case, to the liberation of people of color worldwide.

Working for these two men was, in many ways, the pinnacle of my career and the apex of my years covering, reporting, and communicating the work of Black liberation activists. My experiences with both were certainly among the most exciting of my professional life. I hope that when the history of these liberation struggles is written, and written truthfully, that Jesse and Marion will be remembered for their monumental and world-changing contributions. Future liberation activists can learn many things from the playbooks of both men.

CHAPTER 14

POST-JESSE, PRE-BARACK

Florence chose to end her account of her time in bipartisan politics with her writings about her involvement in Jesse Jackson's campaign for the presidency in 1983. Although she was to make one more foray into the world of Washington, DC's municipal politics, that experience was a very negative one for her, and one she refused to include in her memoirs. Indeed, her aversion to even the thought of adding it was so severe that she bluntly told me: "I don't even want the name [of that candidate] in the book." Given that significant pause in her journal writing, the following shares some of her other recollections and writings from later years, as well as memories from friends who were with her during those years.

During 1990 and 1991, Florence started writing for LaVerne McCain Gill's DC-based *Metro Chronicle* and *National Chronicle* newspapers. With complete freedom to write what she wanted, her subject matter ranged from the political ("Let Jesse Jackson Do Our Thing," "Can African Americans Help Bring Peace to Angola?" and "A Middle East 'Madman', The Media, and Black Folks") to the cultural ("Buy Black for Spring," and "Public Enemy, 'House Party', 'The Piano Lesson', Essence's 20th").

The post-Jesse Jackson campaign period also included what Florence called her "shopping time," during which she enjoyed the relaxation and sensory satisfaction of consignment shopping and, later, selling. Her love of exquisite fashions and sartorial excellence and her desire to support up-and-coming African American designers would eventually lead her to hold regular "sell-and-swap" events she dubbed "Bygones International Caravan." According to a flyer for one of her 1992 Caravan events: *Bygones International Caravan has arrived with its usual complement of the exotic and exquisite, the beautiful and bold, the fun and fantasmagorical things for your buying pleasure.*

It was, for Florence, a period of restoration:

> During the shopping time, I just made that like a project, almost. It was a personal movement. I didn't just "go into" shopping... but I decided that I would find out all that I could about fashion and style and clothing and just really study that whole area. And then I got into looking at antiques. I might have bought a few little pieces, but I wasn't really heavy into antique shopping.
>
> I would look in the most expensive of the clothing stores, women's stores, all of the high fashion [shops], to learn about it. I started knowing what was good—not just fashionable or stylish—but what was good stuff in terms of how it was made and the materials, and where it was made and the designers. I just made it a study. It wasn't a hobby because I was deliberate about it. I planned and made an avocation of this.

These years also brought new people and fresh experiences into her life post-politics years. Independent film and broadcast producer and promoter Kay Shaw, also a well-known and respected strategic engagement and communications director for organizations including the National Black Programming Consortium/BlackPublic Media and the NAACP Legal Defense Fund, would spend time with Florence in both DC and New York, during periods of celebration and depression.

> **Kay Shaw:** The first time I was in her company for an extended period of time was when she hosted a book party for Greg's book, Flyboy in the Buttermilk; I was close to her other son, Brian, first. I had worked with him at "Taste of DC" and when Mrs. Tate came to the event, Brian would pair us up and I would walk her around the site. And she made a point of being close to the people in her sons' lives that they respected and who they were close to.
>
> In terms of a person who was clinically diagnosed medicated and aware of her depression, she was open, honest about it, even when she was in the hospital, getting electric shock treatment — she really kind of ushered us through it. She wasn't quiet about

or secretive about it, so that you had to try to figure out what's going on, and try to understand it, and [wonder] "is it symptoms of depression or is it her?" You didn't have to do any of that. No mind games.

And I was sympathetic. So, whenever she would have those bouts those periods, I would check in with her periodically. And all I had to do was start talking about her children, saying something silly or something that I heard or saw – like "the last time I was at Greg's show…" — Just add a little bit of a spark to take her out of her depression or get her to do her 'tee-hee." So, I would do that periodically, because I understood and knew what joy her children brought to her.

I saw her ups and downs. When she was fine, she could touch the sky and you would have to just get out the way! It would tickle me, sometimes, how people would react to her. Sometimes she would say things and people would shocked. And I would be like, "I thought you knew Mrs Tate!"

Omo Misha Mcglown: *I loved her sense of humor. And obviously you know Miss Tate was an older woman and a mother figure, and she shared those motherly wisdoms with me. Not in any kind of admonishing way, or as if she was given me advice. It was always just very organic and usually pretty funny. But for the most part, I related to her like the girlfriend. You know, because there was a part of her that was ageless, part of her that was a little girl. I was one of the younger people that was close to her and it was a relationship that grew so organically and effortlessly. And again, I think of her as ageless in a sense. She was older and she possessed and shared the wisdom and experience of an older woman, but she also was still very in tune on all these other levels. Some people they're twenty, and then they're forty, and then they're not connecting with their twenty-year-old self anymore. I think she was still definitely connecting with her ten-year-old self, her twenty-year-old self, her forty-year-old self… so wherever you were, she was still able to connect with you.*

She loved to bring women together. I built a lot of relationships with people through her — there were so many extensions, sisterships, extending from Mrs. Tate and some of them got passed on to me. When we made this jewelry connection one of the first things she wanted to was have me bring some jewelry down and invite people over to see it. So, we set a date made some plans, I brought a lot of jewelry. She took it and put it all over the house — living room, dining room, den, draped on the couch. It became a kind of a scavenger hunt. She set up refreshments invited people, we had a great turnout and it was amazing. I admired the relationships she had with so many women, and I admired sometimes just watching her connect with those people. It was, it was inspiring and magical.

Then in early November 1996, Florence began hand journaling the early frame of reference for this book project:

I finally got a handle on which to hang a book. Last night proved to be a very fortuitous one for me. For years, friends (and family, particularly Greg) have asked me after I have regaled them with some tales, "Florence, you ought to write a book." But I always demurred. When I seriously would think about the possibility, I couldn't think of a way to reconcile the variety of people, places, things I had been involved with in a way that would make any sense. Should I write about my thirty-five-year struggle with depression? Should I write about the famous and well-known people that I'd served as press agent, communication director, press secretary? The most interesting parts of those experiences were tales that could not be told—at least, not by me. My son Greg and grandson Samori have repeatedly asked me about writing about my history growing up. I still want to do that but just find it impossible to put pen to paper to get started in any serious way. I have started and stopped accounting for my childhood in a chronological way. I hope to resume that at some point, just don't have the initiative, motivation, perseverance, patience, et al., to really do it. But last night's events may prove to be a turning point in my resistance to writing about my life's experiences. [A friend] directed me to sit down and write for

*fifteen minutes every day. No more, [no] less. "Can you do that?"
I, of course, said I could do that.*

Not long after Thanksgiving that year, however, her depression had grown much worse. Even though the following year, in February, she had enrolled in a creative writing class, noting in her journal, "It's gratifying, at a time when little pleases me, to receive praise from my classmates, teachers and family members," she did not make another entry to her diary until March 1997. As she wrote then: "Today is the first day since my hospitalization that I've mustered the wherewithal to sit down and write again. Late November and December proved to be too much for me and I ended up in [the hospital] for a series of shock treatments. ECT, the treatment is called...which finally brought me out of my depression."

Over the course of the next year-and-a-half, Florence journaled steadily. By November 1998, she felt she had covered enough territory, reflecting upon and writing about her experiences, to begin wondering about her ability to approach a very difficult period in her life: her UNITA years. As she noted: "[I need] to get back into my writing. The next phase is difficult and complex because of personal relationships, political pain, ostracism, denunciations, betrayals, etc. Don't know if I can do it justice—or if it would send me into a tailspin. Maybe I can just skip over and come back to it. Start with Marion Barry years and end with Jesse Jackson years."

There followed another significant break in her writing. Her next entry would not be until July 2000, when she would share an account of happy events: a trip to Santa Fe to see Charles's sister, Audrey Dandridge. Which turned out to be a refreshing and exhilarating experience.

She later wrote humorously about receiving her first computer in January 1999. She hoped it would speed her writing but, by her account, it did just the opposite: "I bought a computer and have been surfing, reading, and sending e-mails ever since. In fact, I deluded myself into thinking that getting a computer would accelerate my memoir writing. It cancelled it." Not long after, she returned to her handwritten journal, writing summarily about the UNITA period but with significant gaps between entries.

Five years later, in February 2005, Florence would write about Charles's and her experiences relocating as retirees from Washington, DC, to Sarasota, Florida, in 2002, as she tried to acclimate herself to the new environment and address her concerns about leaving her family and friends. This would be followed by another lengthy journaling hiatus until March 1, 2007, when she recounted the details of a party that her friend Kay Shaw threw for her for her seventy-fifth birthday that was attended by family and many of her longtime friends including the Meislers, Michael Warren, Mae Jackson, Joan Thornell, LaVerne McCain Gill, and Hedi Butler.

> **Kay Shaw:** *Every time she came to New York, I would go down to Bergdorf's with her, you know, to her do her favorite shops. She would go shopping on Madison Avenue and we would have lunch somewhere. So, she always took time to do that when she came to New York, when she could still move around well. She enjoyed fine things, quality. She enjoyed that. And she knew how to take care of it and preserve it, and she knew the labels and all that. And she had her own style. And she was beautiful! She made sure that she was always – she's a southern girl! — her hair was done, her nails were done. She had her jewelry. You know nothing over the top or ostentatious, but just refined.*

Florence also wrote happily about Brian's marriage to his wife, Maureen Mahon; and a "Queen for a Day" party thrown for her by Mae Jackson the year before. Her journal writing then fast-forwards to 2007, during which she wrote of her ongoing efforts to find a community of like-minded and like-spirited individuals in Sarasota as well as ongoing concerns about the health and well-being of family.

I would meet Florence in 2010 at a women's outing in Sarasota. Soon after, I would begin documenting and recording her reflections on the years not covered by her handwritten journal.

She would not write again in her journal until February 2012, when she commented on her brother Henry's death and the significant depression she was experiencing at the time. That particular round of depression, she would note, would be the most severe she had experienced since 1996. She would undergo ECT therapy again in 2009 in DC under the care of her physician. Soon after she would be hospitalized for what was first believed to be pneumonia but would ultimately be diagnosed as renal failure. Afterward, she would begin kidney dialysis, which she would continue to undergo, albeit with much resentment, for several years.

In 2012, Florence penned an article for a pamphlet her longtime friend LaVerne McCain Gill—by then an ordained minister—was compiling on spiritual care for patients experiencing end-stage renal failure. In the article, Florence expressed her fear, anger, and frustration with the disease and the havoc it was playing on her body.

It was the week before Christmas 2010. I woke up that Saturday morning feeling funny; I turned to my husband Charles and told him that it felt like I had pneumonia. Why? I self-diagnosed because I had contracted it a few years back; the feeling was the same as the onset of that prior bout with the respiratory illness, which was cured with antibiotics. I called my family internist, who sent me to the medical lab for an x-ray, which indicated to him that I, indeed, had water on my lungs.

Charles drove us to the local hospital, where the doctor had already made an appointment for me. The next thing I remember after the battery of various tests – the usual, heart, lungs, blood, urinalysis and so forth— is being semi-conscious, and hooked up to a respirator, an intravenous feeding tube, and hovered over by who, I later learned, were my internist, a cardiologist, and the nephrologist, whom I had been seeing off and on for three years. The nephrologist explained that he and the medical team had been trying everything, all kinds of diuretics, to remove the water from my lungs, to no avail. Finally, as a last resort, he wanted to try dialysis, as my breathing was becoming more labored and my condition more critical.

The next thing I remember was being put on a gurney to be wheeled to wherever in the hospital dialysis was done. It was not an uncomfortable procedure. Apparently, the water was being successfully removed from my lungs, and I received two more treatments before being discharged.

Upon discharge, my nephrologist gave me a card and indicated that I should go to that address the Monday morning following Christmas. And I did.

Mind you, I had no idea that I had been placed on permanent dialysis. Nothing had been explained to me about the procedure, and I was unaware that a catheter was placed in my chest, to be used for dialysis at the center where I had been assigned.

One day I told the technician who was administering the dialysis treatment that I felt like there was a rope in my chest, and he explained about the catheter, what it was, and how it was being used. I began to feel angry and deceived—like someone had "tricked" me. Meanwhile, several weeks passed before I had an in-center visit from my nephrologist. At that meeting, with my husband and me, the doctor confirmed that I would be permanently on dialysis, that this was not a temporary situation. I was shocked, and started crying, feeling and saying that I'd rather be dead.

"I can't go through with this the rest of my life!" He tried to assure me that I would become adjusted to it.

Florence next shared how she came to the decision to "choose life" and submit to the three-times-a-week dialysis treatment that she loathed for the sake of her loved ones:

The clinic made the appointment for me to see Dr. Nair, the Indian American surgeon, who proved to be of more assistance than any of the other medical personnel in helping me to come to terms with my condition. He explained what each were—the fistula and the graft—and how he would help me decide which was preferable for me, all things considered. We decided on the graft because it would make it possible to remove the catheter sooner—the catheter is more problematic because of its proximity to the heart. My veins are small, making a fistula not a good choice—also a surgery in 2005, involving the removal of twenty lymph nodes due to breast cancer, made the use of my right arm unavailable for medical procedures.

In my treatment center discussion with the nephrologist, I had asked him if I decided to forego dialysis and "let nature take its course" if my death would be painful. He told me that this wasn't a decision that I should make alone, and that my family should be a part of such a discussion. He advised me that if I decided on that course, I would simply become weaker and weaker, go to bed, and I would be kept comfortable until I

```
died—probably from a heart attack. After
careful and soul-searching consideration,
I decided to stay on dialysis because of my
husband and family.
```

During the four years Florence and I worked to record her memories, she had neither the time nor the desire to add anything to her journal. As one who traveled with her to the dialysis clinic often, I can attest to her less-than-dutiful acceptance of the gradual failing of her body. But she was a fighter until the end, buoyed by the love of her family and friends; and even towards the end, she was attentive to issues of power, race, and sex—even in her analysis of her own treatment – as noted in the same article:

```
Thankfully, I have had good to excellent
care, using a variety of treatments and
doctors, psychotherapy, drugs, and ECT
(electroconvulsive treatment, or shock therapy).
I have had the best results so far with a
wonderful psycho pharmacologist, who combines
drug therapy with talk therapy.
    I am still trying to come to terms with
the permanence of end-stage renal failure.
I realize that I have a lot of irrational,
displaced and unresolved anger—with the
nephrologist, who had not diagnosed imminent
kidney failure during the three years that
I saw him, and had offered no advice or
prescriptions to retard the process; at my
family, who gave consent for me to be placed on
confining and life-changing dialysis (which I
undergo for three hours, three times weekly);
and the various dialysis technologists who
sometimes cause me severe pain by inexpertly
```

placing the needles. And ultimately, I suppose I am angry with the higher power—although I'm afraid to admit it. I long for the kind of faith experienced by my sister Lucille Knowles, and my friend LaVerne Gill, both of whom know me very well, and continue to pray for my peace of mind...for which I am very thankful.

Through it all I have been blessed with an extraordinarily loving, caring, and supportive husband, who has gone "beyond the call of duty"; my daughter Geri; my sons Greg and Brian; grandchildren Samori, Nzinga, Kilamba, Chinara, and Callie; great-grandchildren, Elias, Salome, and Nile, have brought much love and joy; they have all been a blessing.

Hindsight tells me that before discharging me and sending me to the dialysis center, the nephrologist should have explained to me that he had placed a catheter in my chest and how it was going to be used at the dialysis center. I am particularly sensitive to the issues of racism and sexism, as studies have shown how they can sometimes impact health care decisions made by doctors, the current debates and proposed legislation regarding women's reproductive health care and abortion are examples of how sexism is manifest in the arena. One need only mention the Tuskegee Experiment to raise the specter of racism in medical care.

So, despite the health challenges, including end stage renal failure and the resulting dialysis, I can't really complain.

LIMA Headquarters, Huambo 1976

UNITA training camp 1976

CHAPTER 15

A LUTA CONTINUA

Note: This chapter returns to Florence's words and memories on a variety of matters, compiled from interviews held during 2012 and 2013.

Thirty years after working on Jesse's presidential campaign, we have managed to elect a Black President of the United States. Still, it seems like the landscape of the United States has continued to be rocky, at best, for Black Americans. As of 2013, I can only say that now, in President Barack Obama's second term, my favorite analogy for Black folks in America continues to be that of a hamster scurrying to get next-to-nowhere in its hamster wheel.

The cycle of oppression under white supremacy only allows us Black folks to move so far upward on the wheel before it drags us down again. Any highs for us are followed by equally and often more devastating lows. For instance, in the 1960s, the apex of that cycle was the passage of the 1964 Civil Rights Act. Immediately after, all kinds of opportunities to try and elevate Black Americans to their proper and equal citizenry followed: affirmative action programs, housing desegregation, and more political representation, among them. We believed we were moving in the right direction, and we held high hopes for eventually attaining freedom, justice, and equality.

Then, suddenly, the cry became, "Hey, you've gone too far!" During the post-Civil Rights Movement decades of the 1970s and 1980s, the powers-that-be arranged for various drugs to be released into our communities as community support programs and funding dried up. During the 1990s, the War on Drugs began eviscerating our community. Gains in Black prominence and visibility in the entertainment and sports world were accompanied by the growth of the prison industrial complex in the 2000s. Then, just as it seemed we had reached a new apex, Barack Obama's election as the first Black President in 2008 another inevitable downward crash occurred, sending us back to the nadir at the bottom of the wheel.

Of course, it's never just us who suffer. The entire world is now paying the price of global capitalism, which has long been propped up by—and continues to prop up—global white supremacy. Evidence of this includes the various uprisings, global strikes, and recessions we are seeing worldwide.

These days, I often tell my friends, "I'm glad I'm going out and not coming in." And, more often than not, those with whom I share this sentiment have also lived through the pre-, during-, and post-Civil Rights and Black Power Movements, and have had to weather decades of storm, both personal and political, as have I. Many of these same friends are as disgusted, frustrated, and near-to-exhaustion as I am from viewing oppression and living with being oppressed by the relentlessness of white supremacy in action.

Many people have provided me with gracious, nonjudgmental emotional support during my terrible periods of depression and my "politically embargoed" years. I have been truly blessed by their energizing and enduring friendships. Their love, respect, and admiration remained constant, even if we weren't able to see each other or spend physical time together the way I would have liked. A number of those people took the time I requested of them to be interviewed for this book; the conflicting schedules of many more made their cooperation impossible; and of course, several of them have gone on to "the other side." But all of them kept me afloat, educated me, inspired my work, and "had my back" when I couldn't or didn't have the good sense to do so. I thank you all and love you all, truly, from the deepest part of my heart.

Before, during, and beyond my politically active years, I've fully experienced the greatest joy of my life: watching my children become wonderful people and do wonderful things. People often ask me, "Florence, how did you raise such accomplished, intelligent, interesting people?" I always defer, admitting, "I don't know. I don't think I had much to do with it." Of course, Geri, Greg, and Brian refute my statement and credit our family's supportive home life and the people and influences that Charles and I exposed them to as directly responsible for who and what they've become.

Recently, however, someone stumped me with the question: "What would you say your calling has been?" After initially balking at the inquirer's choice of words, I protested, claiming, "I've never *had* a calling!" Since then, I have thought more deeply about that question, and I have come to understand the importance of *passion* in finding one's calling.

I look especially at my children, who have discovered their own passions in their various pursuits, which they have turned into their careers and callings. Whatever they are doing, they're passionate about it! My oldest, Geri, has sustained a long-term, passionate affair with Pan-Africanism, cross-cultural studies, and education. She is an international scholar, educator, community builder, and mother—and now grandmother to a new tribe of amazing humans: Samori, Nzinga, and Kilamba, my brilliant grandsons. Samori and his wife Josefina have a beautiful family and have made me a great-grandmother with the addition of their children, Elias and Salome.

My second child, Greg, has turned his passion for music into a variety of callings. He has become a well-respected bandleader, author, and cultural critic. He's also a father and grandfather. His daughter, my granddaughter Chinara, is well on her way to becoming a health advocate and PhD herself. Her son Nile is a delight, imaginative and outspoken and sure to be another "Race Man" in the mold of his Grampa Greg, his great-grandfather Charles, and my own father—his great-great-grandfather, Henry Grinner.

Brian, my youngest, is thoroughly engaged in bringing arts and community together in the work he does advocating for nonprofit and cultural institutions. His passion and dedication are evident in the inspiring number of new programs, partners, and audiences he creates and joins together via innovative and thought-provoking projects. He has become an accomplished community builder and is in great demand as a marketing expert and nonprofit director. Like his older brother, he is also a musician; and, to my great joy, Brian is deeply connected to his church and spiritual community. He has rounded out our rich and colorful tribe of Tates with his equally accomplished wife, educator Maureen, and their daughter, my little granddaughter Callie, named after my mother.

All of my children, and grandchildren, have brought joy, support, inspiration, and so much more to my life. During my suffocating depressions, picturing their faces lifted me like buoyant currents that pierced the foggy muck, as their love tethered me to the earth. Conjuring their images anchored me, encouraging me to wade through the ocean of negative and self-defeating thoughts until I could experience the joy of being with them again. They have been my best friends and have put up with so much of my incessant worrying. I really can't begin to thank them all enough for allowing me to be the best mother, grandmother, and great-grandmother I could manage to be to them over the years.

And, of course, Mr. Charles E. Tate, whom I am wont to call "Himself"—has been my lifetime partner, closest friend, co-conspirator, and coworker in the Movement. Charles has spoiled me beyond belief, and he is directly responsible for bringing me the support, loyalty, and devotion that allowed me not only to be able to pick up and leave jobs at the drop of a hat but also to travel, to continue to create bridges, and to do the political work that has been my life's blood. Charles has also always been passionate about the work he has done in the areas of Black economic development, communications, and education. And to this day, he can still run you ragged talking about the economic development of Black people and Black communities!

Between Charles's work and my own, my children grew up in an environment of intense connection to a cause, movement, or profession. Geri and I were conversing one night about her commitment to her work and her ability to connect deeply to it, and she matter-of-factly offered, "Well, "Mom, I got *that* from you, of course." I thought about that for a bit, then acknowledged her with, "I'll accept that *some* of your passion you got from me. But where do you think I got *mine* from?" To which she responded, "Well, *you* have to figure that out!"

I pondered the question, then noted, with more than a hint of pride in her accomplishments, "Geri, you've always been so creative, imaginative, and open to new ideas. I haven't had half the different, exciting experiences that you have. What I did have was on the other end of things."

I was referring, of course, to the way my childhood had shaped me; how being frequently circulated around in the family had taught me to adjust and adapt to various rules, regulations, and ways of doing things. I wanted also to explain how I had to learn quickly to do things this way, that way, or the other because being flexible allowed me to fit in and be accepted into whichever home or community I happened to be in.

My upbringing left me with both an open mind and an awareness of how people learn to function within different lifestyles, cultures, and conditions. I'm sure my upbringing contributed both to my acceptance of and desire to learn about other folks' ways of being and modes of operation. It also might have made me more apt to root for the less fortunate, "the underdog"—those who, like me, had to develop a nimble mindset to survive, who learned to nurture ourselves regardless of how fragile and tenuous our family bonds were.

These were the skills that supported my penchant for communication and contributing to teams, increased my capacity to organize complex events, and helped hone my skill at managing many moving parts within a community. And of course, I *wanted* community, badly.

Considering all this, I've come to realize that, indeed, if I had a calling, it was to develop and nurture webs of communication and community. I like making connections, recognizing something in one person, and identifying something else in another person—seeing where the two connect, and bringing them together.

My early introduction to the racial dynamics of our country and to studying the relationship between those "at the top" and those "at the bottom" fostered my enduring fascination with politics. The draw of being a part of the political process also became a lifelong passion. As a result, that too became part of my calling.

People ask me all sorts of questions these days, expecting pearls of wisdom to usher forth. Though I can't guarantee such pearls, I will attempt to address some of the inquiries.

For example, I'm asked quite frequently whether I believe that today's young folks are less politicized than they should be. To that, I answer: "Definitely!" I would, however, like to tack onto this conclusion the realization that I don't blame young people for *not* being as politicized as they could be. I think of it more as we—meaning their elders—didn't do *our* job. We did not succeed in keeping them apprised of where we'd come from and how hard it was, every step of the way, for us to get where we are to make it possible for them to get where they are. We kept that from our children, I believe, because we did not want them to experience the horror we lived through.

The whole point was to get free of all the stuff white folks had put on us, so why would we want to put that on our children? Our idea or attitude was, "We worked so you could have the advantages we didn't have!" Why would we want to beat our children over the head with, "Well, the white folks did this to me, and I couldn't do this, and I couldn't do that?" In this shielding and protecting and providing for our children to receive and achieve, I think we went too far the other way. So, I don't blame the young people. We didn't do our job, and along the way, some of us got sucked into "the Man's" status quo in one way or the other. And we paid less attention to the struggle.

Of course, in the coming storm that seems to be building in the face of the numerous impending crises facing our world, we may see our children being forced to return to a more political and revolutionary mindset. This, I hope, is where the lessons and strategies of the Movement can be reshaped and recontextualized so that the work my generation and those before me will be able to help guide and direct our youth.

Upon occasion, I'm also asked about the state of the Black family or, more specifically, the relationship between Black men and Black women and how that affects the future of the Black family. In addressing that subject, I usually caution the person asking the question—who is most often a younger Black woman—by stating that my views may not be popular nowadays. I am not someone who considers myself a feminist, mostly because that term wasn't even in use when I was coming up. In fact, if pushed, my response is that I self-identify first as a Black person, then as a woman. My Blackness always comes first in my book. Therefore, my views may not be popular with women who used the term *feminist* to describe their politics and the impact their feminism has on their relationships.

That being said, I believe that if there exists a strain between Black men and Black women, as I've heard from both sides over the years, something will have to change between the sexes to fix that. If the relationship between the two sides is possible to fix—and worth it to both sides to try—then, unfortunately or not, women will probably find themselves being the ones forced to make whatever sacrifices are necessary to salvage those relationships. I say this mostly because I don't believe that men, regardless of race, can accomplish this. They just don't seem to be constructed to make sacrifices for relationships or, at least, they seem less inclined to sacrifice personal goals to build strong families. This again, is my personal observation.

Today's women, however, are becoming less and less willing to compromise any part of themselves or the things they have achieved simply for the sake of a relationship. And honestly, even I find myself questioning my view, is it right to ask them to go in reverse—to give up their independence, goals, or desires to encourage mating relationships with men—simply to perpetuate the race? Getting married and staying married has its virtues but, of course, I've made compromises to keep my family together, and I'm glad that I did and that Charles and I have our children and grandchildren.

But every relationship is different. My relationship with Charles was always different than that of my other friends and their husbands. For example, when I first started actively supporting SNCC, traveling to fundraisers or attend events with them, my friends would say, "Oh, Charles is so good! You're so lucky that he lets you go and do those kinds of things." I was like, "Lets me? How's he going to let me? Charles can't let me do anything!"

I remember one friend who was always taken aback at my busy life outside the home saying, "My husband doesn't even want me to visit my mother! He just wants to tell me what I can do and where I can go!" That was the case for many of the women I knew at that time; they had to be *allowed* to do things by their husbands. I never had that frame of mind. My attitude was that I was free to do what I wanted, even while doing my best to get along in my marriage. When I think about it, I'm sure I got that from my mother, who sure as hell didn't let no man run her life or keep her from doing what she wanted to do. So, looking back on my choices and how I led my life, I guess I wasn't willing to sacrifice that kind of freedom either.

Yet, as fate would have it, Charles's upbringing in a large family meant that he understood that everyone, male and female alike, had to do their share. Therefore, in our house, I never had to complain, like many women I knew, that I had to do all the housework while he just comes home and sits down. I never was left to do this and do that, plus the children! That was never a question in our house. Charles and I never even had to discuss it. When we both worked, whoever got home first would start dinner, and if the clothes needed washing, whoever was available would do them. It was never a question of my role versus his role.

On top of that, both Charles and I wanted our marriage, and it had primary importance in both of our lives. I always said I needed a man—not to tell me what to do and where I could go—but to have someone in my life who was emotionally available to me when I needed it. Charles was there for me, and I didn't have to go looking for anything. I had somebody who cared about me and who was making a life with me. It's like the expression the kids use nowadays: "He has my back." We both wanted it.

In my generation, both women and men were indoctrinated to believe in the importance of having a family with a husband and a wife. We were raised knowing or rather, believing, that we needed somebody, that men and women needed each other. There was no, "I don't need you" or "What do I need with a man?" And yes, in some marriages or relationship, somebody had to be willing to take on a diminished role because they wanted the relationship and were willing to do whatever they had to do to keep it.

Back then, everyone wanted to be married or in a serious, committed relationship. No matter how independent or how educated or how beautiful you might have been, you wanted *somebody*. And men knew, not just that you loved them or wanted to have sex with them, but that you needed them in certain kinds of ways. They were proud of having that kind of position; and they were proud to take care of, look after, and support their wives. They had an investment in their marriages that was mutually beneficial. There also wasn't this issue of so many of our Black men being locked up in jail or suffering so many of the other ills plaguing them in today's society. They were available; there was no "male shortage," so they couldn't go around being "king of the walk" with the attitude that because Black women outnumber Black men ten to one, they have the "pick of the litter."

When we women became liberated, so to speak, in the 1970s, we gained access to better jobs, which was the good part. But seemingly, however, the bad part was that men ended up feeling unnecessary and threatened. Then, with women's sexual liberation, women did not have to get married to have sex anymore, which really diminished the necessity for marriage.

Today's Black women are educated and talented and beautiful as never before in our history. They are busy doing, being, and becoming. They're accomplished and have a lot on the ball. The problem is, between many of our young men and women, we now have vast differences in educational levels and the accompanying differences in salary and resources that come with education. As a result, there are fewer men in the "pool" for women looking for a mate with a similar economic and educational background. Add to that the mindset of both men and women today that they don't have to put up with anything they don't like or don't want or don't feel like they have to have. In any long-term marriage—and mine has been *really* long—you have put up with something about the other person. When I hear young people saying they don't need to put up with something going on in their relationships, I really want to point out that sometimes, somebody, has to "put up with that"—for the sake of the relationship.

In my case, because of my background, after my first marriage ended, my attitude was, "If I get married again, that's going to be it, unless he beats me or is a drunk. I'm going to make it work and be committed to the marriage and the family!" I wanted a family, and to me it was worth it to make it work as long as nothing completely intolerable was going on in our home. And that's about what I have done.

Around our fiftieth wedding anniversary, I began to joke that if someone had ever asked me, "How have you managed to stay married for fifty years?" my response would be, "Honey, the question is not how—but *why*?" And, of course, that was just me being humorous! It's been a wonderful life with Charles. I couldn't have been blessed with a better husband, but sacrifices were required on both our parts.

Are today's young folks willing and able to make those sacrifices to support Black relationships, Black marriages, and Black families generally? I cannot, in all honestly, answer that question. But I believe sacrifices are necessary if we are to see the Black family survive and thrive in the coming years.

> **Omo Misha Mcglown:** *I loved their marriage. I loved the interactions between Mr. and Mrs. Tate. You know I loved how she always called him "Mr. Tate," or "himself." I remember being at their house, and, she would get in a giddy mood and I went right along with it, because I'm silly! And we could be in that kitchen just a-giggling and a-cackling. And Mr. Tate — it might be a Sunday morning, he's just trying to get his morning cup of joe — is completely oblivious to it, which makes whatever we're cackling about even more funny! I really enjoyed the dynamic between the two of them, and being able to be in their midst.*

Another question people ask me quite often is, "What do you think about what's happened, and will happen, to the Black community?" That's a huge question, and I tend to break it down into separate ideas when trying to address it, so here goes.

In some ways, so many of us are better off materially and better educated than ever before, but I truly feel we've lost our original sense of community. We don't seem to be with each or for each other like we were before integration. We don't seem to care for each other and look out for each other the way we used to. We don't seem to believe that we're in this together; we're more divided in terms of class and education. I know I don't feel the warmth we used to feel among each other. Yes, there are clumps of community here and there, where Black folks seem to be taking care of and looking out for each other, but on a whole, the Black community of yesteryear had more oneness and greater unity.

Our sense of shared values no longer remains. In times past, the values of community and family were very important to us. Building, nurturing, and protecting our communities was, in fact, necessary to our survival, but I don't see that kind of community building happening now. Our values today seem to be more personal- and individual-oriented; we seem to lack the power to bond to any Black person outside our immediate family circle.

We have attained so much in terms of material worth, however. Black families spend billions of dollars annually, but we are not spending that money in our communities. And all that wealth certainly doesn't seem to be bringing us together or keeping us any safer from the ills and dangers specific to Black people in America. The weakening of our communities seems to ensure that we're less safe than we've ever been.

Before integration, Black people were not separated by class or position. Given housing segregation, we all lived together. Someone might have more money or might have been able to travel or do more for their children, but even poor Black children had opportunities to get to know the Black doctor or teacher because those role models lived down the street from them. They were their neighbors, they were in their communities, and they went to the same churches. We were together, whether we wanted to be or not. The Black community offered Black children protection. They knew they were surrounded by loving, caring environments and that their neighbors were people from every position in society.

Today, a great many of our poor Black children are trapped in areas where the only people they see and live around are welfare recipients, and high rates of crime are the norm. Schooling in Black communities also seems to have been negatively affected by integration. In the name of integration, the best Black teachers were siphoned off to teach at white schools that had been "integrated." White people's idea of educational integration, and their implementation of it, meant taking the best Black teachers out of the Black schools and placing them into white schools—not moving the white students into Black schools.

That reminds me of something my father predicted when I was at CORE. Under desegregation, he said, there were no more "excellent Black teachers making sure Black children felt good about themselves and learned about their culture." Integration was, he believed, the beginning of our *dis*-integration. Under segregation, he continued, the Black principals and teachers cared about the Black children entrusted to them in a different way, with a pride and concern that touched every level of the school building. They never believed that Black children couldn't learn or that students in Black schools needed to be segregated into classes for slow learners or for special education or gifted students. Everybody was just with everybody: you went to school, and if anybody needed special attention, they'd get it from the teacher, who would stay after class to teach, if necessary. Black children whose families were economically challenged often were supported or taken home by their Black teachers on the weekends. As *teachers-cum-parents*, they would do or provide things for their students that those students wouldn't have access to otherwise.

According to my principal-father, if you were an exceptionally smart student, Black teachers in those days would do whatever they had to do to make sure you got a quality education. I know I got all kinds of support from my segregated community and especially from my teachers. When I needed new boots to participate in band activities, for example, my teachers helped. The family of a good friend of mine, the daughter of a janitor, was very poor and her teachers put together a fund to get her into college. I too received scholarship support from my community to attend LeMoyne because finishing Manassas High and going to college was not the usual thing.

All that to say that, in my day, Black students were recognized and praised for doing well, even in their segregated schools. We were pushed to do and be as much as we could and always pushed forward to do more. I do think that desegregation has had something to do with a lessened focus on the importance of education among Black communities. When I was coming up, every family I knew held and believed that education was a huge goal. Everybody wanted their children to receive the best education that could be provided, and they would make all kinds of sacrifices so their children could be educated. We were indoctrinated into the belief that education was the answer to our problems, that getting an education was the answer and the key to a good life. And for a long time, education seemed to be the answer. If you got an education, we reasoned, you'd get a better job and provide for your family in a better fashion; the world would open up to you in terms of your interests and desires.

Of course, now we see that while education is good and still necessary for a better life, our communities' problems haven't changed just because more and more Blacks have gained an education. Today, educated Blacks, by and large, continue to face the institutional racism that uneducated Blacks encounter generally. While education remains a vital component of attaining and having a good life, it doesn't deliver for you in this society if you are Black. You won't reach the promised land just because you're educated.

Prior to integration, those of us in the Black community also had to rely on each other more frequently. We took care of each other. If you were sick, you knew someone down the street would be bringing you a pot of something to eat or come take your children to the zoo so you could rest. There was friendship, kinship, and comfort in being "with your own kind." You knew you would be accepted, and not discriminated against, in your own community.

Another reality of that period was learning to do more with less—there was no "I can't do this, and I can't do that." If there was something you wanted or needed or had to do, then you would just marshal your internal or community resources to get it done. It wasn't a culture in which poverty meant failure.

But desegregation changed all that. When those among us who had more education and brighter horizons scattered and could go live and attend school outside the Black community, the examples we had of what was possible in life were scattered and demolished. Integration was *dis*-integration for us. It was never true integration for most of the community in terms of equal access and equitable resources. Relatively few of us benefitted from what integration offered. Those who could, fled the Black community, particularly those in inner-city areas, and left behind all of the downsides of poverty and neglect. The wealthy Blacks went to live elsewhere. It's no accident that poverty, crime, and poor Black people are all concentrated in areas with poor services and schools. Those areas were simply left to fester.

Integration was poor medicine for Black people, as far as I'm concerned. We lost the positive things about our communities and what we gained, the opportunities that were offered, were meted out to only some of us. Individuals like me were able to move up economically because the old type of workforce discrimination was no longer in force. *If,* any only if, you had the right training, the right "appeal," and the right "attitude," You could get ahead. There certainly was more access to government jobs, post-integration. For instance, Charles got in on a program that allowed him to rise to the top in his field in the government, and it afforded us a better life than we would have had before integration. Ultimately, in my opinion, the integration experience was a net loss for Black folks. It was not a success, by and large. At least partly because of it, our communities are not in good shape today. I'm also unconvinced that under the current policies and actions in and outside our communities, our communities will ever be able to thrive.

A "what-if" question was put to me recently: "If you were the president of the United States, what would you do to improve our country?" Assuming that what the inquirer really wanted to know was what my "vision for a future America" would be, I believe that, while it would be ideal for all people, regardless of race, to have and get paid for work that they hopefully enjoyed, I would settle for every person having access to a living-wage job, quality healthcare and education, and decent housing. This is what I want for *my* people—Black people— and really, for everyone. It's the same thing people all over the world have wanted from time immemorial. A decent life.

However, rich people cannot exist without poor people to exploit; and frankly, no president can do anything about that as long as this capitalist system keeps things such that there are poor people and rich people. No president can fix that; what we're talking about, then, to get there, is *revolution.*

If the system remains the same, no matter who the president is, all one will be able to do is tinker around the edges and do a little tweaking here and there. You can make it sound better or look prettier, but exploiting the world's resources—especially those found in the planet's darker nations—hey, that's gonna rock on. It doesn't matter who's in the White House: Democrat, Republican, whatever. Unless there is some kind of real revolution—I'm talking about fighting to overthrow the system, and I don't see that in any kind of near future—a president's hands are tied.

Although we have managed to elect a Black man to the highest office in the nation, President Obama has been useless, at least as far as the hopes we might have held for his impact on the fate of Black people in the U.S. and around the globe are concerned. I have yet to see him stand up to for anything that would be of specific benefit to Black people.

Today, his inability to close the detention camps at Guantanamo Bay irks me, but tomorrow it will be something else. In the years since he's been in office, there certainly were other opportunities for him to make change to happen that have not happened. Of course, an obstructionist Congress has stood firmly in his way and probably made it near to impossible to do much of anything he may have promised in his "change"-filled campaign speeches. Still, having backbone and principles—being truly *about something*—should mean that folks just can't blow you over or make you submit to whatever they want you to because you're scared that this, that, or the other thing is going to happen.

People have given their lives for you to be about something, Mr. President! So you don't get reelected, so what? That ain't nothin'! Get a job, Negro! Go back to teaching school; you don't have to be the president to effect the kind of change we need to see.

Of course, now, none of this is to say that I was not as thrilled and excited and proud as any other Black person in the world that Barack Obama managed to get elected. On election night 2008, Charles and I were in Washington, DC, at the home of Doll Gordon, a friend active in Democratic Party politics in the city. She had invited a group of us over to watch the returns, and it was a powerful night for all of us. I recall thinking that night about how I've been passionate about the political process from a young age and have voted in every election since 1952 when I voted for Adlai Stevenson II. Suffrage came early for Blacks in Memphis; we were allowed to vote before Blacks in other Deep South states because of our longstanding loyalty to the political machine of Mayor E. H. "Boss" Crump in the early years of the twentieth century. Since the Fifties, I'd made it a point to exercise my right to vote in every election I could, whether I was writing somebody in (which I'd done) or voting against my party (which I'd also done).

That evening in 2008, Doll had high hopes. "It's going to be a victory party!" she kept saying. I, on the other hand, was less hopeful, even though I had been very enthusiastic about Obama and his campaign from the outset. I was one of the first Black people to volunteer to work for his campaign in Sarasota, the city to which Charles and I recently had retired. I'd worked the phone bank at Obama's get-out-the-vote office, and I held a fundraiser for his campaign at our house. When Obama came to speak at a campaign rally sixty miles away in Tampa, I joined three busloads of people traveling to see him. Believe me, standing with a cane for the entire time, with an arthritic hip, at age seventy-seven, it wasn't easy. I remember how he bounded up the steps—this youthful, extraordinarily intelligent Black man—it was exhilarating! My childhood friend Jo Bridges, who was not a religious person, was convinced he was a gift from above, and proclaimed, "I don't know where he came from, and I don't care — he is perfect! God *must* have sent him!"

When the returns were all in on election night, and Barack Obama stepped onstage as the newly elected forty-fourth President of the United States of America with his wife and their two daughters, tears rolled down my cheeks, just as I'm sure they did for many other Black Americans. Those tears might have been tears of joy, but they might also have been tears of release, as we shed ourselves of the anxiety of months of holding out hope that it might actually happen—that he might actually win!

I don't think anyone actually believed Obama would be able to resolve the myriad issues facing our nation: the inherited, ongoing wars; record unemployment; and a near-depression masked behind a gentler term: "recession." It seemed unlikely that the young, barely experienced senator-turned-president would be able to deal with what

W. E. B. DuBois had once summed up, in his now-famous statement, as "the problem of the color line." But I had hoped he would have done better than he did—or rather, was *allowed* to do.

In any case, to get back to the question of what I would do if I was the leader of this country, here's what I believe: What I want is for this nation to finally achieve some kind of communalistic system in which people pool their resources and help each other and keep anybody and everybody from falling under. I don't know what kind of economic model that would be, but something should be put in place to ensure that Americans can be more altruistic toward one another.

I remember when I was a young mother, I was chatting one day with another friend who was also a mother. We were talking about how everybody we knew was working hard but still strapped for cash and without enough money to do this, that, and the other. In our neighborhood, every little house had a little yard that required some kind of lawn mower. On that particular day, my friend and I began wondering: "Why do we *both* need a lawn mower? We live in the same neighborhood; it's not something we need to use every day. So, why couldn't a few families share a lawn mower? Or what about sharing just one big freezer? Or maybe we only need one washing machine!"

My friend and I later discussed our musings with another friend, who seemed dubious. Not only was it going against the grain for many of our folk to think like this, she said (this was before the hippie communes and all that stuff), but we had missed something important. "For instance," she mused, playing devil's advocate, "if everybody went and did that—if you just bought one lawn mower for the whole neighborhood— wouldn't you be depriving somebody of a job making more lawn mowers, freezers, and washing machines?"

Even then I realized that we, as Black people, were entering into a more modern and individualist mindset. We were confronted with the reality that, in America, everybody wants their own *everything*. Although I would like to think that women think more in terms of sharing and not having such fierce pride of ownership, I'm not convinced men would easily be persuaded to think like that. Still, a more socialistic way of living—a more communal way of being—is what my vision of America would be.

What more can I say? *A luta continua* (the struggle continues). And in the immortal words of Adam Clayton Powell, Jr.: "Keep the faith, baby!"

Florence Louise Grinner Tate
June 21, 1931–December 14, 2014

AFTERWORD

MY HEART AND JUST BEHIND IT

BRIAN TATE

Ma and I were having a laugh one morning about the horrendous state of the world and other affairs when the conversation veered to my health. My doctor had learned there was something wrong with my heart, an anomaly that made my blood pump backwards. A variation of the heart murmur I had inherited from Mom that blossomed into a deadlier shape for me. So I had a heart surgery on the calendar, preceded by a tough battery of tests. I had surrendered to those circumstances – what else was there to do? – but they worried her. She didn't let on but I could tell.

A bit deeper into our call she grew suddenly quiet and said:

"Son, I'm so sorry I never introduced you and your brother to the church. It's one of my greatest regrets as a mother."

Did she say regrets? She might have said failings. She could be hard on herself, hovering at the threshold of a dark room. I said, "Wait, what are you talking about? Seriously?"

"Yes, seriously."

I can't quite recall what she described as the reasons for this self-perceived lapse. That Black Power movement politics had moved her and the Old Man away from the church. Or that she, as the cast-out daughter of a deacon, had never had an uncomplicated relationship with religion. Possibly both.

"Oh, Mom," I told her, "I go to church all the time."

"You do?"

From the sound of her voice it sounded as if she was already leagues away, pulled down some unlit corridor toward a flight of steps. But she paused and turned.

"Yeah," I said. "Every Sunday. Lafayette Avenue Presbyterian, it's just up the street. Brooklyn is the borough of churches, you know."

"You're a Presbyterian?"

"Well, no. But I go to service there. It's a good place, with good people. The pastor is very political, you'd love his sermons. Used to be a union organizer for migrant workers out in California.

"But… how? How did this happen? I never took you or Greg to church at all."

She was coming back to herself now. And I said without pause: "Oh, Ma. Don't you know that everything there is that's good about me came from you and the Old Man? Because of something you said or showed me, or just the way you handled yourselves? Where else would I have absorbed those qualities except from you?"

"Oh, son… Really?"

The darkness cracked and the years tore away. She was the girl out in a sunlit field but also the adult woman watching the girl. Her voice was small and full of wonder, as if she had flipped over a flat black rock and found a prism, a new way of looking at life that cast her in a very different and brilliant light.

"Well, of course, really. C'mon!"

And I laughed. Which immediately worked its charm. Soon she was laughing again too, and that sound teemed up from my phone and filled the room, animating my oddly beating heart and just behind it, hers.

Charles and Florence

INDEX

291121-750-2-60W